D1175093

Spirit-Baptism

A BIBLICAL INVESTIGATION

by

Howard M. Ervin

PEABODY, MASSACHUSETTS 01961-3473

P.O. Box 3473
Peabody, Massachusetts 01961-3473

Printed in the United States of America

ISBN 0913573–79–5

This book is a revision of *These Are Not Drunken, As Ye Suppose* (Logos International, 1968, © Howard M. Ervin).

The elder unto the elect lady and her children,
whom I love in truth (2 John 1, ASV)

To

Marta
Gretchen, Deborah, Judith

and to
the third generation

Elizabeth
Rebekah
Michael
Jacob
Jon Michael

Table of Contents

Preface

THE PRESENT VOLUME was first published in 1968 by Logos, International under the title *These Are Not Drunken, As Ye Suppose*. This marked the culmination of a task begun some six years earlier. In spite of the fact that this earlier edition has been out of print for a number of years, inquiries continue to be made relative to its current availability. The persistence of these inquiries suggests that its message is still relevant to a new generation of Pentecostals/Charismatics.

The apologetic tone of the original publication was symptomatic of its identification with the early stages of the Charismatic renewal in the second half of the twentieth century. The acerbity of the Fundamentalist/Evangelical controversy with the emerging Pentecostal/Charismatic phenomenon made dialogue next to impossible. In the intervening decades, however, the worldwide Pentecostal/Charismatic renewal in both Protestant and Catholic churches has achieved a considerable measure of respectability. Its validity no longer seriously challenged by external critics, its real dangers arise from within. The pressures that put it at risk now are twofold.

First of all, those who would impose upon it their private agendas threaten its integrity, for without accountability there is no integrity. The Lone-Ranger syndrome, operating under charismatic sanctions, is a serious threat to the health and wholeness of the entire Church. Secondly, those who seek to demonstrate the charisms of the Holy Spirit theologically and denominationally threaten its vitality. The charisms of the Spirit resist accommodation to sectarian theological sensitivities. The present work is an invitation to friend and foe alike to examine afresh the biblical and theological foundations of a Pentecostal spirituality. Consequently, the apologetic tone that marked the original text has largely disappeared from the present volume. This change in focus argued convincingly for a change in the title to reflect the changed orientation of the discussion.

As suggested above, the initial impetus for the book was provided by the Fundamentalist/Evangelical polemic directed against the Pentecostal phenomenon then emerging in many of the traditional Protestant denominations. My own experience with a personal "Pentecost" placed me in the midst of the controversy. The pressing need for an explicit and reasonably comprehensive statement of the case from a Pentecostal/Charismatic perspective soon became obvious. My Pentecostal experience, coupled with my denominational identity (Baptist), suggested to me that I might undertake the role of advocate for the Pentecostal/Charismatic cause. My conservative and evangelical theological training emboldened me to address the growing Fundamentalist/Evangelical polemic.

Thus the book was directed primarily to an Evangelical and Pentecostal audience–a refutation of the harsher criticisms of the former, a defense of the Pentecostal hermeneutics for the latter. Now in a more irenic climate, the audience to which it was originally addressed remains substantially the same. Its purpose is to engage dialogically Evangelicals and Pentecostals (hopefully without the rhetorical pyrotechnics that blemished their past encounters) in an examination of the biblical and theological foundations of the Pentecostal baptism in the Holy Spirit.

The initial decision to write for publication was undertaken as an additional agenda in the midst of pressing pastoral responsibilities, numerous speaking engagements, and an increasing involvement in a Charismatic ministry on an ecumenical level. This left little time for the needed research and writing. The process was complicated by the realization that there were few, if any, mentors to whom one could look either among the Pentecostals or the Evangelicals. This made the question of even minimal documentation a pressing one. Lacking convenient access to a theological library, documentation was largely confined to those resources available on a working pastor's bookshelves.

There were, in addition, other pressing considerations. Would this consistent application of a traditional grammatical-historical exegesis really support a Pentecostal hermeneutics? Or did the immediacy of the experience of Spirit-baptism involve subjective interpretative categories that resisted a consistent application of contextual exegesis? It was a charge frequently made that the experience dictated the exegesis. It soon became apparent, however, that while the experience informed the exegesis, it was the hermeneutics that dictated the exegesis, a fact overlooked by both sides in the controversy.

On the other hand, it was my observation that the anti-pentecostal polemic did not itself represent a consistent application of grammatical-contextual exegesis. Its frequently ad hominem character was a tacit acknowledgment of the a priori theological propositions upon which it was predicated. Any challenge to these a priori constructs must, therefore, be buttressed by sources whose orthodoxy could command respect in those theological circles I hoped to impact. It is understood, of course, that the task was undertaken from within a conservative, evangelical theological orientation.

This posed another problem. Was there a sufficient body of orthodox opinion that would support exegetically crucial points in a Pentecostal hermeneutics? Thus the scope of the project was determined by the problems it proposed to address and by the resources at my disposal. This was clearly stated in the original prologue, e.g., "The ambitions it embodies are modest indeed. It makes no pretense of being definitive, merely provocative."

There was a further personal consideration. I had completed a doctoral dissertation in 1962, the year in which this project was formulated, and I had no desire to begin immediately the rigors of another such endeavor, even if my circumstances would have encouraged it. I am aware, of course, that the sources quoted herein are vulnerable to the charge of being "dated," as though that fact, without further consideration, somehow impugned the integrity of the sources and/or the present author's credibility. Irenaeus, Luther, Calvin, et al. do have contemporary significance. The accumulated wisdom of the past does speak to the present. No attempt has been made to reflect the voluminous, and growing literature that the renewal has generated in the intervening years. That is a task for someone with greater skills than mine and the time to invest in such a project.

In one sense, the present volume is a republication of the former text. In another sense, it is a new book. The former text has been largely rewritten. Previous insights have been refined exegetically and theologically. However, the fundamental theses of the former work remain unchanged. New material has been added, some in response to criticisms directed at the former publication, some as a result of reflection and experience after more than twenty-five years of a "Pentecostal" walk in the Spirit.

Those who are acquainted with the former text will note significant differences in the organization of the present one. In the interests of clarity, technical details, wherever possible, have been placed in the footnotes. Those interested will have ready access to them, while the general reader need not be burdened with them. Hopefully, this will make it more attractive to a wider readership.

In conclusion, it is a welcome privilege to acknowledge the contributions, both direct and indirect, of those who have assisted in the successful completion of the present volume. The perceptive, and at times critical, interaction with successive classes of students at every level, from the baccalaureate through the doctoral levels, has aided in the clarification of the issues involved. I regret that my pedestrian prose does not convey the no-holds-barred vitality of those discussions. A special work of appreciation is due the following students in GTHE 692 Pneumatology who during the spring semester of 1987 collated the indexes, viz., Ed Crawford, Andrea Crider, Gary L. Kern, Deanne Klug, John T. Phillips, Timothy John Seigler and Eric Titus.

The interest and expertise of Hendrickson Publishers, and in particular the editorial competence of the associate editor, Mr. Patrick H. Alexander, M.A., are also gratefully acknowledged. To my wife, Marta, I express a special sense of gratitude for her constant support and encouragement even when the domestic routine was coopted by literary priorities, not to mention the nocturnal clatter of the typewriter.

Foreword

When my esteemed friend Dr. Howard M. Ervin requested that I write a foreword to his new book, *Spirit Baptism: A Biblical Investigation,* I felt greatly honored but somewhat overwhelmed. Upon second thought however, I came to see it as fitting that a first-generation classical Pentecostal should evaluate a volume written by a present-day Pentecostal/Charismatic theologian.

Providing a brief historical backdrop might encourage the reader of this volume to follow the intricate path of the exegetical and theological reasoning of the author to the very last, extremely satisfying, end. In the spring of 1963 I had the exciting experience of meeting Dr. Howard M. Ervin, a Baptist minister who was pastoring a church in Atlantic Highlands, N.J., who had been baptized in the Holy Spirit a short time before. I was informed that he had graduated from the Eastern Baptist Theological Seminary in Philadelphia with a Bachelor of Arts/Bachelor of Theology degree, that he had received the Master of Arts degree from the Asia Institute in New York, that he had received the B.D. degree (cum laude) from the New Brunswick Theological Seminary of the Reformed Church in America, that in addition he had also earned the degree of Doctor of Theology at Princeton Theological Seminary. I was deeply impressed.

He informed me at the time that he was seriously considering writing a book in which he would present sound biblical and theological foundations for Pentecostal spirituality. This was like music to my ears, as I came from a first-generation Pentecostal background where higher education was frowned on. This anti-educational attitude stemmed from the fact that after being baptized in the Holy Spirit, most Pentecostal pioneers were excommunicated from the institutional churches, at the insistence of "scholarly" ministers.

As a consequence of the vital leadership roles in the Pentecostal movement both in South Africa and abroad of my parents and my brother, David du Plessis, I was brought in contact with world leaders of this Renewal from my earliest youth. Since I was fairly fluent in English and Afrikaans, the two official languages of my country, I was frequently called on to act as interpreter for distinguished visiting preachers such as Donald Gee, Howard Carter, Smith Wigglesworth, Noel Perkins, Ralph Riggs, and numerous others. Those were pioneering days!

The lack of theological training proved no obstacle to our evangelistic outreach, our missionary endeavor, or to our rich experience in the realm of the divinely supernatural. The baptism in the Holy Spirit certainly proved to be the supernatural enduement of power from on high for effective ministry.

As early as 1940 I was ordained to the ministry in "The Apostolic Faith Mission of South Africa," the oldest and largest Pentecostal church in the country. In my private endeavour to equip myself more effectively for ministry, I built a substantial personal theological library. During this process I was confronted with the disturbing reality that when it came to teaching on the Holy Spirit from the Pentecostal perspective, there was an empty space on the shelves of my library. Yet, the need for the Church to give account of its doctrine to other Christian bodies was becoming more and more apparent to me.

Up to the sixties a number of books on the subjects of the Holy Spirit, the baptism in the Holy Spirit, and the gifts of the Holy Spirit were written by Pentecostal authors. These however, having been written primarily for the instruction and edification of early Pentecostals, were presented in simple layman's language and style. With the advent of the Charismatic movement, literally hundreds of books on all aspects of the Holy Spirit, began to flow from the presses of many countries of the world. Yet, most of these lacked sound exegetical, theological expression.

In 1968 the book Dr. Howard M. Ervin envisioned in 1963 was published by Logos International under the title *These Are Not Drunken, As Ye Suppose*. It was gratefully received by a new generation of Pentecostal/Charismatic pastors as the most scholarly enterprise on the baptism in the Holy Spirit—a masterful exegesis of those passages from the Bible especially held dear by them. For me personally, it carried marks of exegetical and theological genius.

Howard M. Ervin emerged as one of the most erudite apologists of twentieth-century Pentecostalism! This volume, which can be found on the shelves of almost every theological library of any significance anywhere in the world, has done much to convince even the most ardent critics, that the Pentecostal/Charismatic movement is not the sectarian and effervescent passing phenomenon that they had originally judged it to be. The movement has made a significant impact on the Church universal, and there is abundant evidence that a more charitable and more objective evaluation is presently being made.

This latest book could not have been published at a more opportune time. There has been a steady and growing demand for a reprint of the original volume. Instead of merely a reprint, the author has blessed the ecclesiastical world with a totally revised version.

I have had the great privilege of reading through the page proofs, and in the limited time at my disposal, of making a comparative study. It afforded me many hours of joy. The new presentation is fresh, rich, less polemical and more comprehensive than its predecessor. I discerned in it the author's great love for the body of Christ, and therefore, his desire to impart to the reader the profound depths of the Holy Spirit that he has not only taught, but that he has so richly experienced.

I must confess that I expected nothing less than that, for during the intervening decades I witnessed his ecumenical journey through winding pathways, touching all parts of the body of Christ. In part of that beautiful journey I walked with him, such as in our mutual involvement with the International Roman Catholic/Pentecostal Dialogue, where he has made a rich contribution over a number of years.

The first volume satisfied the dire need of the Pentecostal churches for a biblical and theological foundation for their Pentecostal spirituality. This second volume will serve to convey to the entire body of Christ a spirituality that is both intellectually and theologically accountable, but above all, experiential.

My blessing goes with this book. I give thanks to God that He so richly endowed my friend with the knowledge, the gifts, and the grace to produce this volume for the edification of His body, the Church.

July 25, 1987

Pastor Justus du Plessis
Secretary for Ecumenical Affairs—
The A.F.M. of South Africa
Co-Chairman: International Roman Catholic/
Pentecostal Dialogue

Chapter 1

Filled with the Spirit

"BE FULFILLED WITH THE SPRETE."[1] The translation of Tyndale's New Testament (1525) 1535 sounds quaint, even stilted, to the modern ear. Yet it lends a dimension of freshness the word "filled" has lost in modern translations. "Fulfilled" carries with it overtones of complete realization, or manifestation, neatly illustrated by the inversion of its members. For example, fulfilled = filled full, that is to say, filled to the level of overflowing. It is to be understood as a liquid, rather than a static, metaphor. Spiritfulness is appraised, not by how much one can contain of the Holy Spirit, but by how much of the Spirit can flow through one. In the Johannine metaphor, the Spirit is likened to "rivers of living water."[2]

What significance does this apostolic injunction have for contemporary Christians? Is it merely rhetorical moralizing? i.e., "be not drunken with wine . . . but be filled with the Spirit." Is it, perchance, an archaic vestige of a first-century spirituality of dubious relevance to the twentieth century? Is it incidental to Christian experience, or is it of the essence of biblical Christianity?

The biblical text makes it quite clear. It is not stated as an option. It is first of all an admonition, but more than that, it is an opportunity to experience life abundant. In short, it is an apostolic imperative addressed to every Christian in every age. It is not merely the unique privilege of a spiritual elite, a remote possibility attainable only by the exceptional soul or the spiritual athlete. On

[1] Eph. 5:18; L. A. Weigle, ed., *The New Testament Octapla* (Thomas Nelson & Sons, 1946); cf. also the Geneva Bible (1560) 1562.

[2] John 7:37–39.

the contrary, to be filled with the Spirit is the privilege of every Christian. The Spirit-filled life is, in fact, the norm of Christian experience, and to the interpretation of this proposition the following study is devoted. Granted this premise, it is of considerable practical importance to investigate the prerequisites for, the nature of, and the manifestations of the Spirit-filled life.

In the biblical context, the Christian who has been filled with the Holy Spirit is characterized by a supernatural enablement to witness for Jesus Christ.[3] Peter, for example, before the crucifixion, quailed at the accusing taunt of a serving maid: "You also were with Jesus the Galilean."[4] When the accusation was repeated, despite his denial, "he began to curse and to swear, 'I do not know the man.'"[5] However, after Pentecost, this same vacillating disciple, now filled with (i.e., baptized in)[6] the Holy Spirit, was hauled before the same Sanhedrin that had delivered Jesus to death. With his companion John, he courageously defended their action in the healing of the lame beggar before the temple gates, saying, "in the name of Jesus Christ of Nazareth, whom you crucified, whom God raised from the dead . . . this man stands here before you whole."[7] The effect of these words upon the council was electrifying, for the boldness of Peter and John astonished them.

In the biblical accounts, the testimony of Spirit-filled witnesses was confirmed by the accompanying manifestations of the Spirit's supernatural signs. Nor was this confined to the apostles, for Philip, a Spirit-filled deacon and evangelist, went down to the city of Samaria and proclaimed to the Samaritans the advent of Jesus the Messiah. Centuries of bitter hostility between Samaritans and Jews were disarmed, for they paid attention to Philip "when they heard, and saw the signs which he did."[8] It is this charismatic dimension that sets the Pentecostal experience apart from a merely propositional approach to the Spirit-filled life.

Furthermore, the Spirit-filled community overflowed with supernatural graces bestowed by the Spirit of God. By way of

[3] Acts 1:8; cf., Luke 24:48, 49.
[4] Matt. 26:69.
[5] Matt. 26:74.
[6] In Acts 1:8 and 2:4 the terms are synonymous.
[7] Acts 4:10.
[8] Acts 8:6.

illustration, the men chosen by the apostolic fellowship to dispense alms to the needy were men of good reputation, "full of the Spirit and of wisdom," "full of faith and of the Holy Spirit," and "full of grace and power."[9] To the charism of faith was added by the Spirit "hope and love,"[10] while abounding "joy"[11] characterized the life and worship of the churches.[12]

While the biblical phenomenology of the Spirit-filled life is quite clear, related questions still remain to be asked. Is the biblical pattern valid for today? Was Pentecost a once-and-for-all event, or may Christians today expect to be filled with the Holy Spirit as in the apostolic age? Do the supernatural charisms of God's Spirit function in the Church today, as they did in the days of the apostles? While the fallout from theological polemics has frequently obscured or distorted the answers to these and related questions, nevertheless, it will be the task of this study to answer them from a Pentecostal perspective.

In an effort to present factual and objective answers to these and related questions, the first recourse will be to examine critically texts relating to the subject. Contemporary experience may (and does) illustrate, but only the biblical record adjudicates our conclusions. Whenever, therefore, contemporary witness to the Pentecostal experience is cited, it will be subordinated to the positive judgment of the Scriptures. In the final analysis, however, neither the application of contextual exegesis nor propositional logic to the written Word can infuse our conclusions with the self-validation of personal experience. As a matter of fact, the very concept of witnessing that is intrinsic to the Pentecostal experience is predicated upon a personal experience. Paradoxically, it is the living experience of the truth of God's Word that authenticates these conclusions, for "truth divorced from experience must always dwell in the realm of a doubt." Consequently, a critical evaluation of primary sources within an *empirical* frame of reference is indispensable for an understanding of the biblical injunction, "be filled with the Spirit."

The investigation begins with an examination of the occurrences of the phrase "filled with the Spirit." This expression,

[9] Acts 6:3, 5, 8.
[10] I Cor. 13:13.
[11] Acts 13:52.
[12] Eph. 5:18, 19.

whether as a verb phrase or a noun phrase, is found, with one exception,[13] only in Luke's Gospel and Acts.

There are three instances of the verb phrase, "filled with the Spirit,"[14] and one of the noun cognate, "full of the Spirit,"[15] in the Gospel according to Luke. In the first reference, an angel revealed to Zacharias that his hitherto barren wife Elizabeth would bear a son to be called John. The prophecy specifically stated that "he [John] shall be filled with the Holy Spirit, even from his mother's womb."[16] Thus was the Baptist to be uniquely endowed for his ministry as the forerunner of the Messiah.

Some months later, when Mary visited her kinswoman Elizabeth, it is recorded by Luke that "when Elizabeth heard the salutation of Mary, the babe leaped in her womb; and Elizabeth was filled with the Holy Spirit."[17] In recording this reminiscence the evangelist unmistakably implied that the preternatural activity of Elizabeth's unborn child in the presence of Mary was evidence of the influence of the Holy Spirit upon the child. Thus the prophecy of the angel to Zacharias that John would be filled with the Holy Spirit while yet in[18] Elizabeth's womb was fulfilled. Then at the birth of John, Zacharias himself "was filled with the Holy Spirit, and prophesied."[19]

It is of more than passing interest, in the light of the disciples' Pentecost experience, that in the instances cited above, the fulness of the Holy Spirit was evidenced by prophetic utterance. In the case of Elizabeth, at Mary's greeting she was filled with the Holy Spirit, and "she spoke out loudly."[20] What follows in the narrative is a prophetic acknowledgement of Mary as the mother of "my Lord."[21] So also, when Zacharias was filled with the Spirit at the birth of his son John, "he prophesied."[22] Mary's *Magnificat*[23] was

[13] Eph. 5:18.

[14] Luke 1:15, 41, 67, *πίμπλημι*.

[15] Luke 4:1: "Jesus, full [*πλήρης*] of the Holy Spirit, returned from the Jordan."

[16] Luke 1:15.

[17] Luke 1:41.

[18] Luke 1:15, *ἐν*: W it sy, *Novum Testamentum Graece*, eds., E. Nestle and Kurt Aland, 25th ed. (Stuttgart: Wurtembergische Bibelanstalt, 1963).

[19] Luke 1:67.

[20] Luke 1:42.

[21] Luke 1:43, *τοῦ κυρίου μου* = Heb. *'Adoni* = Yahweh.

[22] Luke 1:67.

[23] Luke 1:46–55.

also a prophetic utterance, the result of the Holy Spirit "coming upon"[24] her. Anticipating a fuller discussion later, it should at least be noted here that prophetic utterance was (and is?) the initial response to the fulness of the Holy Spirit's presence and power.

Despite similarities, however, there are differences between the experiences described by Luke in the incarnation narratives and those described by him in the Acts. The differences are attributable, at least in part, to the eschatological time-frame in which each is set. The Gospel narratives belong to the fulfillment of prophetic time, the Pentecostal references in Acts are set in apocalyptic time. The former represents the fulfillment of linear prophetic time, the kingdom of God at hand. The latter belong to apocalyptic time, the kingdom "not yet."

Prophetic eschatology and apocalyptic eschatology are radically different ways of understanding time in relation to salvation history. For the classical prophets of the Old Testament, time was perceived as linear, a history of revelation and redemption. In the prophetic linear view of salvation history, the ultimate fulfillment of time is the ushering in of the kingdom of God.[25] This view of time dominates the four Gospels until the passion week. However, in the apocalyptic discourses of Jesus[26] the expectations of prophetic time were drastically altered. With His rejection and crucifixion, the realization of the kingdom was indefinitely postponed.[27]

Zacharias, Elizabeth, John, Mary, and one might add Simeon and Anna, all played their roles in the context of linear prophetic time. In the fulness of the Holy Spirit each in his or her own way bore witness to the imminent fulfillment of Israel's messianic hope, "the kingdom of God at hand." After Pentecost the fulness of the Spirit represents a supernatural enablement for worldwide, age-long witness until the King returns. The Gospel narratives breathe the atmosphere of Old Testament expectation, while the Acts is a recital of hope postponed.

[24] Luke 1:35, ἐπέρχομαι, a Lukan metaphor for the baptism in/filling with the Holy Spirit; cf. Acts 1:8.

[25] Mark 1:15: "the time is fulfilled, and the kingdom of God is at hand."

[26] Matt. 24:1ff.; Mark 13:1ff.; Luke 21:5ff.

[27] Acts 1:6, 7: "It is not for you to know times or seasons [when the kingdom will be restored to Israel] which the Father has set within His own authority."

The incarnation was a once-and-for-all event in the unfolding of God's redemptive purpose, and these experiences associated with it were an intrinsic part of this unrepeatable event. The old covenant was still in effect. The crucifixion and resurrection of Jesus had not yet ushered in the new covenant. These were Old Testament saints whom Luke described as "filled with the Spirit" for a unique and special mission.

One last reference to the phrase in Luke's Gospel does have a bearing on the New Testament pattern of the fulness of the Spirit. This passage relates the experience of Jesus when the Holy Spirit descended upon Him during His baptism by John in the river Jordan, for "Jesus, full of the Holy Spirit, returned from the Jordan."[28] The descent of the Spirit upon Jesus was *empowerment* for ministry, for "Jesus returned" from the wilderness temptation "in the power of the Spirit into Galilee."[29] This motif is a crux in the interpretation of Jesus' experience at Jordan, for were the theme of power removed from Luke–Acts, or even relegated to a subordinate place, Luke's theology of the Holy Spirit would be largely unintelligible.

As a matter of fact, it is this motif of power that makes Jesus' experience at Jordan the prototype of the Pentecostal effusion of the Spirit upon the infant Church poised on the threshold of its worldwide ministry in Jesus' name, and in the power and demonstration of the Holy Spirit. The book of Acts traces in fuller detail the pattern and progress of the Church filled with the Spirit.

[28] Luke 4:1.
[29] Luke 4:14.

Chapter 2

The New Nation

BEFORE EXAMINING THE WITNESS of the book of Acts, some preliminary hermeneutical and theological presuppositions need statement and clarification. Certain events associated with the transition from the old covenant to the new covenant have an immediate bearing on the subject. It is no exaggeration to say that an understanding of the interrelationships of these events is essential to the interpretation of the experience of Jesus' disciples with the Holy Spirit at Pentecost.

The point of departure in the consideration of these events is a post-resurrection experience of Jesus' disciples frequently identified as the "Johannine Pentecost."[1] The fourth evangelist recorded the circumstances of the event thus: On the evening of the resurrection day, the disciples were huddled behind locked doors fearing arrest as fellow conspirators with a convicted "felon." Suddenly Jesus stood in their midst. Exposing first the tokens of His passion in His flesh to their skeptical gaze, He addressed them with the familiar greeting, "Peace be with you." It was the sight of His wounds that confirmed the fact of His resurrection, and changed doubt into joyous recognition. Their faith thus quickened served as the catalyst for what followed, for "He breathed[2] on them and said, 'Receive the Holy Spirit.'"[3]

Observe the time, the evening of the resurrection day, and the setting, a frightened, doubt-ridden group of disciples cringing

[1] The mooted question of a Johannine Pentecost will be discussed in the next chapter.

[2] Gk., ἐνεφύσησεν, *breathe into/upon, inflate*. H. G. Liddell and R. Scott, *A Greek-English Lexicon*, eds. H. S. Jones and R. McKenzie (Oxford: Clarendon Press, 1940).

[3] John 20:22.

behind locked doors, fearing imminent arrest as followers of the recently crucified Nazarene. For them hope had been turned into despair by the events of Gethsemane, Golgotha, and the garden tomb.

Their personal grief was compounded by the recollection of His prophetic judgment pronounced upon their holy city, Jerusalem.[4] The city that killed the prophets and rejected the messianic overtures of Jesus, would find her "house[5] left desolate."[6] For them the words must have had an ominous ring. Did they signify an impending national catastrophe—perhaps another "Babylonian" exile? How was this pronouncement of doom to be interpreted in the light of the longed-for messianic kingdom? The implied threat to their theocratic hopes could only have intensified their apprehensions.

During the passion week, when confronted with the rejection of His messianic claims by Israel's leaders (their fury shortly to erupt in the mass denunciation, "Crucify, crucify Him"),[7] Jesus had pronounced a solemn sentence of interdict upon the ancient covenant nation, i.e., "the kingdom of God shall be taken away from you, and shall be given to a nation bringing forth the fruits thereof."[8] This was a proclamation of far-reaching consequences for the understanding of the transition from the old to the new covenant.

"We have no king but Caesar," responded the chief priests to Pilate's question, "Shall I crucify your King?"[9] Categorically they rejected Him, and just as categorically "Great David's greater Son"[10] revoked Israel's theocratic status.

With the crucifixion of Jesus, the older covenant promulgated at Sinai ceased to be efficacious. Until the death of Jesus the

[4] Matt. 23:37–39.

[5] Matt. 23:38, *οἶκος*, *house* in a wider sense, *city*; Walter Bauer, *A Greek-English Lexicon of the New Testament and Other Early Christian Literature*, trans. and adapt., William F. Arndt and F. Wilbur Gingrich (4th ed.; Chicago: University of Chicago Press, 1957). Exegetical opinion is divided between *temple* and *city*. Both figure in the context.

[6] Matt. 23:37, 38; cf. the textual variant *ἔρημος*, *a desert*: H(esch.) R(Byz.) D(Bezae) θ pl lat. Nestle–Aland, op. cit.

[7] Luke 23:21

[8] Matt. 21:43.

[9] John 19:15.

[10] J. Montgomery, "Hail to the Lord's Anointed," *Christian Worship, A Hymnal* (Philadelphia: Judson Press, 1941), p. 257.

Messiah, His disciples were as much "saved" as Abraham, Isaac, Jacob, Moses, or any of the other Old Testament believers. Their relationship with, and access to, God were comprehended under the terms of the older covenant. However, the disciples had heard their Master pronounce judicial sentence of excommunication against the nation of Israel. This could mean only one thing to them personally. Their covenant privileges and prerogatives must cease, therefore, with those of the nation of which they were a part. They were suspended in favor of a new nation. They had yet to learn that the "new nation" was the Church.[11] The older theocracy was to be superseded by the new kingdom,[12] the ecclesia of the Messiah. Hence, their bewilderment was compounded not only by the death of Jesus, but also by the portent of spiritual as well as temporal desolation of their beloved nation.

Their preoccupation with the idea of Israel's loss of the kingdom is brought into clearer focus when the edict of Jesus—"the kingdom of God will be taken from you"—is compared with the anxious question the disciples addressed to their risen Lord on the mount of the ascension: "Lord, will you at this time restore the kingdom to Israel?"[13] The urgency of their query is underscored by the circumstances under which they asked it. At such a time, and under such circumstances, one may justifiably assume that there were scores of unanswered questions they would have wanted to ask Him. Why then is such priority given to this one question? It is the only one recorded for posterity out of this last earthly conversation between Jesus and His closest followers. The context suggests the answer.

During the forty days of post-resurrection appearances, Jesus taught them further "the things concerning the kingdom of God."[14] Apparently no additional details relating to the restoration of Israel's theocratic status were given at that time, only the cryptic promise of power[15] through a unique "baptism in the Holy Spirit"[16] that would equip them for a universal mission. Details of

[11] I Pet. 2:9.

[12] Rev. 1:6; 5:10.

[13] Acts 1:6.

[14] Acts 1:3.

[15] Acts 1:8. "you will receive power when the Holy Spirit has come upon you; and you will be my witnesses both in Jerusalem, and in all Judaea and Samaria, and to the end of the earth.

[16] Acts 1:5: "John baptized with water; but you shall be baptized in the

such a restoration must await the fuller revelation promised to the apostles as a ministry of the Paraclete, who would make known to them "the things that are to come."[17] It is the still future restoration which the Apostle Paul declared was contingent upon the appointed time when "the fulness of the Gentiles be come in [i.e., into the Church] and so all Israel shall be saved."[18] Thus by inspiration of the Holy Spirit, he foretold the future conversion of Israel, for "Israel a Christian nation, Israel a nation a part of the Messianic kingdom is the content of his thought."[19]

However, before this can take place, the Church must accomplish its worldwide, age-long ministry of evangelization both to Jew and to Gentile. In His eschatological discourses on the eve of His crucifixion, Jesus declared that the gospel of the kingdom must be proclaimed in the whole world as a prelude to the consummation of the age.[20] Therefore, cryptic though Jesus' answer to their question must appear—"you will receive power when the Holy Spirit has come upon you; and you will be my witnesses . . . to the end of the earth"—His reply contained in germ the fuller answer given later by Paul. True, His answer would not be understood by them beforehand. Only when it became a vital part of their own experience did the answer to their question begin to unfold. In the very act of evangelizing the nations, they were setting the stage for Israel's eventual restoration.

A concrete illustration of this fact is found in Peter's discourse to the curious multitude in the temple after the healing of the crippled beggar before the gate called Beautiful. Calling for repentance is the precondition for sending (again) the Messiah appoinited, that is Jesus, he continued, "whom the heavens must receive until the times of restoration of all things,[21] whereof God spoke by the mouth of His holy prophets."

Holy Spirit not many days hence."

[17] John 16:13.

[18] Rom. 11:25, 26.

[19] J. Denny, *St. Paul's Epistle to the Romans*, ed., W. R. Nicoll, Vol. II, *The Expositor's Greek Testament* (Grand Rapids: Eerdmans, [n.d.]), p. 683.

[20] Matt. 24:14.

[21] Acts 3:21, ἄχρι χρόνων ἀποκαταστάσεως, "wherein the state lost and to be restored is to be conceived as that of the obedience of the theocracy toward God and His messenger": H. A. W. Meyer, *Critical and Exegetical Handbook to the Book of the Acts of the Apostles*, trans. P. J. Gloag, IV (4th German ed.; New York: Funk & Wagnalls, 1883), p. 84.

In conformity with the mission strategy outlined by the Lord himself, the evangelization of the world was to begin with Jerusalem and Judaea, then to branch out to Samaria, and finally radiate throughout the whole world. The evangel His disciples were commissioned to proclaim was the gospel of the kingdom of God, entrance into which was predicated upon individual repentance and a personal acceptance of Jesus by faith. Clearly Peter, and one must logically conclude the whole Church too, had grasped something of the implications in Jesus' answer to their question, when after Pentecost they committed themselves unreservedly to the implementation of the Great Commission.

A digression is in order at this point. If Jesus implied in His answer to the disciples' question that full knowledge of these things was veiled to Him before His ascension, then this limitation of knowledge was removed after His glorification. In the opening words of the book of the Revelation, which bears his name, John stated unequivocally that this is "the Revelation of Jesus Christ, which God gave him to show unto His servants, even the things which must shortly come to pass."[22] After Jesus' ascension all self-imposed limitations of His incarnation[23] were removed, and the Father gave to the Son knowledge of details to reveal to His Church. Consequently, Jesus' teaching before His ascension, "the things pertaining to the kingdom of God," omitted details concerning Israel's future relationship to the kingdom in a national sense. These details were supplied by the Holy Spirit whose function it was to guide them into all truth.[24]

Most important for the immediate discussion is that their question clearly indicates their awareness that the rejection of Israel, the termination of its theocratic status announced by Jesus *before* His crucifixion, was already in effect *before* His ascension.

With the suspension of Israel's theocratic prerogatives, the way was cleared for the inauguration of the new nation. The disciples of Jesus, passing from life under the Mosaic covenant to the new covenant of our Lord and Savior Jesus Christ, were not exempted from the conditions of the new covenant. They too must meet the preconditions for entrance into the new nation,

[22] Rev. 1:1.

[23] Phil. 2:7, ἑαυτὸν ἐκένωσεν, *he emptied himself*, "divested himself of his privileges" [not of His deity] (Bauer, Arndt, Gingrich).

[24] John 16:13.

i.e., "unless a man is born again" he can neither see nor enter the kingdom of God.[25] The incredulous reaction of Nicodemus to the words of Jesus—"how can a man be born when he is old, can he enter a second time into his mother's womb, and be born?"[26]—suggests that "Nicodemus was probably familiar with the notion of rebirth for proselytes to Judaism for the Gentiles, but not with the idea that a Jew had to be reborn."[27]

This concept of an individual spiritual rebirth marked an advance over their previous religious experience under the Old Testament economy. True, the benefits of Christ's atonement are retroactive to the Old Testament believer, for it is written that "Abraham believed God, and it was reckoned unto him for righteousness."[28] However, whatever the quality of spiritual experience deduced from this for the individual under the Mosaic covenant (and one has but to read passages like the moving pentential Psalm 51 to realize how deep and personal was this experience), one must still recognize its incompleteness. The writer of the epistle to the Hebrews, after calling the roll of Old Testament heroes of faith, concluded by saying, "these won a glowing testimony to their faith, but they did not then and there receive the fulfillment of the promise."[29]

In the words of one commentator, "they lived and died in the hope, but not the possession of the spiritual blessings vouchsafed to the days of the manifested Messiah and of the Better Covenant."[30] In sharp contrast is Peter's affirmation; "he has granted to us his precious and exceeding great promises" whereby the New Testament believers "become sharers[31] in the divine nature."

Before Christ's death and resurrection, His disciples were "saved" by faith looking forward to the ultimate reality of His atoning death and resurrection. After His resurrection all the benefits of the atonement, which had been theirs by anticipation,

[25] John 3:3, 5.

[26] John 3:4.

[27] A. T. Robertson, *Word Pictures in the New Testament*, V (New York: Harper & Brothers, 1932), p. 45.

[28] Rom. 4:3.

[29] Heb. 11:39; J. B. Phillips, trans., the *New Testament in Modern English*.

[30] A. C. Kendrick, *Commentary on the Epistle to the Hebrews*, ed., A. Hovey, Vol. VI, *An American Commentary on the New Testament* (Philadelphia: American Baptist Publication Society, 1889), p. 164.

[31] II Pet. 1:4, *κοινωνός* (Bauer, Arndt, Gingrich).

became theirs in experience. This was consummated by their personal identification, by faith, with Jesus Christ in His resurrection life.

Inasmuch as His death and resurrection are events in history, so also the disciples' participation in His resurrection life was effected at a specific point in history. His resurrection is the source of our spiritual regeneration, and it is a personal participation, by faith, in His resurrection life that constitutes the experience of the new birth. Peter speaks to this very point in the following words: "Praise be to the God and Father of our Lord Jesus Christ, who in his mercy gave us *new birth* into a living hope *by the resurrection* of Jesus from the dead."[32]

The apostolic community was no exception to the rule enunciated by Jesus. It too must be born again of the Holy Spirit in order to enter the kingdom of God. The new nation to whom the kingdom is now committed, is not a homogeneous ethnic group. It is an election of God's grace "out of every nation and of *all* tribes and peoples and tongues,"[33] who have "washed their robes, and made them white in the blood of the Lamb."[34]

[32] I Pet. 1:3, italics added.
[33] Rev. 7:9.
[34] Rev. 7:14.

Chapter 3

The Paschal Impartation of the Spirit

WHEN, THEREFORE, were the disciples of Jesus born again? In other words, when did they pass from the sphere and influence of the old covenant to the privileges and responsibilities of the new covenant?

Some have assumed that this took place before the crucifixion when Jesus said to them, "Rejoice that your names are recorded[1] in heaven." Others have seen in Peter's confession of the deity of Jesus—"You are the Messiah, the Son of the living God"[2]—evidence that he was born again. But all such suggestions ignore the fact that the covenant of Sinai was still in force. True, there is no past, present, or future in the mind of God "who inhabits eternity,"[3] but on the plane of time and space, there is a definite chronological unfolding of the divine purposes, for God himself is the author of times and seasons, of days and years.[4] The new covenant had not yet been promulgated. Even our Lord Jesus was born subject to the conditions of the old covenant, as the Scriptures testify, for "when the fulness of time came, God sent forth His Son, born of a woman, born under the Law.[5]

The foregoing assumptions are, therefore, really anachronistic. They imply that Jesus' disciples entered the new covenant while their Lord was still subject to the provisions of Sinai's legal

[1] Luke 10:20, ἐγγέγραπται, *recorded* (Bauer, Arndt, Gingrich).
[2] Matt. 16:16.
[3] Isa. 57:15. Heb., *šoken ʿad*, *living forever*.
[4] Gen. 1:14.
[5] Gal. 4:4

covenant. This, of course, cannot be true, for "the abolition of the law, the rescue from bondage, was a prior condition of the universal sonship of the faith."[6] This prior condition was accomplished only by the death and resurrection of Jesus Christ. It is only by identification with Him in His death and resurrection that we are enabled to "walk in[7] newness of life."

Still others have equated the outpouring of the Holy Spirit upon the Church at Pentecost with the beginning of the new covenant. It is this assumption that underlies the oft-repeated cliché, "Pentecost is the birthday of the Church." This, however, is tantamount to saying that the disciples of Jesus were born again by the descent of the Holy Spirit on that day.[8] This in turn has led to the self-defeating assumption that at conversion all believers are filled automatically with the Spirit.

As a matter of fact, none of these views quite squares with the biblical evidence. There remains, however, a fruitful avenue of investigation already suggested, and now to be explored. Its starting point is the passage from John's Gospel already cited, viz., John 20:19–23.

Fundamental to the interpretation of this passage is the acknowledgement that the deeds, no less than the words, of Jesus have didactic significance. In other words, the Master taught by His acts as well as by His words. This will be difficult, if not impossible to acknowledge for those for whom truth is exclusively propositional. Nonetheless, it is regarded as self-evident within the context of the present discussion. Justification for this thesis is found in the fact that redemptive truth is not merely propositional, it is essentially incarnational.

Note then that having entered the upper room where His followers were gathered together, He first allayed their quite

[6] J. B. Lightfoot, *Saint Paul's Epistle to the Galatians* (London: Macmillan, 1896), p. 169.

[7] Rom. 6:4, "The state in which one lives or ought to live is designated by ἐν" (Bauer, Arndt, Gingrich).

[8] For a popular exposition of this view see G. C. Morgan, *The Acts of the Apostles* (New York: Revell, 1924), pp. 28, 29.

But here upon the day of Pentecost, that which happened was not merely the renewal of the life of these men; it was the imparting to them of a new germ of life, something they never had before . . . there was given to them the life of Christ, the Incarnate One; so that there came to these men that which made them one with Him and with each other, and constituted their membership in the Church of the first-born.

natural apprehensions, saying, "Peace be with you."[9] Next he exposed the wounds of His passion in His hands and side for their inspection. Thus He authenticated for them the fact of His bodily resurrection. Such tangible evidence was needed since they were reluctant to accept the testimony of those who were the first to see Him after His resurrection.[10] Yet faith in His resurrection is a precondition of salvation, for "if you confess with your mouth Jesus as Lord and believe in your heart that God raised Him from the dead, you will be saved."[11]

With faith in His resurrection powerfully stimulated by this tangible evidence, they were prepared for what followed, for "He breathed on them, and said to them, 'Receive the Holy Spirit.'"[12] In the exposition of this passage, the meaning of Jesus' words must be weighed in their relation to His action in breathing on them. Some interpreters have seen this as "a symbolic act with the same word used in the LXX when God breathed the breath of life upon Adam (Gen. 2:7)."[13] This act of breathing on His disciples "was meant to convey the impression that his own very Spirit was imparted to them."[14] The universal and natural symbol of life is breath, and "in the Bible it is used as a symbol of divine life."[15] Yet in a more realistic sense, it was much more than merely symbolic,

[9] In the light of the context—"for fear of the Jews" (v. 19)—the traditional greeting, *šālōm lākem* meant more than a casual greeting, e.g., Hello!

[10] Mark 16:14: "And afterwards He was manifested unto the eleven themselves as they were reclining at table; and He upbraided them with their unbelief and hardness of heart, because they did not believe them that had seen Him after He was risen."

[11] Rom. 10:9.

[12] John 20:22.

[13] Robertson, *Word Pictures*, V, p. 314.

[14] M. Dods, *The Gospel of St. John*, ed., W. R. Nicoll, Vol. I, *The Expositor's Greek Testament* (Grand Rapids: Eerdmans, [n.d.]), p. 865.

He breathed on them, "ἐνεφύσησε"; the same word is used in Gen ii.7 to describe the distinction between Adam's "living soul," *breathed* into him by God, and the life principle of the other animals.

[15] L. Abbott, *An Illustrated Commentary on the Gospels* (New York: A. S. Barnes & Company, 1906), p. 230.

God breathes into man the breath of life (Gen. 2:7); in the vision of Ezekiel the wind breathes on the dry bones and clothes them with life (Ezek. 37:9, 10); in Christ's conversation with Nicodemus the life-giving power of God is compared to the breath of wind (ch. 3:8), and it is significant of the extent to which this symbol underlies Scripture that the Greek word used for spirit is the one also used for wind, which is poetically represented as the breath of God.

for the natural sense of the expression implies that "some gift was offered and bestowed then and there."[16] Consequently, by a direct impartation Jesus infused His disciples with "that divine life which man never *acquires*, which God alone can give."[17]

This experience was not simply a promise, an anticipation of the greater effusion to be poured out upon them at Pentecost. The word here translated "receive"[18] "cannot *merely promise* a reception belonging to the *future*, but expresses a reception actually present."[19] The force of this verb in the aorist tense, imperative mood is "receive right here and now,"[20] thereby "implying that the recipient may welcome or reject the gift: he is not a passive receptacle."[21] What Jesus bestowed on them, and they received, "is not a simple promise, but neither is it the fulness of the Spirit. . . . As at Pentecost He will initiate them into His ascension, so by breathing on them now He associates them with His life as the Risen One."[22]

The resurrection day, therefore, marks the beginning of the new creation. As in the former creation, man received life by the breath of God, so at the beginning of the new creation His disciples received new, spiritual life—they were born again—by the breath of God, the Son. It is this breath of the risen Son of God that is not only the source, but also the pledge of that eternal life[23] bestowed on all who subsequently "believe on the Son."[24]

There is one objection to this view that requires an answer.

[16] A. Plummer, *The Gospel According to St. John*, Vol. XXXVI, *The Cambridge Bible for Schools and Colleges* (Cambridge: University Press, 1923), p. 362.

[17] Abbott, loc. cit.

[18] λάβετε, aorist imperative, *receive*; H. E. Dana and J. Mantey, *A Manual Grammar of the Greek New Testament* (New York: Macmillan 1955), p. 300.

The Aorist Imperative in Commands. When the aorist imperative is used it denotes *summary* action—"an action that is either transient or instantaneous . . . or to be undertaken at once" (W. 313).

[19] H. A. W. Meyer, *Critical and Exegetical Hand-Book to the Gospel of John*, trans. W. Urwick, III (5th German ed.; New York: Funk & Wagnalls, 1884), p. 533.

[20] Dana and Mantey, loc. cit.

[21] Plummer, op. cit., p. 362.

[22] F. Godet, *Commentary on the Gospel of St. John*, trans. S. Taylor and M. D. Cusin, Vol. III Clark's Foreign Theological Library, 4th series, LVI (3rd ed.; Edinburgh: T. & T. Clark, 1900), p. 321.

[23] Chr. Wordsworth, *The New Testament of Our Lord and Saviour Jesus Christ, in the Original Greek*, I (7th ed.; Rivingtons, 1870), p. 321.

[24] John 3:36.

This is the proposition that John 20:19–23 "is Pentecost itself, so far as it was known to the evangelist."[25] In support of this view, it is claimed that "this scene is for John almost certainly the counterpart of Pentecost; for . . . he 'telescopes' Resurrection, Ascension, and Pentecost into one event of 'glorification.'"[26] But the same writer concedes that there are "occasional hints . . . of the survival of the point of view of the Synoptists, who regard Resurrection, Ascension, Parousia, as three events distinct in space and time."[27] By parity of reasoning then, Pentecost is also an event distinct in space and time, and is not to be conflated into a Johannine Pentecost.

Such assumptions reflect an attempt to unravel the prehistory of the biblical text. The methodology is frequently flawed by its unproven assumptions about the "free creation and flow of tradition"[28]—the hypothesis of independent and often contradictory sources of the biblical narratives. A cogent rebuttal to such a hermeneutic is the recognition of the regulative influence of the apostles themselves upon the biblical tradition. The visit of Paul to Jerusalem to confer with "those who were recognized[29] as pillars" in the Church—among whom James, Peter, *and* John are singled out for special mention—illustrates the point that "there was an authoritative source of information about the facts and doctrines of Christianity in the apostolic collegium in Jerusalem."[30] It cannot be conceded, therefore, that John in his account of the resurrection day makes a concession to the more primitive(?)[31] tradition of the synoptists, which he preserved in

[25] Bauer's view according to Godet, op. cit., p. 321. This view is generally accepted today among biblical scholars.

[26] G. H. C. Macgregor, *The Gospel of John*, ed. J. Moffatt, Vol. I, *The Moffatt New Testament Commentary* (New York: Harper & Brothers [n.d.]), p. 365. W. F. Howard *The Gospel According to St. John*, ed. G. A. Buttrick, et al., Vol. VIII, *The Interpreter's Bible* (Nashville: Abingdon-Cokesbury Press, 1952), p. 796. "This gift of the Spirit could be bestowed only after the glorification (i.e., the resurrection) of Christ, according to the view of the evangelist."

[27] Macgregor, op. cit., p. 360.

[28] C. H. Pinnock, "The Case Against Form Criticism," *Christianity Today*, IX, 21 (July 1965), pp. 12, 13.

[29] Gal. 2:9, οἱ δοκοῦντες, *be influential*, *be recognized as being somth.*, *have a reputation* (Bauer, Arndt, Gingrich).

[30] Pinnock, op. cit., p. 12.

[31] W. F. Albright, *From Stone Age to Christianity* 2nd ed.; Garden City: Anchor Books, 1957), p. 383. Cf. his appraisal of C. C. Torrey's thesis of Aramaic originals for the Gospels. "Torrey concludes that all the Gospels were

form, but spiritualized to such an extent that he virtually denied its substance.[32]

John was present with the rest of the apostles on the day of Pentecost, and it is hardly likely that the dramatic events of that day should be confused in his mind with the equally momentous happenings on the resurrection day. The Holy Spirit, the Paraclete, is presented in Jesus' farewell discourse "as practically equivalent to the presence of the risen exalted Jesus—His alter ego (vi. 16–18; xvi. 7)."[33] In point of fact, John stated clearly that Jesus' ascension was the precondition for the coming of the Holy Spirit. "It is to your advantage," said Jesus, "that I go away, for if I do not go away, the Paraclete will not come to you; but if I go, *I will send Him to you*."[34] In the Paraclete sayings, John looked beyond the resurrection to the ascension of Jesus for the coming of the promised Holy Spirit. It is in His absence that He is to *send* the Spirit to them, an apparent reference to the Pentecostal effusion of the Spirit poured out by Jesus after His ascension.[35]

Thus when John 20:22 is compared with the Paraclete sayings, especially John 16:7, it is indeed probable that "John would know of two bestowals of the Spirit, though recording only one, and the promised baptism in the Spirit (1.33) could easily be referred to the unrecorded Pentecost."[36] The facts of the case are

---

written before 70 A.D., and that there is nothing in them which could not have been written within twenty years of the Crucifixion." More recently J. A. T. Robinson, *Redating the New Testament* (Philadelphia: Westminster Press, 1976), has dated all four Gospels between A.D. 40 and A.D. 65+. The Dead Sea Scrolls have also been thought to point to an early date for John's Gospel. Cf. G. A. Turner, "A Decade of Studies in John's Gospel," *Christianity Today*, IX, 5 (Dec. 1964), 5, 6.

[32] Macgregor, quoting Scott op. cit., p. 362.

[33] R. H. Strachan, *The Fourth Gospel Its Significance and Environment* (3rd ed.; London: SCM 1941), p. 288.

[34] John 16:7, italics added.

[35] Acts 2:33.

[36] J. D. G. Dunn, *Baptism in the Holy Spirit* (Philadelphia: Westminster Press, 1979), p. 177.

> It may be best, therefore, to interpret the Paraclete promises of 14.16, 26, 15.26 and 16.7 *not of 20.22* (which is not naturally described as a 'sending' of the Spirit, especially by or from the Father), but to a later bestowal of the Spirit, following Jesus' final return to the Father after his various appearances to the disciples. John's account could then dovetail chronologically into the Acts narrative: John would know of two bestowals of the Spirit, though recording only one, and the promised baptism in the Spirit (1.33) could easily be referred to the unrecorded

succinctly summarized thus: "there was therefore a Paschal as distinct from a Pentecostal gift of the Holy Spirit, the one preparatory to the other."[37]

In addition to the evidence of the Johannine Paraclete sayings, two other objections to the idea of a Johannine Pentecost merit consideration. (1) There is a clear time-lapse between the resurrection and Pentecost[38] that can only be harmonized by introducing a radical disjuncture into the intention of the context. (2) As already noted, the Paschal bestowal of the Holy Spirit was ontological; it involved a change of nature, a new birth. The sending of the Spirit upon the disciples at Pentecost was functional, i.e., empowerment for service.

John 20:19–23 is, therefore, of crucial importance for an understanding of the Holy Spirit's ministry to the Church. It is not a record of a Johannine Pentecost; rather, it marks the transition from the terms of the old covenant to those of the new covenant. As God imparted life by breathing His breath into Adam on the day of the former creation, so also God the Son imparted a new spiritual life to His followers by breathing the Holy Spirit into them on the resurrection day, the day of the new creation.[39] Accordingly, His disciples enter the new covenant through the new birth. The new nation whose responsibility it now became to bring forth the fruits of the kingdom of God, thus displaced the older theocracy. The stage was now set for the acting out of the next scenes in the drama of redemption.

It is essential to note further, that the transition in theocratic status from Judaism, as an ethnic and political entity, to the Church was accomplished before the book of Acts opens. Acts

---

Pentecost. (Italics added)

In the light of Dunn's antipentecostal polemic, this concession to the Pentecostal hermeneutic is all the more remarkable. His attempt, however, to evade the consequences of these admissions by dispensationalizing their significance is examined and rejected in my critique of his position. See my ***Conversion-Initiation and the Baptism in the Holy Spirit*** (Peabody: Hendrickson Publishers, Inc., 1984).

[37] Plummer, op. cit., p. 362.

[38] Dunn, op. cit., p. 362. "On any reckoning the οὔπω (20.17) preserves a clear enough time-lapse between resurrection and ascension."

[39] John's preoccupation with the (new) creation motif is clearly foreshadowed in the Prologue with its pregnant allusion to the creation account in Genesis (John 1:1–5).

does not contain such a transitional phase. There is no second offer of the kingdom to national Israel in its pages, for the transition from Judaism to the Church involved not only Israel's rejection of Jesus as her sovereign, but also Messiah's rejection of Israel as the theocratic nation[40]—a rejection consummated in the crucifixion of Jesus. Therefore, when the disciples preached the gospel in Acts, they were not addressing the good news to Judaism as a corporate entity. They addressed the gospel to them individually and ethnically. To miss this distinction is to miss an important point in Peter's quotation of the prophecy of Joel, viz., "whoever calls on the name of the Lord shall be saved."[41] Observe closely that it is an appeal for individual rather than corporate decision.

Thus beginning with this, the first public proclamation of the gospel by the apostles, the appeal is addressed to individual Jews, and not to the Jewish nation corporately. The Apostle Paul placed this interpretation beyond a reasonable doubt. He explicitly divested it of any exclusively national application. This is all the more noteworthy since it occurs in a context in which he dealt at length with the mystery of Judah's excommunication, and ultimate restoration; "For there is no distinction between Jew and Greek; the same Lord is Lord of all and bestows His riches upon all who call upon Him. For, 'whoever calls[42] upon the name of the Lord will be saved.'" Paul characteristically declared that the *whoever* of the gospel does not distinguish between Jew and Gentile.

[40] Matt. 21:43.
[41] Acts 2:21, *ὅς ἐὰν ἐπικαλέσηται.*
[42] Rom. 10:12, 13, *ὅς ἄν ἐπικαλέσηται.*

Chapter 4

The Promise of the Father

THE GOSPEL OF LUKE CLOSES with the pledge of Jesus to His disciples: "Behold, I send the promise[1] of my Father upon you; but stay in the city, until you are clothed with power from on high."[2] The book of Acts opens with a reaffirmation of the promise, for He charged them again "not to depart from Jerusalem, but to wait for the promise of the Father, which He said, 'you heard from me, for John baptized with water, but before many days you shall be baptized with the Holy Spirit.'"[3] To what does the promise refer? The context makes it clear that it is the baptism in the Holy Spirit. More precisely "the promise is the Spirit spoken of in prophetic oracles,"[4] for "the Holy Spirit is the divine promise par excellence."[5] It is the same "promise of the Spirit" we receive through faith;[6] the same "Holy Spirit of promise" in whom we are sealed[7] now poured forth in Pentecostal fulness.

[1] ἐπαγγελία, "*what was promised, namely the Spirit* Ac 2:33; Gal 3:14. Followed by the gen. of the one who promises ε. τοῦ πατρός Luke 24:49" (Bauer, Arndt, Gingrich).

[2] Luke 24:49.

[3] Acts 1:4.

[4] A. B. Bruce, *The Synoptic Gospels*, ed. W. R. Nicoll, Vol. I, *The Expositor's Greek Testament* (Grand Rapids: Eerdmans, [n.d.]), p. 651. "(Is xliv.1; Joel ii.28)." Cf. also Ezek. 36:27; 39:29. Also H. K. Luce, ed., *The Gospel According to Luke*, Vol. XXXV, *The Cambridge Bible for Schools and Colleges* (Cambridge: University Press, 1936), p. 255.

> What was the promise referred to? One would expect a direct reference to something in the Gospel. If so it must be the prophecy of John the Baptist, "He shall baptize you with the Holy Spirit and with fire. . . ." Otherwise it must be thought that the reference is to various passages in the O.T., which promised the gift of the Spirit (Lake, p. 106).

[5] F. Godet, *A Commentary on the Gospel of St. Luke*, trans. M. D. Cusin, Vol. II, Clark's Foreign Theological Library, 4th series, XLVI (2nd ed.; Edinburgh: T. & T. Clark, 1878), p. 361.

[6] Gal. 3:14; "ἡ εὐλογία τοῦ 'ABρ. the salvation (by the Messiah) promised

Immediately after the Pentecostal effusion of the Holy Spirit, Peter, interpreting the significance of the event in the light of the resurrection and ascension, declared that Jesus "having received from the Father the promise of the Holy Spirit, He has poured out this which you see and hear."[8] Luke is not here referring to the work of the Holy Spirit in conversion and regeneration. The things "which you see and hear" can only be understood in the light of the supernatural and charismatic phenomena accompanying the Spirit's descent; e.g., "the rushing mighty wind," "divided tongues as of fire," "speaking in other tongues."[9]

In reply to the conscience-stricken inquiry of the bystanders, Peter stated the conditions for the reception of the promise: "Repent . . . be baptized (in water) . . . and you shall receive the gift of the Holy Spirit.[10] For the promise is to you and to your children

---

to Abraham." Gimmm's Wilke's, *A Greek-English Lexicon of the New Testament*, trans. & rev., J. H. Thayer (New York: American Book Company, 1889). Cf. also H. A. W. Meyer, *Critical and Exegetical Hand-Book to the Epistle to the Galatians*, trans. T. H. Venables, VII (5th German ed.; New York: Funk & Wagnalls, 1884), p. 119.

> This by no means accidental emergence of the first person [λάβωμεν], after τὰ ἔθνη had been previously spoken of in the *third*, is incompatible with our taking the reception of the Spirit as *part* of the εὐλογία (Wieseler), or as essentially *identical* with it Hofmann). The charismatic dimensions of the promise of the Spirit is spelled out in v. 5; "He who supplies (ὁ ἐπιχορηγῶν, pres. act. part.) the spirit to you and works (ἐνεργῶν, pres. act. part.) miracles among you."

[7] Eph. 1:13. A question at issue here is whether the seal of the Spirit is to be identified with the initial action of the Holy Spirit in conversion, or with the subsequent baptism in the Holy Spirit. Both interpretations have been suggested. On the one hand, Eph. 1:13 is interpreted "of those who enter the Christian fellowship as being sealed with or by the Holy Spirit" (Bauer, Arndt, Gingrich). This would make πιστεύσαντες and ἐσφραγίσθητε contemporaneous. However, Meyer (op. cit., p. 331), comments that πιστεύσαντες "is not to be taken, with Herless, as contemporaneous with ἐσφραγ. . . . but it contains that which is prior to the σφραγίζεσθαι." In II Cor. 1:22 "σφ(ραγισάμενος) obviously means more than just 'provide w(ith) a mark of identification.' Rather it = 'endue with power from heaven,' as plainly in J(ohn) 6:27" (Bauer, Arndt, Gingrich). This may well be the intent of Eph. 1:13, in which case Gal. 3:14 (above) and Eph. 1:13 offer support to the Pentecostal view.

[8] Acts 2:33.

[9] Acts 2:2–4.

[10] Acts 2:38. The thesis of a Johannine Pentecost implies a univocal harmonization of John's theology of the Spirit with Luke's pneumatology. Its conclusions are implicit in its assumptions, namely that both John and Luke share the same perspective on the person and work of the Holy Spirit. That is to say, that the Johannine insufflation of the Spirit on the resurrection day (John

and to all that are far off, every one whom the Lord our God calls to Him."[11] Here again the Apostle Peter described the Pentecostal gift of the Holy Spirit as the promise, i.e., "the promise made by Jesus (1:4) and foretold by Joel (v. 8)."[12] Each reference to the promised gift of the Holy Spirit in Luke's Gospel and the Acts must be interpreted contextually with full recognition of the supernatural and charismatic phenomena accompanying it. To subordinate the context to an a priori theological overlay is to distort the author's intention.

In the Pentecostal hermeneutic, repentance, faith, and water-baptism constitute conversion and initiation into the new covenant community. Repentance and faith are the results of the Spirit's action in the spiritual experience of the convert. These elements are the conditions for the new birth from above,[13] for apart from the Holy Spirit convicting of sin[14] there can be neither repentance nor faith. They are, therefore, sequentially prior to the Lukan gift of the Holy Spirit.

Only by an arbitrary harmonizing of Luke's theology of the Spirit with John's theology of the Spirit can the Lukan gift of the Holy Spirit be equated with the Johannine new birth from above. John's primary concern is with the work of the Spirit in creation and life, and this theme is introduced in the beginning of John's Gospel.[15] Luke, on the other hand, stresses the Pentecostal gift of the Holy Spirit for power in life and witness.[16]

On the one hand, John's new birth from above is ontological.

20:22) is identical with the Lukan "gift of the Holy Spirit" (Acts 2:38) on Pentecost. Such assumptions, however, serve only to trivialize the hermeneutical task. In John's pneumatology, the action of the Holy Spirit is *ontological*. Those who receive the incarnate Word receive also the right (ἐξουσίαν) to be born (ἐγεννήθησαν) children of God (John 1:12, 13). In Luke's theology of the Spirit, the effect of the Pentecostal gift of the Spirit is *functional*. The key word in John is *γεννάω*, *to beget*. In John 3:5 the phrase *γεννηθῇ ἐξ ὕδατος καὶ πνεύματος*, is "an expression which denotes the commencement of a new personal life, traceable to a (creative) act of God." H. Cremer, *Biblico-Theological Lexicon of New Testament Greek*, trans. D. W. Simon and W. Urwick (Edinburgh: T. & T. Clark, 1872), p. 120. In Luke the key word is *δύναμις*, *power in action* (Cremer, op. cit., p. 200).

[11] Acts 2:38, 39.

[12] Robertson, *Word Pictures*, III, p. 36.

[13] John 3:3.

[14] John 16:8f.; cf. Acts 11:18.

[15] John 1:1–17.

[16] Acts 1:8.

It is a change of nature; the Lukan gift of the Spirit is functional. By its very nature, spiritual rebirth is observable only in and through the attributes of a transformed life, a life characterized by the fruits of the Spirit.[17] On the other hand, the Pentecostal gift of the Holy Spirit is manifested in the charisms of the Spirit, e.g., tongues, prophecy, healings, et al. These are substantive distinctions that must not be blurred in the interpretation.

It should now be self-evident that "the promise of my Father,"[18] "the promise of the Father,"[19] "the promise of the Holy Spirit,"[20] and the promised "gift of the Holy Spirit,"[21] are all allusions to the Pentecostal experience,[22] which Jesus described as being "baptized in the Holy Spirit."[23] Luke, though, characterized the Pentecostal experience as being "filled with the Holy Spirit."[24] Things equal to the same thing are equal to each other. Contextually, the terms baptized in the Holy Spirit and filled with the Holy Spirit are used interchangeably as related aspects of the same experience. Suffice it then to say, that the baptism in the Holy Spirit results in one being permeated by, and filled to overflowing with the presence and power of the Holy Spirit.

In addition, Luke recorded the phrase "baptized in the Holy Spirit" only twice in the book of Acts: (1) in the passage already referred to, Acts 1:5, and (2) in Acts 11:16. In the latter instance, Peter quoted these words of Jesus in his own defense to those, "of the circumcision party"[25] in the church at Jerusalem, who contended with him for breaking the ritual law[26] by entering the house of the Gentile centurion, Cornelius. In every other place where Luke made reference to the Pentecostal baptism in the Holy Spirit, he employed such phrases as "the Holy Spirit came

[17] Gal. 5:22. The fruits (καρπός though singular in form is a collective noun) are a graphic metaphor of spiritual life.

[18] Luke 24:49.

[19] Acts 1:4.

[20] Acts 2:33.

[21] Acts 2:38, 39.

[22] Acts 2:4.

[23] Acts 1:5.

[24] Acts 2:4.

[25] Acts 11:2.

[26] Acts 11:3; "*kashruth* (ritual lawfulness, especially of food)" (R. Alcalay, *The Complete Hebrew-English Dictionary* [Jerusalem: Massada Publishing Co., n.d.], p. 1073). Peter was accused of having countenanced table fellowship with the uncircumcised.

upon,"[27] "filled with the Holy Spirit,"[28] "received the Holy Spirit,"[29] "the Holy Spirit fell upon,"[30] and "the gift of the Holy Spirit was poured out."[31]

A fundamental point of disagreement among interpreters is the question of the repetition, hence the continuity, of the Pentecostal baptism in the Holy Spirit. *Was it*, as some affirm, a once-and-for-all event in the Church's history—a sort of cosmic shove to get things rolling? Or *is it* a contemporary experience that can, and does, recur in the experience of successive generations of believers? To those engaged in the present Pentecostal dialogue, this issue is often sharply drawn. On the one hand, it is axiomatic to Pentecostals, that the baptism in the Holy Spirit did not expire with Pentecost, nor even with the close of the apostolic age. They believe, and their experience confirms, that it is the birthright of every Christian and represents the biblical norm for the Spirit-filled life. On the other hand, there are those who categorically affirm, that "the baptism of the Holy Spirit which it was the Lord's prerogative to bestow was, strictly speaking, something that took place once for all on the day of Pentecost when He poured forth 'the promise of the Father' on His disciples and thus constituted them the new people of God."[32]

The foregoing assertion, that the baptism in the Holy Spirit was "something that took place once for all on the day of Pentecost," is often repeated, but it is none the less erroneous. For instance, some ten years after the Jerusalem Pentecost,[33] Peter visited the home of the Roman centurion, Cornelius, in Caesarea. He, with his now believing household, received "the gift of the Holy Spirit."[34] Confronted with the hostility of certain of the

[27] Acts 1:8; 19:6.

[28] Acts 2:4; 4:31; 9:17.

[29] Acts 8:17.

[30] Acts 8:39, cf. the alternate reading of the Western text, *ἅγιον ἐπέσεν ἐπι τὸν εὐνοῦχον, ἄγγελος* (Nestle–Aland).

[31] Acts 10:45.

[32] F. F. Bruce, *Commentary on the Book of the Acts*, ed. F. F. Bruce, *The New International Commentary on the New Testament* (Grand Rapids: Eerdmans, 1964), p. 76. I have already argued that the disciples entered the new covenant on the resurrection day when they became "the new people of God," and not, as above, on the day of Pentecost.

[33] Ca. A.D. 40. P. Schaff, *History of the Christian Church*, I (New York: Charles Scribner's Sons, 1887), p. 220.

[34] Acts 10:45.

Jewish believers in Jerusalem who objected strenuously to Peter transgressing the ban on fraternization with Gentiles, he fended off their accusation by saying in part, "as I began to speak, the Holy Spirit fell on them, just as on us at the beginning."[35] Obviously, Peter was thus alluding to their own baptism in the Holy Spirit on the day of Pentecost. The very language used to describe both the outpouring of the Spirit in Jerusalem at Pentecost, and the pouring forth of the Holy Spirit in Caesarea more than a decade later, coupled with the charismatic phenomena evident in both cases, places the claim beyond cavil, that Pentecost was repeated in the house of Cornelius. Some have even called it "the Gentile Pentecost."

However, the baptism in the Holy Spirit bestowed upon Cornelius and his household is not the only recurrence of the Pentecostal experience in the Acts. As already demonstrated, the phrase, the gift of the Holy Spirit, is one of several synonymous designations used by Luke for the Pentecostal baptism. Cornelius and his household received "the same gift"[36] of the Holy Spirit as the first disciples at Pentecost. By his choice of words, Peter thereby stressed the identical nature of the two experiences. So also, the Samaritans "received the Holy Spirit . . . the gift of God,"[37] when Peter and John laid their hands upon them. Each of these instances constitutes a repetition of the Pentecostal "gift[38] of the Holy Spirit," in His charismatic fulness. This is the promise that Peter said is "to all that are far off,[39] every one whom the Lord our God calls to Him." Manifestly God is still calling, and by parity of reasoning, the promise of Pentecost is still in effect.

[35] Acts 11:15.

[36] Acts 11:17, *τὴν ἴσην δωρεάν*, *the same gift* (Bauer, Arndt, Gingrich).

[37] Acts 11:17, 20.

[38] Acts 2:38, "*δωρεάν* 'free gift': used of the Holy Spirit in viii.20; x.45; xi.17" (F. F. Bruce, *The Acts of the Apostles* [Grand Rapids: Eerdmans, 1960], p. 98).

[39] Acts 2:39. Certainly more than diaspora Judaism is intended as the "all flesh" of Acts 2:17 indicates. "Those 'afar off' from the Jews were the heathen (Isa. 49:19; Eph. 2:13,17). The rabbis so used it" (Robertson, op. cit., III, p. 36).

Chapter 5

Baptized into One Body

THE PENTECOSTAL SIGNIFICANCE of the phrases, the *gift* of the Holy Spirit, and the *promise* of the Father, as these are used in the book of Acts, is clearly established in each context. Unequivocally, Peter declared that the gift of the Holy Spirit is synonymous with the promise of the Father that is extended "to all that are far off, every one whom the Lord our God calls to Him."

However, dogmatic presuppositions constrain many interpreters to ignore, or to blur this evidence for the repetition and continuity of the Pentecostal baptism in the Spirit in the experience of subsequent generations of converts to the Christian faith. The gift of the Spirit, the promise of the Father, and the baptism in the Holy Spirit are thereby arbitrarily identified with conversion and the new birth from above. Two biblical texts are usually cited in support of this position. One, Acts 2:38, has already been discussed. A second supposedly biblical basis for this identification is found in Paul's words, "For by/in one Spirit we were all baptized into one body . . . and all were made to drink of one Spirit."[1]

This identification of the "baptism by/in one Spirit into one body" with conversion and regeneration prompts the somewhat rhetorical question: "Are not, then, all converts baptized by/in one Spirit into Christ's body, the Church?" The obvious inference is, "Of course they are!" It follows then that they have been baptized in the Spirit at the moment of their conversion. Therefore, the baptism in the Holy Spirit is synonymous with conversion and the new birth from above. This syllogism rests, however,

[1] I Cor. 12:13, ἐν ἑνὶ πνεύματι, *in one Spirit.*

upon the fallacious assumption that the word *baptism* is used univocally.

Because of the vehemence with which the question is often posed, one might be led to suspect that there is a hidden agenda behind such questioning. All too frequently, such questions are asked defensively to parry the implication that the Pentecostal experience is something subsequent to the experience of conversion, hence, it may not have been the experience of all converts. However, when such questions are asked in a contemporary frame of reference, it must be pointed out that they are being posed in a context of Christian experience considerably different from the one in which, and to which, Paul wrote. Such questions have currency only where the activity of the Holy Spirit is considered terminal in conversion and the new birth. Hence, the often quoted cliché: "We received all there is of the Holy Spirit in conversion."

From the proposition that Paul's words refer to the activity of the Holy Spirit in regeneration—a baptism by/in the Holy Spirit common to all believers—it is advocated as a truism that every Christian has been baptized in the Spirit in a Pentecostal sense at conversion. The truth, or error, of such deductions rests upon the meaning of Paul's words in their context and in their relation to the references to the baptism in the Spirit found in the Gospels and in the Acts.

The difficulty of the task of interpretation is compounded by the fact that this is the only text in the Pauline epistles that speaks unambiguously of a Spirit-baptism. The answers to two questions are crucial, therefore, for an understanding of the passage. (1) Is the preposition ἐν, variously translated as *by* or *in* one Spirit, to be understood as instrumental or locative? (2) Are the two verbs, "we were baptized" and "we were given to drink,"[2] to be understood as a synonymous or a synthetic parallelism?

In the translation of the preposition ἐν, the versions are divided between the instrumental *by* and the locative *in*.[3] A prec-

[2] ἐβαπτίσθημεν, *we were baptized*; ἐποτίσθημεν, *we were given to drink*. Both verbs are aorist, passive, indicative.

[3] Representative of those favoring the instrumental *by one Spirit* are: Great Bible (1539) 1540; Geneva Bible (1560) 1562; Bishop's Bible (1568) 1602; KJV 1611; RSV (1945) 1960; Phillips Modern English 1958; NASB 1960; NEB (1961) 1970; NIV (1973) 1978; NKJV (1979) 1982. The locative *in one Spirit*

edent favoring the instrumental *by* is provided by the context. It is used with πνεῦμα (Spirit) once in v. 3 and twice in v. 9 where the instrumental probably interprets best the intention of the passage. By analogy then, in v. 13 "the reference is patently that of the very common instrumental use of *en,* meaning 'with,' or 'by means of.'"[4] But is it?

The preposition *with* suggests that the Spirit is the instrument used to effect the baptism. Alternatively, the prepositional phrase *by means of* implies that the Spirit is the effectual agent of the baptism, for "baptism receives significance only if there is an activity of the Spirit."[5] In that case, activity may well be construed as agency; the Spirit is then the baptizer. However, such a usage is not consistent with Greek grammar.[6]

It may be urged against this interpretation that making the Holy Spirit the agent deprives the context of an element in which the baptism takes place. If, however, one assumes that an allusion to water-baptism is implied,[7] the force of this objection may be blunted. A sacramental potency is thereby imparted to the water by the action of the Holy Spirit. The assumption is itself consistent with Paul's use of the verb *to baptize*, and is consistent with the initiatory significance of water-baptism. In this interpretation, the convert is initiated "into the one body" by means of water-baptism which, from the spiritual viewpoint, is made efficacious by the power of the Holy Spirit.

However, the instrumental use of the preposition with the verb *to baptize* has been vigorously challenged. In the opinion of A. T. Robertson, "all the N.T. examples of *en* can be explained

---

is represented by Tyndale (1525) 1535; Rheims 1582; RV 1881; ASV 1901; Jerusalem Bible 1966; NAB 1971.

[4] M. F. Unger, *The Baptizing Work of the Holy Spirit* (Findlay: Dunham Publishing Co., 1962), p. 80: "It is proper to say 'baptism *with* the Spirit' or 'baptism *by* the Spirit,' but not 'baptism *in* the Spirit'" (p. 70).

[5] F. W. Grosheide, *Commentary on the First Epistle to the Corinthians*, ed. F. F. Bruce, *The New International Commentary on the New Testament* (Grand Rapids: Eerdmans, 1953), p. 293.

[6] "Greek: not ὑπό but ἐν, because baptism as such is not performed by the Spirit. But baptism is only valid if there is a working of the Spirit. Therefore ἐν πνεύματι is employed." (Grosheide, loc. cit., fn. 12). The Spirit *works* in baptism, but does *not perform* the baptism. Clearly the application of the instrumental to ἐν in I Cor. 12:13 is ambiguous.

[7] "εἰς ἕν σῶμα, to unite together into one body by baptism, I Cor. 12:13" (Grimm, Wilke, Thayer).

from the point of view of the locative."[8] Two ancillary sources lend support to this thesis.

In the Synoptic Gospels, Jesus is the baptizer, the Holy Spirit is the element[9] in which the baptizand is immersed. Clearly the analogy is with water-baptism. John the Baptist testified: "I indeed baptize you in water . . . he shall baptize you in the Holy Spirit and fire."[10]

In Acts 1:5, Jesus compared the baptism in the Spirit with baptism in water. His words echo the synoptic tradition noted above: "John indeed baptized in water; but you shall be baptized in the Holy Spirit not many days hence." In John's baptism, John was the administrator, the water was the medium, or element in which the baptism took place. By analogy then, Jesus is the baptizer and the Holy Spirit is the element in which the baptism takes place. In these instances, the locative is preferable to the instrumental sense of the preposition.

The second exegetical question, crucial for an understanding of I Cor. 12:13, now demands attention. Are the two verbs, *we were baptized* and *we were given to drink*, to be interpreted as a synonymous or a synthetic parallelism?[11]

Several interpretations have been proposed for this verse. (1) Both verbs refer metaphorically to baptism. (A variation of this theme refers both figures of speech to the Pentecostal baptism in the Spirit, a suggestion that will be discussed later.) This assumes a synonymous parallelism between the verbs. (2) The first image refers to the initiatory rite of baptism, the second to "the outpouring of spiritual gifts after baptism."[12] This suggests a synthetic

[8] *A Grammar of the Greek New Testament in the Light of Historical Research* (Nashville: Broadman Press, 1934), p. 590.

[9] "ἐν defines the *element* and *ruling influence* of the baptism εἰς the relationship to which it introduces": G. G. Findlay, *St. Paul's First Epistle to the Corinthians*, ed. W. Robertson Nicoll, Vol. II *The Expositor's Greek Testament* (Grand Rapids: Eerdmans, [n.d.]), p. 890. Cf. also A. T. Robertson and A. Plummer, *A Critical and Exegetical Commentary on the First Epistle of St. Paul to the Corinthians*, ed. S. R. Driver et al., *The International Critical Commentary* (Edinburgh: T. & T. Clark, 1863), p. 272.

[10] Matt. 3:11, ASV. Cf. also Mark 1:8; Luke 3:16.

[11] The nomenclature is drawn from Hebrew poetry. Its usage here is considered appropriate, even though the N.T. is in Greek, for Paul was a Hebrew of the Hebrews, thoroughly imbued with the religious and literary idioms of the O.T.

[12] Robertson and Plummer, op. cit., p. 272. Cf. also A. Clarke, *The New Testament of Our Lord and Saviour Jesus Christ*, II (New York: T. Mason and G. Lane, 1873), p. 260.

parallelism in which the first metaphor is supplemented, but not repeated in the second. (3) Baptism is referred to in the first verb, the second is an allusion to the Eucharist.[13]

As noted above, the first of these interpretations refers the entire verse to Christian baptism under two separate metaphors—"being immersed in the Spirit, and made to drink of the Spirit as a new elixir of life."[14] In favor of this view is the aorist indicative tense of both verbs—"we were baptized" and "we were given to drink"—which points to a definite event in past time, the former, "the outward badge . . . the symbol of an inward change already wrought in them by the Holy Spirit."[15] It may be objected to this view, that neither figure of speech refers to "the outward symbol of an inward change," but both figures speak of spiritual realities in Christian experience.

It may be observed also that under the first interpretation, a curious mixed metaphor emerges. Inasmuch as baptism in the Spirit initiates the convert into the one body (the Church), then by parity of reasoning drinking of the one Spirit must also be initiatory. The imagery of drinking one's way into the one body is, on second thought, more than a curious mixing of metaphors.[16]

It may be noted in passing that the third interpretation does not accord well with the context. As already observed, both verbs are aorist indicatives referring to a definite past event,[17] and not to a repeated action as in the celebrating of the Eucharist.

It is the second interpretation that, with some nuancing of terms, is compatible with the Pentecostal point of view. First Corinthians 12:13 stresses two aspects of the Holy Spirit's relationship to the Christian initiate. To be baptized in the Spirit is to be placed in the sphere of the Holy Spirit, that is to say, at conversion. To be given to drink of the Spirit places the Spirit's fulness

[13] Wordsworth, op. cit., p. 128.

[14] Robertson and Plummer, loc. cit.

[15] Robertson, *Word Pictures*, IV, p. 17.

[16] Cf., however, the statement that since "ποτίζειν is used of irrigating lands there is perhaps not much change of metaphor" (Robertson and Plummer, loc. cit). It may be objected that this introduces yet a third metaphor into the text without contextual justification. The baptizands are now likened to plants and fields.

[17] The aorist tense "has time relations only in the indicative, where it is past and hence augmented" (Dana and Mantey, op. cit., p. 178).

within the believer. This fulness is normally attested by charismatic manifestations, e.g., tongues, prophecy, healings, et al.

That Paul here speaks of a baptism in the one Spirit *into* the one body, the Church, argues for the initiatory significance of this baptism. It is faulty methodology, however, to read Paul's usage of the phrase into the book of Acts, and to assert on that basis that Luke used the phrase with exactly the same meaning. A critical comparison quickly reveals the fallacy of such a methodology. Nor can it be argued from the same premises that every convert's experience of conversion is tantamount to a Pentecostal baptism in the Spirit for power in mission. Paul's addition, "and were given to drink of one Spirit," indicates that more than conversion and initiation is involved. Rather, conversion and initiation are followed by a Pentecostal fulness of the Holy Spirit.

If it is objected that this introduces ambiguity into the use of the phrase baptized in the Spirit, it must be pointed out that such ambiguities are inherent in the use of language. It is the task of exegesis to unravel such equivocal terminology. For instance, words are not used univocally, that is in one sense only. In common language usage, they are used equivocally, that is with more than one meaning depending on the context. For example, the common word *ball* may mean either a spherical toy, a formal dance, or in a colloquial sense, a good time. The context is decisive for the final meaning of any word, or phrase, and not the dictionary definition.

The interpretation adopted above receives support from another context. Helen Barrett Montgomery's paraphrase of Eph. 5:18—"Do not be drunk with wine . . . but drink deep in the Spirit"—suggests an interesting parallel to Paul's words in I Cor. 12:13.[18] Her paraphrase of the more literal "be filled" as "drink deep" is defensible as a synonymous parallelism with the first half of the verse, "do not be drunk." How does one become drunk? By drinking wine to excess. In the context of the parallelism, how is one filled with the Spirit? By "drink(ing) deep in the Spirit." Thus "drink deep in the Spirit" is another way of saying "be filled with the Spirit." The parallelism of metaphors, in the light of Paul's own experience (Acts 9:17), suggests that fulness of the Spirit is the intent of "we were given to drink of one Spirit."

[18] *Centenary Translation of the New Testament.*

The conclusion implicit in the foregoing is, or ought to be, self-evident. Baptized in one Spirit *into* one body is initiatory, while being given to drink of one Spirit is another metaphor for the Pentecostal fulness of the Holy Spirit.

A fourth interpretation, already alluded to, refers both figures of speech to the Pentecostal baptism in the Spirit. It regards the baptism in the Spirit in I Cor. 12:13 as the sign or seal of one's prior membership in the body of Christ.[19] Support for this thesis is adduced from the interpretation of the preposition "*into* one body" as "with reference to (the) one body." The resultant translation reads thus: "For in *one* Spirit we were all baptized with reference to (the) one body . . . yea, we all were given to drink one Spirit."

As noted above, this view equates both figures of speech with the Pentecostal baptism in the Spirit. That is to say, the convert enters into relationship with the body of Christ in conversion, and this subsequent baptism with reference to the body "marks us out, or seals us as members of the one and the same body."[20] Stress is also laid on the claims that Jesus is the one who joins believers to His body at conversion and that membership in the body of Christ is prior to the baptism in the Spirit.

Support for this interpretation is drawn analogically from water-baptism "unto repentance" by calling attention to the fact that repentance precedes baptism. Thus biblical baptism is not "for the purpose of repentance," but "on the basis or ground"[21] of a prior repentance.

Attractive as this view may seem, at least from a Pentecostal point of view, there are problems it does not solve convincingly. The most cogent objection to this view derives from grammatical considerations. On these grounds, the translation "with reference to" is dubious in this context. The usual idiom is with verbs of motion. Combined with the accusative case, it gives the resultant meaning *into*.[22] Thus the preposition is used "to indicate effect . . .

[19] Called to my attention in a personal correspondence by a colleague, Dr. John Rea. Refer to chapter 4, note 8 for a discussion of the seal of the Spirit.

[20] John Rea, loc. cit.

[21] Robertson, *Word Pictures*, III, p. 35.

[22] "The usual idiom with εἰς was undoubtedly with verbs of motion when the motion and the accusative case combined with εἰς ('in') to give the resultant meaning of 'into,' 'unto,' 'among,' 'to,' 'towards,' or 'upon,' according to the context" (Robertson, *Grammar*, p. 593).

to unite together into one body."[23] The interpretation "with reference to" was anticipated and rejected by at least one commentator a century ago, who wrote, "not 'in reference to one body,' but 'into one body.'"[24] It is preferable, therefore, to understand the baptism here referred to as initiatory.

For some biblical exegetes, the Pentecostal position still faces a formidable obstacle. Does the identification of the baptism in the Spirit in the Corinthian passage with conversion and initiation prejudice the Pentecostal hermeneutics? More pointedly still, does the "*one* baptism" of Eph. 4:5 obviate the Pentecostal claim of a baptism in the Spirit subsequent to conversion? This objection loses its force, however, when the Ephesian passage is seen in its historical context.

If the suggestion is correct, and there is weighty evidence to support it, that this epistle was written as a corrective to incipient Gnostic heresies within the Church, the "one Lord" is in contrast to the Gnostic series of aeons; "one faith" confesses one way of salvation for all (not faith for the vulgar, but a sophisticated γνῶσις for the Gnostic initiate); "one baptism" is the one Christian rite of initiation, in contrast to additional Gnostic initiatory rites.[25] The objection is itself representative of the confusion caused by the tendency of expositors to interpret univocally the phrase, baptism in the Holy Spirit.

Apropos of the present discussion, Luke's choice of words to describe the Pentecostal experience is illuminating. In the book of Acts, he used the phrase, "baptized in the Holy Spirit," twice,[26] each time as a quotation of the words of Jesus. Contextual evidence supports the conclusion that Luke avoided the phrase elsewhere, and described the experience by a variety of synonymous expressions. The disciples were "filled with the Holy Spirit" at Jerusalem. The converts in Samaria "received the Holy Spirit," while upon the household of Cornelius at Caesarea, "the gift of the Holy Spirit was poured out." Yet in each instance, it is the Pentecostal experience that is described.

[23] Grimm, Wilke, Thayer, p. 94.

[24] T. C. Edwards, *A Commentary on the First Epistle to the Corinthians* (2nd ed.; New York: A. C. Strong & Son, 1886), p. 325.

[25] Robertson, *Word Pictures*, IV, p. 535.

[26] Acts 1:5; 11:16.

One might theorize that because of current ambiguities in the use of the phrase, "baptism in the Spirit," Luke used various circumlocutions to distinguish the Pentecostal baptism in the Spirit from the Holy Spirit's operation in conversion and the new birth. Are some such ambiguities revealed in Paul's equivocal use of the expression? Did his use of the phrase as practically identical with conversion and initiation prompt Luke to avoid it when describing the Pentecostal effusion of the Spirit subsequent to the new birth? Or is the answer to be found in Luke's preoccupation with the phenomenology of Spirit-baptism, i.e., tongues, prophecy, healings, etc.? Suffice it to say here, that by whatever name it is designated in the book of Acts, the Pentecostal baptism in/fulness of the Spirit is not confounded with the Holy Spirit's activity in conversion. Rather, the new birth from above is prerequisite to the Pentecostal baptism in the Holy Spirit.

For the apostolic community at Pentecost,[27] the Samaritan converts,[28] and Paul,[29] the baptism in the Spirit was separated from their conversion and new birth by an appreciable interval of time. For Cornelius and his household,[30] as well as for the twelve disciples of John the baptist whom Paul met at Ephesus,[31] however, their Spirit-baptism followed immediately upon their conversion. According to a variant reading of the text,[32] the same may be said of the Ethiopian eunuch. In the latter instances, conversion and the baptism in the Spirit were almost simultaneous, but nonetheless distinct administrations of the Holy Spirit. This suggests that conversion, with its attendant water-baptism, and the baptism in the Holy Spirit belong together as "two sides of one great act, whereby men were brought into the Church, the Body of Christ."[33] They are what a colleague[34] has aptly termed "a unit whole." The significance of these two baptisms is not, however, identical. They are still "two sides" of the Spirit's ministrations. As

[27] Acts 2:1–4.

[28] Acts 8:44ff.

[29] Acts 9:1ff.

[30] Acts 10:44.

[31] Acts 19:1–6.

[32] Acts 8:39. "The Holy Spirit fell upon the eunuch, and an angel of the Lord snatched away Philip" (Western text, Nestle–Aland).

[33] A. C. Winn, *Acts of the Apostles*, ed. B. H. Kelly, Vol. XX, *The Layman's Bible Commentaries* (London: SCM Press Ltd., 1960), p. 107.

[34] Dr. Charles Farah in a private communication.

such, they represent a progression in the spiritual experience of the individual believer.

The cogency of this interpretation may be tested by the answers to two questions. (1) Within the context of their own experience, how would the Christians to whom Paul wrote understand his words, "for we were all baptized in one Spirit into one body . . . and we were all given one Spirit to drink?" In Jerusalem, Samaria, Caesarea, and by implication at Corinth also, they had been converted and subsequently baptized in/filled with the Holy Spirit. The manifestation of the supernatural charisms of the Spirit in their midst—tongues, prophecy, healings, exorcisms—testifies to the fact that they knew experientially the power that accompanies the Pentecostal baptism in the Spirit. It is a matter of record that Jesus commanded His disciples not to leave Jerusalem until they had received the Holy Spirit's enduement with power. Clearly then, their new birth from above, received on that first Easter day, was *not* all that they were to expect from the Holy Spirit of promise.

(2) In the light of his own experience of conversion and Spirit-filling, what did Paul mean in I Cor. 12:13? The answer is obvious. One needs but to recall that Paul was converted on the Damascus road in his encounter with the risen Christ, a fact to be explored further in another place,[35] and three days later in Damascus he was filled with/baptized in the Holy Spirit when Ananias laid his hands upon him in the name of Jesus. It is apparent then, that the Spirit's activity in conversion was not terminal in Paul's experience. His personal Pentecost followed his conversion by three days.

[35] Cf. my critique of Dunn's rebuttal of this interpretation. Ervin, op. cit., p. 41ff.

Chapter 6

The Purpose of Pentecost

THE CHARISMATIC NATURE of the Pentecostal baptism in the Holy Spirit is implicit in the purpose for which it is given. Luke recorded the promise of Jesus thus: "you shall receive power when the Holy Spirit has come upon you; and you shall be my witnesses in Jerusalem, and in all Judea and Samaria, and to the end of the earth."[1] The purpose of Pentecost is unmistakably world evangelism, and the progress of the gospel is determined by the outline given above. Acts 1–7 record the initial Jerusalem, Judean phase. This is followed in chapters 8 and 9 by the record of Philip's successful mission in Samaria. Finally, chapters 10–28 record in considerably more detail the spread of the apostolic witness to the Gentile world. What is particularly germane to the present discussion is the fact that the purpose of the Pentecostal empowerment with the Spirit has not yet been fulfilled. Jesus' commission is still in effect, and so too is the charismatic enduement with power given to realize this purpose.

Inasmuch as the human faculty preeminently used in witnessing is the power of speech, it comes as no surprise, nor should it jar one's aesthetic sense of propriety, that on the day of Pentecost the Spirit's fulness was manifested in supernatural speech, "as the Spirit gave them utterance."[2] And in each subsequent recital of the experience of believers being baptized in/filled with the Spirit, whether explicitly stated or implied, the initial manifestation of the Holy Spirit's presence and power is divinely inspired utterance, or tongues.

This is the thorniest question in any discussion of the Pente-

[1] Acts 1:8.
[2] Acts 2:4.

costal experience. Perhaps an understanding of the rationale of tongues would obviate some of the stock objections to it. Speech is a unique manifestation of personality. It is not extrinsic to humanity; it is rather intrinsic in human personality. It is in fact evidence of personality. The perceptive comment of Eduard Thurneysen underscores this: "Only the fact that man can speak and does speak makes him man. . . . In the last analysis, the mystery of speech is identical with the mystery of personality, with image of God in man."[3]

God is personal, and as Person manifests himself in speech. This is the predicate of all revelation. God, who of old spoke through the prophets of Israel, has "spoken unto us in *his* Son."[4] In the divine personality, speech is a fundamental attribute. More than simply being functional, it is expressive of the essential nature of Deity. It was by speech that God created the world.[5] John the evangelist described Jesus as the incarnate Word, and this Word is God.[6] The divine "speaking" is the essential secret of the cosmos, for thus was the primeval chaos tamed. And according to the writer of the epistle to the Hebrews, the cosmos is sustained by the incarnate Word "upholding the universe by his word of power."[7] The prophetic phrase, "the Spirit said,"[8] is an acknowledgement of the Holy Spirit's personality. Speech and personality are inseparable in God.

It is an article of the Church's faith that God can and does speak to His people in their own languages, but such communication is always limited by two human factors. When God addresses humanity (or conversely, humanity addresses God) in the languages learned, communication is limited (1) by the conceptual categories in which the individual structures his thoughts, and (2)

[3] *A Theology of Pastoral Care*, trans. J. A. Worthington, et al., (Richmond: John Knox Press, 1963), p. 103. Cf. Ervin, op. cit., p. 73.

The biblical account makes it clear that the image replicates the divine likeness within the limits of man's creaturehood. The divine-human relationship is not, therefore, a symbiotic one. Rather the similitude of the image predicates a mutuality of being in both God and man.

[4] Heb. 1:2, ASV.

[5] Gen. 1:3ff.

[6] John 1:1.

[7] Heb. 1:3. If the new physics says what it means, and means what it says, then this is neither myth nor metaphor. Cf. V. S. Owens, *And the Trees Clap Their Hands*, (Grand Rapids: Eerdmans, 1983).

[8] Acts 8:29; 13:2.

verbally by the vocabulary with which one is conversant. By the way of contrast, when the Spirit-filled Christian prays or speaks in tongues, he is speaking a language he has never learned. The vocabulary is controlled by the mind of the Spirit. It may be one language or many languages, at the Spirit's discretion, and all restrictions of conceptual categories and vocabulary are surpassed. Paul described his own experience of glossolalia in such terms. "For if I pray in a tongue," he wrote, "my spirit prays but my mind[9] is unfruitful." Nor does the apostle deprecate this, for he added: "What am I to do? I will pray with the spirit [i.e., in tongues as the Spirit gives utterance], and I will pray with the mind [i.e., in the languages he had learned], I will sing with the spirit [i.e., in tongues] and I will sing with the mind also [i.e., in the languages he knew]."[10]

Jesus promised His disciples power when the Holy Spirit came upon them, and the *first* distinctively personal manifestation of the Spirit's power was supernatural utterance in other languages. Thereby, the Holy Spirit demonstrated His sovereignty over the organs of human communication involved in fulfilling their responsibility as witnesses. Tongues are the unique charismatic manifestation of the divine Spirit's presence and power on the day of Pentecost. Every charismatic manifestation of the Holy Spirit can be paralleled before Pentecost, with the exception of tongues. They were, and are (and herein is their scandal) normative evidence of the Pentecostal power in the lives of Christians.

A further word is indicated here to clarify the relationship of the tongues at Pentecost with Peter's quotation from the prophecy of Joel wherein prophecy is the distinctive feature of the outpouring of God's Spirit "upon all flesh."[11] Was it simply a loose accommodation, dictated by homiletical expediency, of the ancient seer's words to the Pentecostal phenomenon? Or is there a more precise link between Joel's *prophesying* and Pentecost's *tongues*? The answer is suggested by the Greek word translated in our English versions as "utterance." In the Septuagint the same word is "used not of ordinary conversation, but of the utterance of prophets."[12]

[9] I Cor. 14:14, νοῦς, *the understanding* (Bauer, Arndt, Gingrich).
[10] I Cor. 14:15.
[11] Acts 2:17.
[12] R. J. Knowling, *The Acts of the Apostles*, ed. W. R. Nicoll, Vol. II, *The*

The use of this word may also have been suggested by the unusual conduct of the disciples who were mockingly accused of being "filled with new wine."[13] Their conduct was analogous to the ecstatic state of ancient Israel's prophetic guilds.[14] Peter apparently interpreted the tongues at Pentecost as prophetic utterance.[15] In this sense then, the tongues were a literal fulfillment of Joel's oracle: "And in the last days it shall be, God declares, that I will pour out my Spirit upon all flesh, and your sons and your daughters shall prophesy."[16]

When the apostolic community spoke in tongues "as the Spirit gave them utterance" on the day of Pentecost, they were speaking by divine inspiration languages they had not previously learned. To them it was tongues, but to the bystanders who heard and understood them speaking in their dialects,[17] it was not tongues, but prophecy. They heard them extol "the magnificence of God"[18] with prophetic ardor. This same manifestation of praise in tongues occurred later in the house of Cornelius when "they heard them speaking in tongues and extolling God."[19]

Expositor's Greek Testament (Grand Rapids: Eerdmans, [n.d.]), pp. 4, 5.

ἀποφθέγγεσθαι—a word peculiar to Acts, cf. v.14 and xxvi.25; in the LXX used not of ordinary conversation, but of the utterances of prophets; cf. Ezek. xiii.9; Micah v.12, I Chron. xxv.1, so fitly here: (cf. ἀποφθέγματα, used by the Greeks of the sayings of the Wise and philosophers).

[13] Acts 2:13.

[14] *nābi*, who prophesied in an ecstatic state. F. Brown, S. R. Driver, and C. A. Briggs, eds. *A Hebrew-English Lexicon of the Old Testament* (1907 rpt; Oxford: At the Clarendon Press, 1959).

[15] This same aspect will be referred to again in the exposition of I Cor. 14:6.

[16] Acts 2:17.

[17] Acts 2:6.

[18] *τά μεγαλεῖα*, in our literature only substantively, *greatness*, *sublimity* (Bauer, Arndt, Gingrich). Cf. A. T. Robertson and W. H. Davis, *A New Short Grammar of the Greek New Testament* (New York: Harper & Brothers, 1933), p. 205: "The articular neuter adjective is often used in the same sense as an abstract."

[19] Acts 10:46.

Chapter 7

The Pattern of Pentecost

IN THE FOREGOING DISCUSSION, sufficient was said to formulate a normative pattern of the baptism in the Holy Spirit. By way of recapitulation, the following five propositions may be affirmed with reasonable confidence as regulative of this experience. Each is derived from the historical accounts of the various groups and individuals whose baptism in the Spirit has been recorded in the book of the Acts. Since it is only in the historical narratives of the Acts that Spirit-baptism is recorded in detail, such a formulation must depend upon these records.

The allusions to the baptism in/filling with the Spirit in the epistles interpret theologically the significance and subsequent manifestations of the Holy Spirit in the lives of Spirit-baptized Christians. The epistles do not record the initial experience, they presuppose it. However, in an effort to negate the Pentecostal's paradigm of a baptism in the Spirit subsequent to conversion and the new birth, an appeal is frequently made to the Pauline epistles, especially Rom. 8:9: "Any one who does not have the Spirit of Christ does not belong to him."[1]

On the basis of this text, it is assumed as self-evident that the Johannine new birth and the Lukan gift of the Spirit for power in mission are one and the same. The assumption rests, however, upon two methodological fallacies. (1) As previously noted, John's theology of the Spirit cannot be combined univocally with Luke's theology of the Spirit. The error is simply compounded when John, Luke, and Paul are combined without regard for individual contexts. (2) Every text has a context, and Rom. 8:9 is no

[1] For a critique cf. Ervin, op. cit., pp. 25ff.

exception. In the context Paul is not alluding to Luke's gift of the Spirit for power in mission. One might more cogently argue that his contention that "by the power of signs and wonders, by the power of the Holy Spirit . . . I have fully preached the gospel of Christ,"[2] is such an allusion. However, the Romans 9 context reflects the Johannine emphasis upon the new birth. The subject of the context is life in the Spirit (v. 4) versus life according to the flesh (v. 5).

As a consequence, a normative pattern for the baptism in the Spirit cannot be derived from these sources. Nowhere in the epistles is one told how to be baptized in/filled with the Holy Spirit. It is assumed that the readers already know this. One must, therefore, turn to the book of Acts for this information. Accordingly, any reconstruction of the circumstances, and details of the baptism in the Spirit must be derived from the records of those who experienced this baptism.

(1) John the Baptist's baptism supplied the type for the baptism in the Spirit. Jesus linked the two when He said, "John baptized with water . . . you shall be baptized with (in)[3] the Holy Spirit." As the baptism of John placed the candidate in the medium of water, so the baptism of Jesus places the Christian in the Spirit.

(2) Jesus is himself the administrator of this Spirit-baptism. John the Baptizer testified of Him; "he shall baptize you in the Holy Spirit and *in* fire."[4] To this Peter added confirmatory testimony in his Pentecost sermon, saying; "Being therefore exalted at the right hand of God and having received from the Father the promise of the Holy Spirit, he has poured out this which you see and hear."[5] In Jerusalem, as in Caesarea, the effusion of the Spirit was experienced without human mediation. In Samaria and Ephesus the apostles mediated the experience through the laying on of their hands. In every instance, though, the administrator of the baptism in the Spirit is Jesus.

(3) In the next place, the baptism in the Holy Spirit is not synonymous with conversion and the new birth from above. Rather it is subsequent to conversion and regeneration.

[2] Rom. 15:19.
[3] Acts 1:5. Cf. Robertson, *Word Pictures*, III, p. 8.
[4] Matt. 3:11; Mark 1:8; Luke 3:16; John 1:33.
[5] Acts 2:33, ASV.

(4) The normative evidence of this baptism is a charismatic manifestation of the Spirit's personality and power. And the only one documented in Acts occurred first at Pentecost: "they were all filled with the Holy Spirit and began to speak in other tongues, as the Spirit gave them utterance."[6] Tongues-speech as evidence of the baptism in/filling with the Spirit is explicitly stated as taking place in Jerusalem, Caesarea, and Ephesus.

However the question may be begged in other contexts, the evidential value of tongues emerges clearly in the response of Peter's companions to the reception of the Spirit by Cornelius and his household. They were convinced (apparently against their will) that this Roman household had indeed received the gift of the Holy Spirit, "for[7] they heard them speaking in tongues and extolling God." Speaking in tongues was objective evidence that they had truly received the fulness of the Spirit.

(5) The baptism in the Holy Spirit is, for Luke at least, synonymous with being filled with the Spirit.[8] Jesus, speaking prophetically of the Pentecostal baptism in the Spirit, said, "you shall be baptized in the Holy Spirit." Luke, in recording the phenomenology of the event, wrote, "they were all filled with the Holy Spirit." It is no homiletical extravagance to conclude, therefore, that baptism in the Spirit = filled with the Spirit. The message is clear enough. Christians who would experience the (charismatic) fulness of the Holy Spirit must submit themselves as candidates to Jesus the Baptizer.

There is no scriptural evidence for a progressive filling, a process of progressive surrender of oneself whereby commensurate increments of the Holy Spirit are received. It is a full surrender involving obedience[9] to the Trinity in every area of life, surrendering even the *untamed member*, the tongue,[10] to the sovereign manifestation of the Holy Spirit's person and power. Baptized in the Spirit, filled with the Spirit, these are one and the same experience. It follows therefore, that if there is one baptism in the

[6] Acts 2:4.

[7] Acts 10:46. The Greek conjunction γάρ is either causal or explanatory (Dana and Mantey, op. cit., p. 257). Even if the conjunction is taken here as explanatory, its casual significance is seen here as explanatory of the preceding ὅτι clause.

[8] Cf. Acts 1:5 with Acts 2:4.

[9] Acts 5:32.

[10] James 3:8.

Holy Spirit, there is one filling with the Spirit. The cliché, "one baptism, but many fillings," cannot be true. The assertion, "repeated fillings with the Holy Spirit are necessary to continuance and increase in power,"[11] is unfounded. It does not comport well with "filling" as a liquid metaphor.[12] The biblical pattern and provision is a state of constant fulness with the Holy Spirit.[13] The way is now prepared to discuss Luke's use of the phrase, "filled with the Holy Spirit," in the book of Acts.

The first baptism in the Holy Spirit in the Church is described in Acts 2:1–4. As an abiding consequence of this baptism, the disciples "were all filled with the Spirit." Here the word translated *they were filled*[14] is an ingressive aorist tense, "commonly employed with verbs which signify a *state* or *condition*, and denote entrance into that state or condition."[15] Pentecost marked the introduction of the disciples into the state of Spirit-fulness. The significance of both the ingressive aorist tense with the stative verb, *filled*, to describe the inception of the baptism in the Spirit on the day of Pentecost must be underscored. Baptized in the Spirit by Jesus, they entered "into the state or condition" of fulness of the Holy Spirit. It was not a transitory experience that needed to be repeated, but an abiding state or condition of fulness of the Spirit.[16] There are several reasons for this conclusion.

(1) The verb *filled* is a stative verb that describes the state or condition of the recipients of the baptism in relation to the Holy Spirit. The passive voice of the verb reinforces its stative sense.[17]

(2) Luke uses the verb, *πίμπλημι*, exclusively with states or conditions experienced by the subject of the verb.[18]

[11] R. A. Torrey, *The Person and Work of the Holy Spirit* (London: James Nisbet & Co., Ltd., 1910), p. 212.

[12] John 7:38. For a discussion of this metaphor see chapter 1, p. 1.

[13] Eph. 5:18.

[14] *ἐπλήσθησαν*, *they were filled*, aorist, indicative, passive.

[15] Dana and Mantey, op. cit., p. 196, italics added.

[16] This insight will have a bearing on the subsequent interpretation of Acts 4:31.

[17] Cf. Ervin, op. cit., p. 37. The verb *πίμπλημι* is used 22 times in the passive voice, and once in the active voice in Luke–Acts.

[18] In the following examples, note the use of the passive voice of *πίμπλημι* with the genitive of the states or conditions experienced by the subject, e.g.: *πνεύματος ἁγίου*, "of the Holy Spirit" (Luke 1:15, 41, 67; Acts 2:4; 4:8, 31; 9:17; 13:9); *αἱ ἡμέραι τῆς λειτουργίας αὐτοῦ*, "the days of his priestly service" (Luke 1:23; cf. 2:6, 21, 22); *ὁ χρόνος τοῦ τεκεῖν αὐτήν*, "the time for her to give birth" (Luke 1:57); *θυμοῦ*, "of wrath" (Luke 4:28); *φοβου*, "of fear" (Luke

(3) Luke uses the cognate noun[19] of the verb πληρόω, *to make full*, *to fill*, five times in Luke–Acts. Jesus,[20] the first seven deacons (almoners),[21] Stephen,[22] and Barnabas[23] are all described as *full* of the Holy Spirit. The noun, by its very nature, is stative, and underscores the fact that an abiding fulness of the Spirit was the normative result of being baptized in the Holy Spirit.

Shortly after the Pentecostal experience, Luke had occasion to elaborate upon the effect of the Spirit's fulness in the life of Peter. Brought before the ruling council of the Jewish nation, Peter was ordered to tell them the nature of the "power," and the identity of the "name"[24] whereby the lame man at the temple gate had been healed.[25] Luke prefaced Peter's reply with the explanatory comment, "Then Peter, filled with the Holy Spirit, said to them."[26]

At issue here is the interpretation of the word *filled*. The grammatical form of the word is an aorist passive participle. In interpreting the syntax of the passage, the choice rests between the adverbial (circumstantial) and the adjectival (attributive) uses of the participle. If the participle is regarded as adverbial (i.e., as modifying the verb), the aorist tense would simply designate an action antecedent to the main verb,[27] but not necessarily immediately prior to the act of speaking, for "the time relations of the participle do not belong to its tense, but to the sense of the context."[28]

When then was Peter filled with the Holy Spirit? The only answer supplied by the context is on the day of Pentecost when he, along with the rest of 120 disciples in the upper room, was baptized in the Holy Spirit by the ascended Jesus, and thereby entered into the state or condition of Spirit-fulness.

5:26); ἀνοίας, "of fury" (Luke 6:11); θάμβους καὶ ἐκστάσεως, "of astonishment and amazement" (Acts 3:10); ζήλου, "of jealousy" (Acts 5:17; 13:45); συγχύσεως, "of confusion" (Acts 19:29).

[19] πλήρης, "*full* of a power, gift, feeling, characteristic, quality, etc." (Bauer, Arndt, Gingrich).

[20] Luke 4:1.

[21] Acts 6:3.

[22] Acts 6:5; 7:55.

[23] Acts 11:24.

[24] Acts 4:7.

[25] Acts 3:1ff.

[26] Acts 4:8.

[27] Dana and Mantey, op. cit., p. 230.

[28] Ibid.

On the other hand, if the participle is regarded as adjectival (attributive), then it modifies the noun. Since the participle here represents a state or condition experienced by Peter, it may then be interpreted as an anarthrous attributive participle, i.e., "as an adjective without an accompanying article."[29] The clause may then be translated, "the full-of-the-Spirit Peter said."[30] This adjectival sense of the participle is reflected in several translations of this text that read, "Peter, full of the Holy Spirit."[31]

It was a Spirit-filled Peter who was the human instrument in the healing of the lame man at the temple gate. It was to this abiding fulness of the Holy Spirit that he referred when he said to the lame beggar, "I have no silver and gold, but I give you what I have; in the name of Jesus Christ of Nazareth, walk."[32] It was a Spirit-filled Peter who then preached in the temple courts, was arrested, imprisoned, and finally arraigned before the Sanhedrin because of his evangelistic activities.

Precisely the same grammatical construction occurs in Acts 13:9. Paul, while preaching to the proconsul Sergius Paulus, was hindered by the diabolical antagonism of a sorcerer, Bar Jesus. Confronting his antagonist, Luke records that "Paul, filled with the Holy Spirit looked intently at him and said." What follows is a scathing denunciation of the villainy of the sorcerer. Whether one opts for the adverbial or the adjectival use of the participle, the contextual question is the same. When was Paul filled with the Holy Spirit? The answer is, when Ananias laid his hands upon him in the name of Jesus and said, "Brother Saul, the Lord Jesus who appeared to you on the road by which you came, has sent me that you may regain your sight and be filled[33] with the Holy Spirit."

The biblical sources thus indicate that Peter and Paul each entered the state or condition of being Spirit-filled when Jesus

[29] Cf. Ervin, op. cit., p. 39 for a discussion of this point of view.

[30] Another example of this usage is found in Acts 22:3; *ἐγώ εἰμι ἀνήρ* ᾿Ιουδαῖος, *γεγεννημένος ἐν* Ταρσῷ, "I am a man born in Tarsus, a Jew = "a Tarsus-born man, a Jew." Cf. Robertson, *Grammar*, p. 1105.

[31] *Good News for Modern Man.* This translation was anticipated in Tyndale, Great Bible, Geneva Bible, and Bishops' Bible (Weigle, op. cit.). In this translation the participle πλησθεὶς approximates the stative sense of the noun πλήρης.

[32] Acts 3:6.

[33] Acts 9:17, πλησθῇς, aorist passive subjunctive.

baptized them in the Holy Spirit—Peter on the day of Pentecost, Paul later in Damascus; Peter through the spontaneous effusion of the Spirit, Paul through the laying on of Ananias' hands. For both it was an abiding enduement with power by the Holy Spirit to make them effectual witnesses for Jesus, the risen Christ.

Chapter 8

One Baptism, One Filling

THE NEXT RECORDED USE of the phrase "filled with the Spirit" occurs in Acts 4:31: "And when they had prayed, the place in which they were gathered together was shaken; and they were all filled with the Holy Spirit and spoke the word of God with boldness." Although the account of this experience is condensed, there is contextual justification for believing that the pattern of the baptism in the Holy Spirit already outlined was fulfilled in this instance also.

The similarities with the account of the events on the day of Pentecost are succinctly stated as follows: "The description here is reminiscent of the description of what happened on the day of Pentecost, both in the external signs of the Spirit's advent and in the prayerful attitude of the disciples when He came."[1] And one might add, also in the results, for they "spoke the word of God with boldness." As already noted, the purpose of the baptism in/filling with the Holy Spirit is empowerment for witness. One might, therefore, argue that it was more than merely reminiscent; it was a repetition of what happened on the day of Pentecost.

If then this was a repetition of Pentecost, the question presses for an answer. Who were the recipients of this fresh effusion of the Spirit? Were the original 120 disciples present on the day of Pentecost refilled (i.e., re-baptized) in the Holy Spirit?

While agreeing with the judgment that the description is reminiscent of Pentecost, the conclusion drawn from it must be rejected, namely, that "while this was a fresh filling of the Spirit, it could not be called a fresh baptism."[2] But this polarization of the

[1] F. F. Bruce, *Commentary on the Book of Acts*, p. 107.
[2] Ibid.

filling with and baptism in the Holy Spirit is not consistent with the context. It implies a theological definition of *filling* and *baptism* that is not supported by contextual exegesis. In Luke's theology of the Spirit, filled with the Spirit is inseparable from the baptism in the Spirit. In Lukan terminology, therefore, if this were a fresh filling (or refilling, to use a popular phrase), then it would be equally valid to say that they were re-baptized in the Spirit.

However, there is another alternative. As a consequence of Peter's Pentecost sermon, "those who received his word were baptized, and there were added that day about three thousand souls."[3] Subsequently, "the Lord added to their number day by day those who were being saved."[4] This represented a considerable influx of Jewish converts into the Church. The events recorded in Acts 4:31 represent the occasion of the filling with/baptism in the Holy Spirit of the converts won to saving faith in Christ Jesus since Pentecost. Several exegetical considerations lend support to this thesis.

(1) With each subsequent influx of converts to Christ, their reception of the Holy Spirit is recorded. The Samaritans "received the Holy Spirit"[5] after baptism when Peter and John laid their hands upon them. The Holy Spirit "fell on all who heard the word"[6] as Peter spoke to the Roman household of Cornelius. In the cosmopolitan city of Ephesus, Paul met twelve disciples of John the Baptist. Having baptized them in the name of Jesus, he laid his hands upon them, and "the Holy Spirit came on them."[7] Thus the advance of the gospel into the Greco-Roman world was heralded by the pouring out of the Spirit in His charismatic fulness. There is a literary symmetry in the record that argues for the thesis presented here. If the Samaritan, Roman, and Ephesian converts received the Holy Spirit in His charismatic fulness after their conversion, then so too did the Jewish converts after Pentecost, and Acts 4:31 is the record of their "Pentecostal" reception of the Holy Spirit.

(2) There is, furthermore, a deeply meaningful variation in nuance between Acts 2:2 and Acts 4:31. In the former place, Luke

[3] Acts 2:41.
[4] Acts 2:47.
[5] Acts 8:17.
[6] Acts 10:44.
[7] Acts 19:6.

wrote: "And suddenly a sound came from heaven like the rush of a mighty wind, and it filled all *the house*[8] where they were sitting." In Acts 4:31 Luke preserved a subtle distinction in the description of these events when he wrote: "And when they had prayed, *the place*[9] in which they were gathered together was shaken." One's understanding of Acts 4:31 will be influenced to some degree by his understanding of *the house* in Acts 2:2, and *the place* in Acts 4:31. If merely synonyms, one could dismiss the contrast on stylistic grounds alone. Granted that "*the place* in which they gathered together" could mean *a house*, nevertheless, there are two facts that argue against their being used synonymously here. (a) *Place* is used in New Testament Greek as a synonym for a tract of unbounded land,[10] and a parcel of (enclosed) ground.[11] (b) Acts 4:4 places the number of new converts at about 5000 men, not counting women and children.

When Peter and John were released from custody by the Sanhedrin, it is said, that "they went to their friends."[12] Did this mean only the initial group of disciples present at Pentecost or were the new converts included? The context clearly implies that *their friends* is "not necessarily limited to their fellow-Apostles . . . but as including the members of the Christian community."[13] More explicit is the comment, "their own people . . . is not merely the apostles (all the disciples)."[14] Confirmation of this view is supplied by Acts 4:32, "the company[15] of those who believed were of one heart and soul." The *company* (multitude) of v. 32 finds its

[8] Acts 2:2, italics added. τὸν οἶκον, *the house*.

[9] Italics added. ὁ τόπος, *place*, "indefinite; a portion of space viewed in reference to its occupance." In Acts 28:7 τόπος occurs together with its synonym χωρίον, a *parcel of ground* (Grimm, Wilke, Thayer).

[10] χώρα, "*region, country*, extensive space yet unbounded" (Grimm, Wilke, Thayer).

[11] χωρίον, *parcel of ground* (Grimm, Wilke, Thayer).

[12] Acts 4:23, τοὺς ἰδίους, *fellow-Christians* (Bauer, Arndt, Gingrich).

[13] Knowling, op. cit., p. 132.

[14] Robertson, *Word Pictures*. III, p. 54.

[15] τοῦ πλήθους,

> *of the multitude*, i.e., *the mass of believers*. These are designated as πιστεύσαντες, *having become believers*, in reference to ver. 4; but in such a way that it is not merely those πολλοί, ver. 4, that are meant, but *they* and at the same time *all others who had till now become believers*. This is required by τὸ πλῆθος, which denotes the Christian people generally, as contrasted with the apostles.

(Meyer, *Critical and Exegetical Hand-Book to the Acts of the Apostles*, p. 99).

antecedent in the ***many*** (i.e., the 5000 men) of v. 4. It is to this larger group that Luke referred in v. 31.

Such an increase in the numbers of the Christian community argues for the need of the larger meeting area implied in Acts 4:31. Paul's later experience at Phillipi where he found "a place of prayer"[16] by the side of a river reflects an established Jewish custom, and provides an illustrative parallel. The customary "place of prayer" of the Jews may have supplied the pattern for such a Christian gathering place apart from the temple and the synagogues of Jerusalem. For instance, Josephus quoted a decree of those of Halicarnassus guaranteeing the right of the Jews "to make their prayers at the seashore, according to the customs of their forefathers."[17] These places of prayer were described by Epiphanius "as places of a semi-circular form . . . without roofs, and outside the cities."[18] There is an explicit allusion to such a place in I Macc. 3:46 as follows: "And they gathered themselves together, and came to Mizpah, over against Jerusalem; for in Mizpah there had been aforetime a place of prayer for Israel."[19]

(3) The grammatical form of the word filled[20] provides inductive evidence in support of the conclusion that Acts 4:31 refers to the filling with/baptism in the Holy Spirit of new converts added to the Church since Pentecost. In Acts 2:4 and 4:31 the identical form of the word is used. As already pointed out, Luke used the ingressive aorist tense in Acts 2:4 to describe the experience of the disciples on the day of Pentecost. It bears repeating here, that "this use is commonly employed with verbs which signify a *state* or *condition*." It is, therefore, analogically sound reasoning to interpret Luke's use of the aorist tense as *ingressive* in Acts 4:31. As the Samaritan, Roman, and Ephesian converts were subsequently to receive the Holy Spirit in His charismatic fulness, so also did these

[16] Acts 16:13, *προσευχή*, *place of* (*or for*) *prayer*; "the πρ(οσευχή) in our passage may have been an informal meeting place, perh(aps) in the open air" (Bauer, Arndt, Gingrich).

[17] W. Whiston, trans., *The Works of Josephus* (Hartford: S. S. Scranton Co., 1905). *Antiquities*, XIV, 10, p. 434.

[18] Quoted by Wordsworth, op. cit., I, p. 119.

[19] R. H. Charles, ed. *The Apocrypha and Pseudepigrapha*, I (Oxford: Clarendon Press, 1963), p. 78. The reference to an old tribal shrine suggests the origin of the *προσευχή*, in antiquity. Cf. also III Macc. 7:20, "and having dedicated a place of prayer on the spot where they had held their festival, they departed unharmed, free, and full of joy" (op. cit., p. 173).

[20] *ἐπλήσθησαν*, *they were filled*.

first Jerusalem converts, and Acts 4:31 is the record of their "Pentecostal" reception of the Holy Spirit.

On the other hand, the burden of proof rests with those who deduce another meaning from the aorist tense in Acts 4:31. For example, the interpretation that this passage represents a refilling with the Holy Spirit of those present at Pentecost arbitrarily assumes the sense of repeated action in the verb *filled*, i.e., "they were all filled *again*." But the aorist tense does not convey the iterative sense. If this had been what Luke intended to say, he could have used an iterative imperfect, but not the aorist which represents the action of the verb as "punctiliar (point action)."[21]

It is the use of the word "all" that has proven a stumbling block in the interpretation of this verse, i.e., "they were *all* filled with the Holy Spirit." Recognition of the force of the aorist tense in Acts 4:31 mitigates this objection. If it is objected that the ingressive use of the aorist cannot be pressed in this verse, a related use of the *aorist* tense reinforces what has already been said. The use of the tense here may be regarded as a dramatic aorist.[22] "This idiom is a device for emphasis. It is commonly used of a state which has just been realized,"[23] and once again it is the stative sense that is conveyed by both the verb and the aorist tense.

It is in the following sense that the comprehensive "all" may be reconciled with the view propounded here. The apostolic company of disciples had entered the state or condition of Spirit-fulness on the day of Pentecost. When the events recorded in Acts 4:31 transpired they were still filled with the Holy Spirit. Note that in the same context[24] (presumably earlier the same day), *a Spirit-filled Peter* stood before the Sanhedrin to answer for his conduct in the healing of the lame man, and his consequent proclamation of the gospel in the temple precincts. As already argued,[25] this was not a new filling (or refilling) with the Holy Spirit for Peter. Rather the idiom used refers to Peter's prior filling with the Spirit at Pentecost. Logically then, this was equally true of the rest of

[21] Robertson and Davis, op. cit., p. 295.

[22] Dana and Mantey, op. cit., p. 295. Robertson agreed with Moulton that in the dramatic aorist, "we have probably to do . . . with one of the most ancient uses of the aorist."

[23] Op. cit., p. 198.

[24] Acts 4:8.

[25] See chap. 7, fn. 31.

those present who had been filled with the Spirit of God at Pentecost. Now the converts won to faith in Christ through their Spirit-filled witness were also introduced into the same state or condition by this fresh effusion of the promised Holy Spirit. It was no longer the unique privilege of those who had been present at Pentecost, for now *all* were inducted into the Spirit's fulness. The Spirit-filled state has now been realized by *all* the Christians.

For those who read Acts 4:31 as a refilling of the initial apostolic company with the Holy Spirit, the pointed reference to Peter's Spirit-filled status in Acts 4:8 is an anomaly. What then happened to Peter's Spirit-filled experience between the events recorded in Acts 4:8 and Acts 4:31? Was it an incremental fulness added to fulness? Or did Peter, in a manner not described, lose the fulness of the Spirit he exemplified in his defence before the ruling council of Judaism? If so, then it is in order to ask, How? When? Where? and Why?—and until these questions can be answered by grammatical and contextual exegesis, there is no support for the thesis that Peter was refilled with the Holy Spirit in Acts 4:31. And no matter how one looks at the evidence, Peter's experience in Acts 4:8 abridges the comprehensive force of the *all* in Acts 4:31. If then this exception is admitted for Peter's experience, it cannot be denied with consistency in the case of the rest of the disciples present with Peter on the day of Pentecost.

The Converts[26] Were Filled with the Holy Spirit

In the next occurrence of the phrase there is a grammatical usage of considerable importance for this inquiry; i.e., "he [Stephen] full of the Holy Spirit gazed into heaven and saw the glory of God."[27] Here the phrase "full of the Holy Spirit" is represented by a present participle with a predicate noun.[28] It is the present participle of the verb meaning *to exist*, and is widely used in Hellenistic Greek for the present infinitive of the verb *to be*.[29] In the context, the verb (participle) may be translated "*who is, since he is*,"[30] thereby recognizing that one's present state or

[26] Acts 13:52, NEB.
[27] Acts 7:55.
[28] ὑπάρχων δὲ πλήρης, *who is full.*
[29] εἶναι, Bauer, Arndt, Gingrich.
[30] Op. cit., p. 846.

experience is the result of an antecedent cause. For instance, this usage is illustrated in Acts 3:2; e.g., "a man lame[31] from birth." The participial construction here alludes to the antecedent lameness of the man. He did not become lame that day. He had been lame from birth, and was still lame when Peter and John encountered him. This is precisely the intent of the phrase in this place.

The same grammatical construction occurs again in Acts 17:24: "The God who made the world and everything in it, being[32] Lord of heaven and earth, does not live in shrines made by man." God did not, at that moment, become Lord of heaven and earth—or what is even more bizarre, become Lord again. He is the Lord, and has always been the Lord. These illustrations make it clear that this participial construction refers to the antecedent existence of some present matter of fact.

What light does this grammatical detail throw upon Stephen's experience? A great deal indeed, for it "shows his antecedent spiritual state."[33] Stephen was no more refilled with the Holy Spirit at this time than that the lame man became lame that day, or that God became Lord again, as noted above. Rather, the idiom used refers to his filling with the Spirit at some prior time. This is further attested by the context.

In Acts 6:3, "seven men of good repute, full[34] of the Spirit and of wisdom" was the precondition set by the apostles for the choice of the first seven "deacons" (almoners) of the Church. Verse 5 says that "they chose Stephen, a man full of faith and of the Holy Spirit." Stephen was not filled again with the Spirit at this time to discharge these responsibilities. Men already ***full*** of the Spirit were chosen to fill this office. Stephen ***had been*** filled with the Spirit of God on a prior occasion. He ***was*** full of the Spirit when he was chosen as a "deacon." He ***continued to be*** filled with the Holy Spirit right up to the moment that he sealed his testimony in martyrdom.

Parenthetically, it is appropriate to note that the two preceding uses of the phrase "full of the Holy Spirit"[35] are noun phrases,

[31] Acts 3:2, *χωλὸς . . . ὑπάρχων*. Cf. also Acts 22:3, *ζηλωτὴς ὑπάρχων*.

[32] *ὑπάρχων κύριος*, *who is Lord*.

[33] Wordsworth, op. cit., I, p. 73.

[34] *πλήρεις* nom. and acc. pl. masc. The use of the noun here underscores again the stative sense.

[35] Acts 6:3, 5.

and the noun, by its very nature, underscores a continuing state of fulness. Another instance of the same kind reports an identical experience of Barnabas, "for he was a good man, *full*[36] of the Holy Spirit and of faith."

In each instance, the genitive phrases "of the Spirit" and "of faith" qualify the subject which it "defines by attributing a quality of relationship to the noun it modifies."[37] Moreover, those who were filled with the Spirit entered into an abiding *charismatic* relationship with the Third Person of the Trinity. These examples also show that the charismatic fulness of the Spirit is complemented by (though not contingent upon) abiding gracements of the divine Spirit, e.g., wisdom, faith, good reputation, and personal integrity. These spiritual endowments are epitomized in Stephen's case as "grace and power," that is to work "great wonders and signs among the people."[38]

The only example in the book of Acts of the phrase "filled with the Holy Spirit" that could be pressed to substantiate a theology of repeated fillings with the Spirit is Acts 13:52: "the disciples were filled with joy and with the Holy Spirit." In this text, the word translated *were filled* is in the imperfect tense, passive voice.[39] Granted, the imperfect tense in Greek may describe repeated action in past time; this constitutes the so-called iterative use of the imperfect tense.[40] If the verb *were filled* is understood as an iterative use of the imperfect tense, however, two choices are open to the interpreter.

(1) It may then be translated, "and the disciples were filled *again* and *again* with joy and with the Holy Spirit." This sense could then be adduced to support the teaching of repeated refillings with the Holy Spirit. However, even if it is taken as an iterative imperfect, such an interpretation is neither mandatory, nor consistent with the evidence of collateral passages dealing with the subject, as has already been shown.

(2) The second choice is then to translate the text, "and the

[36] Acts 11:24, *πλήρης πνεύματος ἁγίου*.

[37] Dana and Mantey, op. cit., p. 74.

[38] Acts 6:8.

[39] *ἐπληροῦντο*. There is no essential difference in meaning between *πίμπλημι* in Acts 4:31 and *πληρόω* in 13:52.

[40] Dana and Mantey, op. cit., p. 187: "The iterative imperfect . . . may be used to describe action as recurring at successive intervals in past time."

disciples were filled *one after another* with joy and with the Holy Spirit." And this is apparently the intention of the New English Bible translation which reads, "and the *converts* were filled with joy and with the Holy Spirit."[41]

This may be illustrated graphically by the use of the iterative imperfect of the word *baptize* in Matt. 3:6; "and they were baptized[42] by him [John the Baptist] in the river Jordan." Obviously, John was not baptizing the same candidates over and over again. Instead, he was baptizing (iterative imperfect) the *converts one after another*.

Not all commentators are agreed, however, that the word translated *were filled* in Acts 13:52 is an iterative imperfect. Some authorities regard it as the descriptive imperfect (durative), also called the progressive imperfect.[43] For instance, A. T. Robertson translated it, "they kept on being filled."[44] This, in essence, is the translation of the New American Standard Bible which renders the passage, "And the disciples were continually filled with joy and with the Holy Spirit." It is also the reading of the New Testament in Modern English (J. B. Phillips): "And the disciples continued to be full of joy and the Holy Spirit."

The weight of the evidence is, therefore, against interpreting Acts 13:52 in favor of the doctrine of repeated fillings with the Holy Spirit. It may be concluded from this examination of the evidence in the book of the Acts, that there is no exegetical support for the theological formulation, "one baptism, but many fillings." Rather, the evidence points to one crisis baptism in the Holy Spirit, whereby the candidate is filled with the Holy Spirit, and inducted into a continuously Spirit-filled life and witness. Anything less than this is a compromise with the scriptural norm.

Be Continuously Filled with the Spirit

A final use of the phrase "filled with the Spirit" is found in Eph. 5:18: "And do not get drunk with wine, for that is debauchery: but be filled with the Spirit." In this text, the word for *be filled*[45] is in

[41] Italics added.

[42] ἐβαπτίζοντο, imperfect, passive.

[43] Dana and Mantey, op. cit., p. 187. Cf. also Robertson, *Grammar*, pp. 838, 883, 884.

[44] Robertson, Word Pictures, III, p. 203.

[45] πληροῦσθε ἐν πνεύματι.

the present tense, imperative mood, and passive voice. Once again, the interpreter is confronted with a choice, for the present imperative when used in commands means either continuous or repeated action.[46]

If the sense of repeated action (the iterative present) is adopted, the clause would then read: "be filled again and again with the Spirit." This then would lend support to the view of repeated fillings with the Holy Spirit. On the other hand, if it is interpreted as a continuous (durative) present, the sense then is, "be continuously filled with the Spirit." In favor of the latter view, it may be urged that this is consistent with all prior uses of the phrase "filled with the Spirit." Against this contention, however, it can be argued that prior usage can yield here only inductive probability. It cannot be completely definitive for the meaning of the phrase in this text. The problem can only be settled by interpreting this phrase *in its context*, for neither the tense nor the "significance of the verbal idea" alone offers a final solution.[47]

The sense in which the verb *be filled* is understood is affected by the antithetical parallelism in this verse between "do not get drunk with wine" and "be filled with the Spirit." This antithesis is not a contrast "between the *instruments* but between the *states*—between two elevated states, one due to the excitement of wine, the other to the inspiration and enlightenment of the Spirit."[48] The verb translated *do not get drunk*, in the first member of the parallelism, is also a present imperative, used here with the negative particle. When the present imperative is used in prohibitions, "the present tense is properly used for expressing continued action."[49] As a matter of record, Robertson found that in a study of the present imperative, and the aorist subjunctive respectively, in prohibitions, "the present imperative was found to be *regularly durative*."[50] Therefore, since the present imperative in the first member of the comparison ("do not get drunk with wine") is a continuous (durative) present, consistency dictates that the pres-

[46] Dana and Mantey, op. cit., p. 300.

[47] Dana and Mantey, op. cit., p. 206. The significance of a particular use of a tense is influenced by "the *basal function of the tense*, the *relation to the context*, and the *significance of the verbal idea*."

[48] S. D. F. Salmond, *The Epistle to the Ephesians*, ed. W. R. Nicoll, Vol. III, *The Expositor's Greek Testament* (Grand Rapids: Eerdmans, [n.d.]), p. 363.

[49] Dana and Mantey, op. cit., p. 301.

[50] Robertson, *Grammar*, p. 890, italics added.

ent imperative in the second half of the parallelism ("but be filled with the Spirit") be interpreted as a continuous present also. The text may be paraphrased thus: "Stop being habitually drunken with wine[51] but be continuously filled with the Spirit."

Since the continuous (durative) idea is grammatically and contextually preferable to the iterative (repeated) sense of the verb *be filled*, it follows that this passage does not teach repeated fillings with the Holy Spirit.

Excursus on πίμπλημι and πληρόω

One further question in relation to the phrase "filled with the Spirit" remains to be addressed. The student of New Testament Greek will be aware that two different words for *filled* have been used in the verses studied. The first word πίμπλημι is used in Acts 2:4; 4:8, 31; 9:17; and 13:9. However, what is especially noteworthy is that it is used *only* in the aorist tense. The second word, πληρόω, is used twice, once in Acts 13:52 in the imperfect tense, and once in Eph. 5:18 in the present tense.

The basic definition of both words is the same, i.e., "to fill full." In addition, the second word, πληρόω, has a secondary meaning, "to perfect, consummate,"[52] i.e., in an absolute sense.[53] Erroneous conclusions may be inferred, on occasion, from an uncritical application of this latter meaning to the texts in question. Any assumption that the filling with the Spirit referred to in Eph. 5:18 is qualitatively different from that described in the book of Acts because πληρόω is used rather than πίμπλημι, is a fallacious inference. The implication, expressed or implied, that Eph. 5:18 means "go beyond the fulness of the Spirit received when you were baptized in the Spirit to a new, or absolute fulness of the Spirit," is likewise in error. It is significant that of the lexicons consulted,[54] all list Eph. 5:18 under the primary meaning of the word. None ascribes the secondary sense, "to perfect, consummate," to the use of the word in Eph. 5:18—and that for a sound grammatical reason.

[51] Dana and Mantey, op. cit., p. 301. "A prohibition in the present imperative demands that action then in progress be stopped."

[52] Grimm, Wilke, Thayer, p. 518.

[53] Cremer, op. cit., p. 519.

[54] Cremer, p. 518; Grimm, Wilke, Thayer, p. 517; Bauer, Arndt, Gingrich, p. 677.

The word used most frequently in Acts, πίμπλημι, has a defective tense system in the New Testament. It is used only in the aorist tense, active and passive voice, and in the future tense, passive voice. When the need arose for another tense to convey a specific shade of meaning, it was supplied by the more complete tense system of the cognate verb πληρόω, or, as in the case of Acts 7:55, by the use of a comparable idiom. For instance, in this latter passage, Luke used a circumlocution for the unused present tense of πίμπλημι. He arrived at the sense of the present by using the present participle of ὑπάρχω, *to exist* (= *to be*), and the predicate noun πλήρης, *full*. Again in Acts 13:52, he filled out the incomplete tense system of πίμπλημι with the imperfect tense of πληρόω. So also in Eph. 5:18, lacking the present tense of πίμπλημι,[55] Paul, or his scribe, simply used the present tense of πληρόω to convey the meaning of πίμπλημι.

The choice, therefore, of πληρόω in Eph. 5:18 was dictated by *grammatical*, and not by *theological*, considerations. The use of one of these verbs over the other in the foregoing instances implies no difference in the degree or quality of the Spirit's fulness. On the one hand, it is a theological fallacy to infer from the secondary sense of πληρόω, i.e., *to perfect*, *consummate*, that the baptism in the Spirit does not result in a complete fulness of the Spirit in the Christian's life and witness.

On the other hand, this does not affirm the opposite extreme. The baptism in the Holy Spirit is not a shortcut to sanctification. Spirit-baptism is not instant maturity; rather, the Pentecostal fulness of the Spirit opens one's understanding to new vistas of spiritual potential set before every Christian. It is an introduction to a charismatic dimension of Christian spirituality, a dimension of spiritual experience filled with new challenges and opportunities. The very phenomenology of the experience restores to Christian experience a sense of the divine immanence often lost in more traditional forms. It provides a powerful stimulus for spiritual growth in communal fellowship, worship, and service.

But, as is so often true in other areas of human experience, its strength may become its weakness. Preoccupation with the phenomena of Spirit-baptism can produce a lopsided emphasis on the external and functional aspects of Christian experience. Cultiva-

[55] Robertson, *Grammar*, p. 317.

tion of the inner graces of the Spirit may be coopted in favor of the functional at the expense of spiritual maturity. However, spiritual maturity is the integration of the fruit(s)[56] of the Spirit with the charisms of the Spirit, of which more will be said later. What may be perceived as a weakness, then, in a Pentecostal spirituality is a failure to cultivate a more traditional, contemplative spirituality. Which is simply saying what the Church must discover anew in each generation. The institutional is renewed by the Spirit's charisms; the charismatic is matured by the institutional disciplines.

[56] Gal. 5:22.

Chapter 9

The Fruit(s) and Gifts of the Spirit

THE PRECEDING DISCUSSION raises the question of the relationship of the fruit(s)[1] of the Spirit to the charisms (gifts) of the Spirit. A colleague defined the relationship thus: "The fulness of the Holy Spirit is much more than a charismatic outflow or empowering . . . the fruit of the Spirit is coordinate with the *charismata* as evidence of the Spirit's control of one's life." What must be underscored here is that this is a theological construct, and not an exegetical datum. In point of fact, it subordinates the exegetical evidence to preconceived theological sensitivities. The definition, however, does provide a convenient paradigm for analyzing the question.

(1) Does the exegetical evidence support the claim that "the fulness of the Holy Spirit is much more than a charismatic outflow or empowering"? At the outset of the inquiry, it should be noted that filled with the Holy Spirit/fulness of the Holy Spirit is a uniquely Lukan concept. This establishes the contextual parameters of the investigation.

In the promise of Jesus, recorded by Luke,[2] He defined the baptism in/fulness of the Holy Spirit as a charismatic empowering, i.e., "you shall receive power when the Holy Spirit has come upon you; and you shall be my witnesses"—and the context makes it clear that this power was demonstrated charismatically in the witness of the disciples.

[1] καρπός, *fruit(s)* in a collective sense. From now on, *fruit* will be used in this sense.

[2] Acts 1:8.

The subsequent evidence of the book of Acts supports this contention. In Acts 2:4, the disciples were filled with the Holy Spirit and "began to speak in other tongues, as the Spirit gave them utterance." In this initial instance, the fulness of the Spirit was evidenced by a charismatic outflowing of His personality in supernatural speech. Shortly after the Pentecostal enduement with the Spirit, a Spirit-filled[3] Peter stood before the council of the Jewish nation, and boldly witnessed for Jesus. The lame man who had been healed at the temple gate was exhibit A at the inquiry.[4] Here also the evidence of the Spirit's fulness in the life of Peter was a charismatic miracle, and a charismatically charged witness.

In like manner, a Spirit-filled Paul countered the attempts of the sorcerer Elymas to divert the proconsul Sergius Paulus from the preaching of the gospel, and pronounced a sentence of blindness upon the magician.[5] In this instance also, the fulness of the Spirit was characterized by a charismatic empowerment of the word and deed. So too, in Acts 4:31 the place where the Christians were gathered together shook under the Spirit's presence; they were filled with the Holy Spirit, and they spoke the word with boldness—all are charismatic manifestations. The martyrdom of Stephen is further evidence of the charismatic nature of the Spirit's fulness, for in I Cor. 13:3, Paul listed martyrdom with the charismatic manifestations of tongues and prophecy in the same context.

In the case of the Church's first deacons, they were "seven men of good repute, full of the Spirit and of wisdom."[6] Stephen, in particular, was singled out from among them as one "full of grace and power" who "did great wonders and signs among the people."[7] Barnabas too was distinguished as "a good man, full of the Holy Spirit and of faith."[8] In each instance, the genitive phrases, "full of the Spirit," "full of wisdom," and "full of faith," modify the noun by attributing certain qualities to each individual. It is noteworthy, that "wisdom" and "faith" are charismatic empowerings for service.

[3] Acts 4:8.
[4] Acts 3:1–8.
[5] Acts 13:6–12.
[6] Acts 6:3.
[7] Acts 6:8.
[8] Acts 11:24.

Only in Acts 13:52 are the fruit of the divine Spirit mentioned as coincident with the Spirit's fulness—"the converts were filled with *joy* and with the Holy Spirit."[9] The combining of the fruit (*joy*) of the Holy Spirit with the fulness of the Spirit is attributable to their experience as converts. The new birth is the precondition for receiving the baptism in the Spirit, and as converts, they had just experienced both.

Fruit is a pregnant metaphor for life, and in the context is evidence of the new birth. The fruit of the Holy Spirit are ontological; the charismata are functional. These are independent and distinct categories. The fruit of the Spirit are the attributes of the divine nature of which believers become partakers through their new birth.[10] They are the attributes of their new, "divine"[11] nature.

What is specifically germane to the present inquiry is the fact that the charismata are sovereign manifestations of the Spirit's power.[12] The fruit of the Holy Spirit are attributes of redeemed nature, and as fruit they may be cultivated. The latter represents a divine-human synergism. Applied to the spiritual state of the individual, this is a parable of growth in spiritual maturity, or sanctification.

(2) Serious consideration of the thesis that "the fruit of the Spirit is coordinate with the charismata as evidence of the Spirit's control of one's life," poses mutually paradoxical conclusions. If the fruit are present in the life, but the charismata are not manifested, then logically one is not under the control of the Spirit. Conversely, if one experiences the charismata of the Spirit, but does not give evidence of the fruit, then one is not under the control of the Spirit. However, it cannot be denied, that many Christians give evidence of spiritual fruit who have never experienced the charismatic manifestations of the Spirit. What is not resolved in the thesis under scrutiny is whether the fulness of the Spirit is to be attributed to the functional category, charismata, or to the ontological category, fruit, or to both. What is tacitly assumed is that it is to be attributed to both equally.

[9] Italics added. Joy is listed as a fruit in Gal. 5:22.

[10] II Pet. 1:4.

[11] Jesus is the Son of God by nature; believers become children of God by grace.

[12] I Cor. 12:11.

In the context of the discussion on the baptism in/fulness of the Spirit, the more important question remains to be asked. Is a lapse in the manifestations of the Spirit's fruit to be interpreted as a loss of the Spirit's fulness? The thesis, as stated, clearly implies this. Remedial action would then require a renewal of the fruit, and a refilling with the Spirit. One must ask, however, whether this is an exegetical datum, or a logical construct. The evidence clearly indicates that it is a logical construct.

For example, Stephen was full of "faith"[13] and "grace[14] and power," which are charismatic enablings of the Holy Spirit. In his denunciation of the Sanhedrin—"you stiff-necked people, uncircumcised in heart and ears"[15]—he transgressed a spiritual principle. Paul, in similar circumstances, when rebuked for his outburst against the high priest, acknowledged that "it is written, 'You shall not speak evil of a ruler of your people.'"[16] Was then this passionate outburst on Stephen's part against the high priest, and the council, evidence that he had lost the fulness of the Spirit? One can hardly claim that the fruit of the Spirit were coordinate with the charismata in this instance. Nevertheless, Stephen, still "full of the Holy Spirit,"[17] sealed his testimony with a martyr's blood.

By analogy, it might further be argued that when Paul and Barnabas engaged in angry controversy over Mark's defection,[18] that this is evidence that they had forfeited the fulness of the Holy Spirit in their lives. But what has been said of Stephen, may also be said of Paul and Barnabas. Human frailty does not disqualify one from manifesting the charismatic fulness of the Holy Spirit in life and witness.

Without belaboring the point, certain conclusions may be reiterated. If the continuing fulness of the Spirit is contingent upon a level of spiritual maturity, then it is conditioned to some degree at least by human effort. If the fulness of the Spirit is initially a free gift of grace, but continuous fulness is contingent

[13] Acts 6:5.

[14] Acts 6:8, χάρις, "is hardly to be differentiated fr(om) δύναμις" (Bauer, Arndt, Gingrich).

[15] Acts 7:51.

[16] Acts 23:5.

[17] Acts 7:55.

[18] Acts 15:39.

upon the cultivation of the fruit of the Spirit, then one's power as witness ought to be in direct ratio to his or her spiritual maturity. To argue that because Barnabas and Paul came to an angry separation over Mark's default, or that because Peter, in a momentary vacillation, dissembled before the Judaizers in Galatia,[19] that they therefore lost the Spirit's fulness in their lives logically implies that they also lost their effectiveness as witnesses. But these are not facts of exegesis.

There is an alternative overlooked in this proposition. While Scripture does not coordinate the fruit of the Spirit with the charismata as evidence of the fulness of the Spirit, Paul does equate *quenching* the Spirit with a willful depreciation of the Holy Spirit's supernatural manifestations, e.g., "Stop quenching the Spirit, stop despising prophesying."[20] It is not, therefore, neglect of the fruit of God's Spirit, but contempt for His charisms that places one at risk spiritually.

This does not deny that the practical consequences of the Holy Spirit's influence in the life of the Christian are reflected in holy impulses and aspirations conducive to spiritual growth. It does deny that the charismatic fulness of the Holy Spirit is commensurate with one's sanctification.

But what of the other side of the coin? Does the absence of the charismata mean that one has lost the fulness of the Holy Spirit? One encounters this attitude frequently in Pentecostal/Charismatic circles. The counsel offered by Paul to his hard-pressed young protégé, Timothy, is to the point: "I now remind you to stir into flame the gift of God which is within you through the laying on of my hands."[21] The gift to which Paul referred was the charism that accompanied Timothy's baptism in the Spirit through the laying on of Paul's hands, namely utterance (prayer) in tongues. This interpretation may be supported analogically by comparison with the experience of the Ephesian converts, who "when Paul laid his hands upon them, the Holy Spirit came on them; and they spoke with tongues and prophesied."[22]

The discussion may be advanced a step further by asking,

[19] Gal. 2:11–14.

[20] I Thess. 5:19, 20. "A prohibition in the present imperative demands that action then in progress be stopped" (Dana and Mantey, op. cit., p. 301).

[21] II Tim. 1:6, NEB.

[22] Acts 19:6.

what, if any, scriptural provision is made for maintaining a Spirit-filled experience? Paul's answer is simple, and direct: "be filled (continuously) with the Spirit, addressing[23] one another in psalms and hymns and spiritual songs."[24]

The personal effects of charismatic worship—specifically speaking (praying) in tongues—are noted by Paul: "He who speaks in a tongue edifies himself."[25] Nor did he denigrate tongues, for he acknowledged their value in his own experience, saying, "if I pray in a tongue, my spirit prays. . . . I will pray with the spirit (i.e., in tongues). . . . I will sing with the spirit (i.e., in tongues). . . . I thank God that I speak in tongues more than you all."[26]

The baptism in the Holy Spirit is not per se an emotional experience, nor can the continuing fulness of the Spirit be equated with transitory emotional experiences, or lack of them—an all too common fallacy on both sides of the charismatic dialogue. Such emotional states are the human response to the fulness of the Spirit's presence. The manifestations of the charismata are the evidence of the Spirit's power. The baptism in and fulness of the Spirit are synonymous terms, and a charismatic dimension to Christian experience is evidence of the Holy Spirit's fulness. Consequently, the nurture of these charismatic manifestations "edifies," that is to say, "maintains," the charismatic flow of the Holy Spirit's fulness. Nor can one improve on Paul's simple formula; "stir into flame the gift of God which is in you through the laying on of my hands."

[23] Eph. 5:18, 19, λαλοῦντες. "The Instrumental Participle . . . may indicate the means by which the action of the main verb is accomplished" (Dana and Mantey, op. cit., 228). Called to my attention by a former student, Phil Windsor.

[24] ᾠδαῖς πνευματικαῖς is reminiscent of Paul's words in I Cor. 14:15: "I will sing with the Spirit" = singing in tongues. The context of Eph. 5:18, 19 echoes I Cor. 14:25ff., with its instructions for charismatic worship.

[25] I Cor. 14:4.

[26] I Cor. 14:14–18.

Chapter 10

To All That Are Far Off[1]

THE LIFE AND WITNESS of the apostolic community may be summarized in a brief, autobiographical statement of Paul: "by the power of signs and wonders, by the power of the Holy Spirit . . . I have fully preached the gospel of Christ."[2] By prophecy and promise, the normal Christian life is charismatic. In walk, witness, and worship, the normal Christian church is a charismatic community. It is, in a word, Pentecostal, for the source of its charismatic enabling is a personal Pentecost.

The normative pattern of the baptism in the Holy Spirit has already been summarized.[3] Of the five theses itemized there, the first two are self-evident, and the fifth has been discussed in detail. Now an exposition of the biblical evidence for the third and fourth propositions will be offered. Because of the nature of the evidence, these will be discussed simultaneously, rather than individually.

The third proposition restated says that the baptism in the Holy Spirit is not synonymous with conversion and the new birth. It is subsequent to regeneration. The fourth thesis says that the normative evidence of the baptism in the Spirit is a charismatic manifestation of the Spirit's personality and power. Simply put, the initial manifestation of the Pentecostal baptism in the Spirit was "speak(ing) in tongues, as the Spirit gave them utterance."[4]

Acts 2:1–4—The Disciples' "Pentecost"

The context of Acts has been examined in sufficient detail to justify only a brief recapitulation here. The disciples of Jesus were

[1] Acts 2:39.
[2] Rom. 15:19.
[3] Chapter 7.
[4] Acts 2:4.

born again on the evening of the resurrection day when He breathed on them and said, "Receive the Holy Spirit."[5] Some fifty days later, "when the day of Pentecost had come,"[6] the promised "gift"[7] of the Holy Spirit was poured out by the ascended Jesus upon those gathered together in the upper room. This was the baptism in the Holy Spirit prophesied by John, and promised by Jesus. As a consequence of this Spirit-baptism, "they were all filled with the Holy Spirit," and in evidence of His overflowing presence, they "began to speak in other tongues, as the Spirit gave them utterance."

The activity of the Holy Spirit in their regeneration was separated from their baptism in the Holy Spirit by an interval of some seven weeks. Furthermore, when they were baptized in/filled with the Spirit, the initial manifestation of His presence and power was speech in other tongues. In fact, His initial self-manifestation is uniformly *speech*, and appropriately so, for the promised power of the Holy Spirit is fittingly manifested first in the organ preeminently associated with witnessing, namely, the tongue. And this is in accord with the purpose of the Pentecostal enduement as announced by Jesus: "you shall receive power, when the Holy Spirit has come upon you; and you shall be my witnesses . . . to the end of the earth."

Acts 4:31—The Jewish "Pentecost"

The Pentecostal effusion of the Spirit was repeated again a short time later, according to Acts 4:31: "And when they had prayed, the place in which they were gathered together was shaken; and they were all filled with the Holy Spirit and spoke the word of God with boldness." In the interim, the number of converts increased to about 5000 men.[8] These were now numbered among the company of believers comprising the growing Church. Subsequent to their conversion, they too were filled with the Holy Spirit. The sequence of events is clear thus far, and though tongues are not explicitly mentioned, attendant circumstances prompt the inference that they were part of the total pattern.

[5] John 20:22.
[6] Acts 2:1.
[7] Acts 2:38, δωρεάν τοῦ ἁγίου πνεύματος; cf. Acts 8:10; 10:45; 11:17.
[8] Acts 4:4.

When Peter and John were released from custody by the Sanhedrin, their recital of the duress and threats to which they had been subjected initiated a prayer meeting of the whole community to meet the challenge. Their prayer contained a threefold request. *One*, "grant to thy servants to speak thy word with all boldness,"[9] i.e., in the face of threatened persecution, the full fury of which was soon to explode in the stoning of Stephen, the first Christian martyr. *Two*, "while thou stretchest out thy hand to heal."[10] This was especially significant since it was the healing of the lame man at the gate of the temple and the resultant evangelistic success of Peter and John that precipitated the confrontation with the Sanhedrin. *Three*, "and signs and wonders are performed through the name of thy holy servant Jesus."

Then followed the second outpouring of the Holy Spirit, as at Pentecost, for (1) "the place in which they were gathered together was shaken"; (2) "they were all filled with the Holy Spirit"; and (3) they "spoke the word of God with boldness."[11] Even a superficial perusal of the ensuing context validates the judgment that "they were thus endued both with courage to declare the word of God and with miraculous power for confirming the truth."[12] In response to their entreaty, there was an immediate divine manifestation, for the place where they were gathered together was shaken, and they were filled with the Holy Spirit. This was followed by a subsequent enablement, for they declared the word of God with boldness, and "many signs and wonders were done among the people by the hands of the apostles."[13] In this regard, the names of two of the first deacons, Stephen[14] and Philip,[15] figure prominently in closely related narratives.

The entire context is a charismatic one of great *signs* and *wonders*,[16] exorcisms and healings. In such a charismatic context, it is more consistent to affirm, than to deny, that the initial

[9] Acts 4:29.

[10] Acts 4:30.

[11] Acts 4:31.

[12] H. B. Hackett, *A Commentary on the Acts of the Apostles*, ed. A. Hovey, Vol. VI, *An American Commentary on The New Testament* (Philadelphia: American Baptist Publication Society, 1882), p. 72.

[13] Acts 5:12.

[14] Acts 6:8.

[15] Acts 8:6, 7.

[16] *σημεῖα καὶ τέρατα*, *miracles* and *prodigies* (Bauer, Arndt, Gingrich).

Pentecost charism of tongues was in evidence among these *signs* and *wonders*. These are, in fact, among the *signs* intended to confirm the preaching of the gospel, according to Mark 16:17–20.[17] Verse 20 of Mark 16 concludes thus: "And they were forth and preached everywhere, while the Lord worked with them and confirmed the message by the signs that attended it." Whether one accepts or rejects the authenticity of this much debated passage, Acts 8:6 explicitly corroborates the confirmatory function of these charismatic signs. Here it is said that the Samaritans responded to Philip's preaching "when they heard him and saw the signs which he did." Paul adds the weight of his testimony in these words: "tongues are a sign not for believers but for unbelievers."[18] Tongues were among the *signs* both heard and seen in Jerusalem, Caesarea, Ephesus, and Corinth. It is, therefore, an inference consistent with an often repeated pattern to infer that these Jerusalem converts also spoke in tongues when they were filled with the Spirit according to Acts 4:31.

Acts 8:14–17—The Samaritan "Pentecost"

The next recorded manifestation of the Pentecostal effusion of the Holy Spirit is related in Acts 8. The martyrdom of Stephen triggered the first general persecution of the fledgling Church. It resulted in the dispersion of all but the apostles from Jerusalem. Philip, one of the seven "deacons"—chosen because he was "full of the Spirit and wisdom"[19]—went down to the city of Samaria and preached "the Christ" (i.e, the Messiah). Revival was the result as the "winds" of the Spirit swept over the people, for

> the multitudes with one accord gave heed to what was said by Philip, when they heard him and saw the signs which he did. For unclean spirits came out of many who were possessed . . . and many who were paralyzed or lame were healed . . . when they believed Philip as he preached good news about the kingdom of God and the name of Jesus Christ, they were baptized, both men and women.[20]

[17] The authenticity of the traditional ending of Mark is not at issue here, for it represents, at least, a very ancient understanding within the apostolic community of its charismatic life and ministry.

[18] I Cor. 14:22.

[19] Acts 6:3.

[20] Acts 8:6, 7, 12.

The sequence of events gives clear evidence that these Samaritan converts had become Christians in the fullest sense of the word. They had believed on Jesus, and they were baptized. This then is an instance of believer's baptism predicated upon saving faith in Christ, the prior condition for the new birth. Their baptism is in itself a witness that these Samaritan converts had experienced the regenerative action of the Holy Spirit in their lives.

The implications of this fact for the sequel needs to be underscored here, for

> when the apostles at Jerusalem heard that Samaria had received the word of God, they sent to them Peter and John,[21] who came down and prayed for them that they might receive the Holy Spirit; for it (He) had not yet fallen on[22] any of them, but they had only been baptized in the name of the Lord Jesus. Then they laid their hands on them and they received the Holy Spirit.[23]

The order of events parallels the pattern of the baptism in/filling with the Holy Spirit already deduced. First, saving faith in Jesus Christ, with its concomitant new birth, followed by believer's baptism in water. Then some time later—i.e., the time necessary for news of the revival to travel from Samaria to Jerusalem, and for the apostles there to send two of their number to Samaria to investigate—Peter and John came down, and "they laid their hands on them and they received the Holy Spirit."[24] It is

[21] "The sending of Peter and John was no reflection on Philip, but was an appropriate mission since 'many Christian Jews would be scandalized by the admission of Samaritans' (Furneau). If Peter and John sanctioned it, the situation would be improved" (Robertson, *Word Pictures*, III, p. 106).

[22] ἐπιπίπτω, *to fall upon, to come upon*. Cf. Acts 8:16, 39 (Western text), 10:44; 11:15. Bauer, Arndt, Gingrich, "*fall upon someth(ing)* . . . Of the Holy Spirit, *who comes upon someone*." He falls upon from without before He wells up from within. One cannot be filled until he or she has been immersed in the Holy Spirit.

[23] Acts 8:14–17. For a critical exposition, cf., Ervin, *Conversion-Initiation and the Baptism in the Holy Spirit*, pp. 25–39.

[24] One might ask, in what sense does the action of the Holy Spirit in regeneration differ from His activity in the baptism? In the new birth one receives Jesus Christ as personal Savior and Lord, and "to all who did receive him . . . he gave the right to become children of God . . . the offspring of God himself" (John 1:12, 13, NEB; cf. I Pet. 1:23). In the baptism in the Spirit one receives power "to do." The new birth is an ontological change of one's nature; the baptism in the Spirit is the "gift of the Spirit" in supernatural enablement for service. This empowerment is "power in operation, in action; not merely *power capable of action, but power in action*" (Cremer, op. cit., p. 200).

noteworthy here that Peter and John did not rebaptize these Samaritan converts in water before laying their hands upon them for the reception of the Spirit, as, for example, Paul did with the disciples of John the Baptist whom he met at Ephesus. Obviously, these two representatives of the apostolic college in Jerusalem were satisfied that these Samaritan disciples were born again in consequence of the Holy Spirit's regenerative work, accomplished through Philip's preaching of the gospel.

The accompanying episode is, in one sense, cryptic, yet nonetheless illuminating; for when Simon the sorcerer saw that they had received the Holy Spirit through the laying of the apostles hands, "he offered them money, saying, 'Give me also this power, that any one on whom I lay my hands my receive the Holy Spirit.'"[25] Signs and great miracles, including healings and exorcisms,[26] were performed by Philip without producing this result in Simon, and so arousing his cupidity. The question remains to be answered: What did Simon *see* that convinced him that these Samaritan disciples had received the Holy Spirit through the laying on of the hands of Peter and John? It is said, that "a man convinced against his will, is of the same opinion still," but this is not the intention of the present author in what follows. However, for the unbiased enquirer, as well as the charismatic Christian, there is considerable value in the answers given to this question by exegetes who cannot be accused of a Pentecostal bias. The more so since their views cannot be discounted as a Pentecostal apologetic.

In Meyer's opinion, "the communication of the Spirit was visible . . . in the gestures and gesticulations of those who received it, perhaps also in similar phenomena to those which took place at Pentecost in Jerusalem."[27] The American editor of Meyer's *Commentary*, William Ormiston, appealed to Calvin's comment in the following vein: "Calvin on verse 16 writes: 'Surely Luke speaketh not in this place of the common grace of the Spirit, whereby God doth regenerate us, that we may be his children; but of those singular gifts, wherewith God would have certain endued at the beginning of the gospel to beautify Christ's kingdom."[28] To this, Ormiston adds his own comment:

[25] Acts 8:18, 19.
[26] Acts 8:7, 13.
[27] *Critical and Exegetical Commentary on the Acts of the Apostles*, p. 171.
[28] Ibid., p. 180. The exception to Calvin's view urged here is that the

> By the *Holy Ghost* we do not understand the regenerating and sanctifying agency of the Holy Spirit in the conversion and renewal of the soul; but the impartation of such a presence of the Holy Spirit as is accompanied with supernatural gifts; the miraculous influences of the Spirit, which were manifested by speaking with tongues, or other visible tokens.[29]

F. F. Bruce's view is unambiguous, for he writes: "The context leaves us in no doubt that their reception of the Spirit was attended by external manifestations such as had marked His descent on the earliest disciples at Pentecost."[30] The terse comment of A. T. Robertson is in the same vein: "This participle (second aorist active of *horaō*) shows plainly that those who received the gift of the Holy Spirit spoke with tongues."[31] Equally succinct and direct is the remark of F. J. Foakes-Jackson: "The gift is manifested openly, possibly (though this is not stated) by *glossolalia*."[32] More recently Johannes Munck added his voice to the consensus above: "Simon . . . was struck by the apostles ability to make the baptized prophesy and to speak in tongues by the laying on of hands."[33]

Thus the analysis of the context justifies the conclusion that these Samaritan converts received the baptism in the Holy Spirit after their conversion, with the probable evidence of speaking in tongues.

Acts 8:38, 39—The Ethiopian Eunuch's "Pentecost"

The normative biblical pattern of the baptism in the Holy Spirit is reflected again in a variant textual reading of Acts 8:39. In place of the accepted reading, several manuscripts and church fathers read, "the Spirit of the Lord fell upon the eunuch, and an angel of the

---

Scriptures do not limit the baptism in the Spirit to a select few in the apostolic age

[29] Ibid., p. 180.

[30] *Commentary on the Book of the Acts*, p. 181. He adds in fn. 34: "The prior operation of the Spirit in regeneration and faith is not in view here." Whether this is a paraphrase of N. B. Stonehouse (the context would suggest that it is), or his own further summary is not clear.

[31] *Word Pictures*, III, p. 107.

[32] *The Acts of the Apostles*, ed. J. Moffatt, *The Moffatt New Testament Commentary* (New York: Harper & Brothers, [n.d.]), p. 73.

[33] *The Acts of the Apostles*, rev. W. F. Albright and C. S. Mann, ed. D. N. Freedman, et al., *Anchor Bible* Vol. 31, (Garden City: Doubleday 1973), p. 75.

Lord caught away Philip."[34] This variant reading probably arose, according to Henry Alford, "from a desire to conform the result of the eunuch's baptism to the usual method of the divine procedure."[35] This simply reiterates the fundamental premise of this study, namely, there is a normative pattern in the Holy Spirit's activity: (1) in conversion with its attendant regeneration, and (2) a subsequent baptism in the Spirit for power in mission.

This is also spelled out in the declaration that "the much more important effect of the longer reading is to make it clear that the Ethiopian's baptism was followed by the gift of the Spirit. However, even with the shorter reading it is a safe inference that he did receive the Spirit."[36] If one may "safely infer" this from the shorter reading, then it is equally valid to infer from the studied conformity of the longer reading, "to the usual method of the divine procedure," that the entire pattern of the Pentecostal enduement with power is implied—including the evidence of *glossolalia*. The context itself suggests that the Ethiopian's immediate reaction to the effusion of the divine Spirit was vocal, for "the eunuch . . . went on his way rejoicing." However, A. T. Robertson's comment in another context is appropriate at this point: "One will believe here as the facts appeal to him."[37]

Acts 9:17—Paul's "Pentecost"

The personal "Pentecost" of Paul (Saul) is related in Acts 9:17. The facts are simply related. Paul met Jesus in a theophany while journeying to Damascus with warrants from the high priest at Jerusalem for the arrest of the Christians residing there. Escorted into the city, blinded as a result of his encounter with the glorified Son of God, he spent the next three days and nights in fasting and prayer. Meanwhile, the Lord appeared in a vision to one of the local community of believers, Ananias by name, whom He commissioned to go to Paul (Saul), and to minister to him as a "chosen vessel." Ananias reluctantly agreed, and v. 17 recounts how he entered the house where Paul was staying, "and laying his hands on him he said, 'Brother Saul, the Lord Jesus who appeared

[34] Bruce, *The Acts of the Apostles*, p. 195.

[35] *The Greek Testament*, II (5th ed.; Cambridge: Deighton, Bell, and Co., 1865), p. 190.

[36] Bruce, *Commentary on the Book of the Acts*, p. 190.

[37] Robertson, *Word Pictures*, III, p. 342.

to you on the road by which you came, has sent me that you may regain your sight and be filled with the Holy Spirit."

From the preceding context, it is clear that Ananias knew who Saul was and why he had come to Damascus—to persecute the believers there. He would never, therefore, have entered Saul's presence and addressed him as "Brother Saul," unless he had been assured in advance that Saul was, in very truth, a "Brother" in Christ.[38] Saul must, therefore, have become a Christian, in the fullest sense of the word, before Ananias came to him.[39]

If the narrative is clear and direct, so also are the conclusions to be drawn from it. It was in the Damascus road encounter that the persecutor of the Christians became a disciple of Christ Jesus. He was saved, and three days later he was healed of blindness, and filled with the Holy Spirit when Ananias laid his hands upon him in the name of Jesus. Here too the Pentecostal pattern is consistent: (1) conversion with its concomitant new birth, and (2) subsequently baptized in/filled with the Holy Spirit.

It should be noted in passing that this is the second instance wherein the Pentecostal enduement was mediated through the laying on of hands by those who had themselves been filled with the Spirit. In this case, it is also noteworthy that the human instrument was not an apostle. He was simply a fellow "disciple." The emphasis is not upon the human instrument, but upon the divine administrator: "Ananias laid his hands on Saul, but it was the power of Christ that in the same moment enlightened his eyes and filled him with the Holy Spirit."[40] It was not apostolic prerogative, but the authority of the divine commission that validated the laying on his hands. Jesus commissioned believers to perform a number of signs in His name, including "laying their hands on the sick"[41] for their healing. This Ananias did, and Jesus both healed Paul and filled him with the Holy Spirit. It is a kind of exegetical double vision that would try to divorce the laying on believer's hands for healing from the laying on of hands for the reception of the Holy Spirit of promise.[42]

[38] Robertson, *Word Pictures*, III, p. 121.

[39] For a critical defense of this thesis, see *Conversion-Initiation*, pp. 41–49.

[40] Bruce, *Commentary on the Book of the Acts*, p. 201.

[41] Mark 16:18.

[42] Knowling, op. cit., p. 237. To say, as Knowling does, that Ananias laid his hands on Paul "not as bestowing the Holy Spirit . . . but as recovering from

It is sometimes urged at this point that Paul did not speak in tongues when he was filled with the Spirit—at least it is not specifically mentioned in the context. On this basis it is argued that the Pentecostal pattern of Spirit-baptism was interrupted short of utterance in tongues, therefore, others too may be baptized in the Spirit without manifesting tongues as evidence. God is sovereign, so the argument goes, therefore, He is not bound by precedent. However, what is in view here is not the exception that proves the rule, but the normative pattern of Spirit-baptism in the book of the Acts.

Before a priori arguments are pressed, and the discussion polarized, Paul's own testimony should be introduced—if not as a rule, at least as an example: "I thank God," he wrote to the Corinthians, "that I speak in tongues more than you all."[43] Whether he spoke in tongues immediately or later is of little consequence to the major premise here. As the record consistently bears witness, there is a causal sequence and connection between being filled with/baptized in the Holy Spirit and speaking in tongues. It is a reasonable assumption then to affirm that Paul also spoke in tongues when he received the Pentecostal gift of the Holy Spirit.

Acts 10:44–46—The Roman "Pentecost"

Some ten years after Pentecost, Peter was summoned to the home of a Roman centurion named Cornelius. In spite of his exclusive Jewish scruples, allayed in part by a prophetic vision, he left Joppa for Caesarea and there proclaimed to Cornelius and his household the message of salvation. Cornelius was in all probability "a God-fearing proselyte"[44] in relation with the synagogue through which he may have acquired the knowledge of Jesus' life that Peter presumed of him.[45] Jesus' baptism, miracles, crucifixion, resurrection—all are touched upon by him.

---

his blindness," ignores both the grammar and the larger context. The adverb ὅπως, used as "a conjunction with the subjunctive . . . indicate(s) purpose (in order) that" (Bauer, Arndt, Gingrich). Ananias was sent to fulfill the twofold purpose of the Lord, viz., that Paul's sight be restored, and that he be filled with the Holy Spirit.

[43] I Cor. 14:18.

[44] Knowling, op. cit., p. 25.

[45] Acts 10:36ff.

The order of events sketched by Peter closely paralleled the sequence given by Jesus himself: "Thus it is written, that the Christ should suffer and on the third day rise from the dead, and that repentance and forgiveness of sins should be preached in his name to all nations."[46] The commission in Luke's Gospel closes with the promise of the Father (i.e., the Pentecostal gift of the Holy Spirit), which Peter declared prophetically on the day of Pentecost is not only for Jewish converts, but "to all that are far off, every one whom the Lord our God calls to him."[47]

The invitation to respond was pressed upon the Roman household in the following words: "To him all the prophets bear witness that every one who believes in him receives forgiveness of sins through his name."[48] Consistent then with the pattern given in the Gospel according to Luke, as Peter preached and Cornelius and his household received the message with saving faith, Jesus poured out the promised gift of the Holy Spirit upon the Roman, now Christian, household.

Was this a repetition of Pentecost? Peter's words before the Jerusalem congregation, in defense of his entering a Gentile home, leave little room for argument, for in his own words, "As I began to speak, the Holy Spirit fell on them just as on us at the beginning."[49] The reference is obviously to the Spirit's advent on the day of Pentecost and not to the Paschal insufflation of the Spirit when Jesus breathed new spiritual life into them on the resurrection day.

Furthermore, the outpouring of the Spirit in the house of Cornelius is described as "the gift of the Holy Spirit."[50] This characteristically Lukan phrase does not refer to the action of the Holy Spirit in regeneration, but to the Pentecostal baptism in the Spirit for power in mission. That tongues are the normative evidence of the baptism in the Holy Spirit is unmistakably clear in this place. In fact, the Jewish believers who accompanied Peter knew that these Gentile converts had received the gift of the Holy

[46] Luke 24:46, 47.
[47] Acts 2:39.
[48] Acts 10:43.
[49] Acts 11:15.
[50] Acts 10:45.

Spirit, "For they heard them speaking in tongues and extolling God."[51]

Acts 19:1-6—The Ephesian "Pentecost"

Almost twenty-five years[52] had elapsed since Pentecost when Paul met certain disciples of John the Baptist at Ephesus. Learning that they knew only the baptism of John, which was a baptism of repentance, he expounded the gospel more accurately to them, pointing to Jesus as the fulfillment of John's ministry. Luke recorded the scene in this fashion in Acts 19:4–6.

> And Paul said, "John baptized with the baptism of repentance, telling the people to believe in the one who was to come after him, that is Jesus." On hearing this, they were baptized in the name of the Lord Jesus. And when Paul had laid his hands upon them, the Holy Spirit came on them; and they spoke with tongues and prophesied.

Once again, the order of events is clearly marked. One can scarcely improve on the observation that "they were therefore baptized again in a Christian sense, and when Paul laid his hands on them, they received the Holy Spirit in Pentecostal fashion."[53] The evidential nature of the glossolalia here is heavily underscored by the comment that "the speaking with tongues and prophesying was external and *indubitable proof* that the Holy Spirit had come on these twelve uninformed disciples now fully won to the service of Jesus as Messiah."[54] The unequivocal affirmation, "external and indubitable proof," is consistent with the norm presented in the Scriptures.[55]

[51] Acts 10:46, γάρ, a conjunction "used to express cause, inference, continuation, or to explain" (Bauer, Arndt, Gingrich).

[52] P. Schaff, op. cit., pp. 220, 221.

[53] Bruce, *Commentary on the Book of the Acts*, p. 386.

[54] Robertson, *Word Pictures*, III, p. 313, italics added.

[55] An appeal to the participle of coincident action in Acts 19:2—"Did you receive (ἐλαβετε) the Holy Spirit when you believed (πιστεύσαντες)?"—does not prejudice the Pentecostal exegesis, even though it is "a characteristic of Luke's style to use frequently the coincident participle . . . placed after the regular verb" (Robertson, *Grammar*, p. 1113).*Coincident action* is not to be construed as "*simultaneous action* relative to the main verb [which] is ordinarily expressed by the present tense" (Dana and Mantey, op. cit., p. 230, italics added). In the context, faith precedes (water) baptism, baptism precedes the laying on of the hands, the laying on of (Paul's) hands preceded the gift of the Holy Spirit. In v. 6, the aorist participle, ἐπιθέντος *precedes* the principle verb, ἦλθε. The laying on

The relationship of this Ephesian outpouring of the Holy Spirit with the effusion of the Spirit at Pentecost is evident in this common denominator: "the Holy Spirit came on them; and they spoke with tongues and prophesied." In the previous discussion of Acts 2:4, it was pointed out that the word there translated "utterance" is used in the Septuagint not of ordinary conversation, but of the utterance of the prophets. One is reminded of the prophesying of the ecstatic prophets of ancient Israel. From this insight, it was concluded that while the newly Spirit-baptized disciples spoke supernaturally in tongues (i.e., in languages they neither knew nor understood), the representatives of the various language groups who heard and understood them, heard not tongues but inspired prophecy in their own languages. They heard the disciples extolling prophetically the "magnificence" of God. Likewise in Ephesus, these two related aspects of inspired utterance are combined, for "they spoke with tongues and prophesied."

In Ephesus the normal pattern of the baptism in/filling with the Holy Spirit was repeated. Hearing from Paul that Jesus was the long-awaited Messiah, they believed and received Christian baptism from him. Certainly their regeneration was a prior condition to their baptism in water. After water-baptism, their baptism in the Spirit followed, mediated by the laying on of Paul's hands. The point to be emphasized here is that Paul did not lay his hands on John's disciples to receive the Holy Spirit until after they had confessed their faith in Jesus in water-baptism. He laid his hands on them only after he was assured that they had become truly Christian. Consistent with the normative pattern of this experience, when they received the Spirit of the living God in charismatic fulness, they manifested His presence by speaking with tongues and prophesying.

Excursus on Tongues as Initial Evidence

Jews, Samaritans, and Romans, Saul a persecuting Pharisee, an Ethiopian eunuch, and twelve disciples of John the Baptist—all called on the name of the Lord Jesus, and all were saved. And after their conversion, each received as a birthright the baptism in the

---

of hands is *antecedent* to the reception of the Spirit. The Pentecostal doctrine (and experience) is therefore found to be compatible with both the context and the grammar of the passage.

Holy Spirit, for the promised gift of the Holy Spirit is "to all that are far off, every one whom the Lord our God calls to him." Whether stated or implied, it is a fair conclusion from the biblical evidence that tongues were the "external and indubitable proof"[56] of their baptism in the Holy Spirit.

A baptism in the Spirit then without charismatic evidence is not a biblical datum. It is a theological construct dictated by subapostolic experience to extenuate the impotence of the Church's life and ministry in the face of secular humanism and atheistic materialism. So it is that other evidences of the Spirit-empowered life have been proposed. Perhaps most noteworthy of these is the often repeated assertion that love is the evidence of the baptism in the Holy Spirit. But this is not scriptural. Love is evidence of conversion and the new birth: "We know that we have passed out of death into life, because we love the brethren."[57] Thus love is not evidence of the baptism in the Holy Spirit; it is a consequence of the new birth.

It is likewise often urged on the basis of I Cor. 12:11—"All these [gifts] are inspired by one and the same Spirit, who apportions to each one individually as he wills"—that the manifestation of any of the charisms listed in the context is sufficient evidence that one has been baptized in/filled with the Holy Spirit. The fallacy of this reasoning, however, is its tacit either/or premise, i.e., *either* prophecy, *or* gifts of healings, *or* discerning of spirits, etc., *instead of* tongues. But the disciples healed the sick,[58] spoke prophetically,[59] and cast out demons[60] before Pentecost. Actually, all of these supernatural manifestations of the Spirit can be paralleled either in the Old or the New Testaments before Pentecost. They were not then evidence of the baptism in the Holy Spirit. The initial evidence manifested with the baptism in the Spirit at Pentecost was "speak(ing) in other tongues, as the Spirit gave them utterance."

What this thesis fails to take into account is that Paul in his Corinthian epistle presupposes their prior baptism in the Spirit. The manifestations of the charisms in their midst were evidence

[56] Robertson, *Word Pictures*, III, p. 313.
[57] I John 3:14.
[58] Matt. 10:8.
[59] Matt. 16:16, 17.
[60] Luke 10:17ff.

that they had already been filled with the Spirit in a Pentecostal manner. These gifts of the Spirit are not presented as a substitute for the initial evidence of Spirit-baptism; rather, they are a consequence of that baptism.

It bears repeating here that of all of the Spirit's supernatural gifts, tongues appeared first in order at Pentecost. The other charisms followed subsequently. There is no convincing evidence that this order has been changed. It was in the context of a tongues-speaking congregation at Corinth that these manifestations of the Spirit proliferated. It is a matter of record that when tongues-speech disappeared from the corporate life and experience of the Church, the other charisms of the Spirit began to disappear also. Account for this as one will, the fact remains that theologians do not rationalize away miracles within the context of a personal charismatic experience.

In the same vein, the apostle's words, "Do all speak with tongues?" are often generalized out of their context in the interest of proving that one can be Spirit-filled without speaking in tongues. A casual reading of the series of rhetorical questions propounded by Paul in I Cor. 12:29, 30 implies a negative answer and thereby lends apparent credence to this assumption. When, however, they are related to their context, this support vanishes. From chapter 11 through chapter 14 of this epistle, the apostle Paul discussed the conduct of the corporate worship of the church at Corinth. The real point of his question, "Do all speak with tongues?" is this: "Do all speak with tongues in the corporate worship of the fellowship?" The implied answer is No! Otherwise, the injunction to interpret tongues, and to discern prophecy is pointless. Paul himself cited as an example the "unlearned,"[61] i.e., "the ungifted people."[62] Paul freely admitted that he could, and did, speak in tongues more than all of them. However, as the context indicates, he preferred to exercise this charism in his private devotions. The praying in tongues to which Paul alluded is for private edification.[63] It is prayer and praise addressed to God, and it is this devotional use of tongues that is an abiding evidence of the Spirit's fulness. On the other hand, the *gift* of tongues, with

[61] ἰδιῶται, "*destitute of the gift of tongues*" (Grimm, Wilke, Thayer); "a kind of proselytes, or catechumens" (Bauer, Arndt, Gingrich).

[62] Robertson and Plummer, op. cit., p. 317.

[63] I Cor. 14:18.

its indispensable companion gift of interpretation, is a public manifestation for the edification of the whole congregation. Through it God speaks to the assembly by way of "revelation or knowledge or prophecy or teaching."[64]

Spirit-baptized believers may pray in tongues as they consciously yield themselves to the Holy Spirit in worship. They cannot, however, speak in tongues the oracles of God unless the Holy Spirit chooses so to manifest himself. Clearly this is the import of Paul's warning to the Corinthians that "If, therefore, the whole church assembles, and all speak in tongues, and outsiders or unbelievers enter,"[65] they risked the accusation of madness. If *all* could not pray in tongues, contrary to the scenario here proposed by the apostle, then his argument has no relevance.[66]

On the day of Pentecost, they *all* spoke with tongues when they were filled with the Holy Spirit. In Caesarea, "the Holy Spirit fell on *all* who heard the word," and Peter and his companions "heard them speaking in tongues and extolling God."[67] A quarter of a century later, Paul met twelve disciples of John the Baptist at Ephesus. After baptizing them in water, the public confession of their faith in Jesus, he laid his hands upon them and *all* twelve spoke with tongues. In Corinth, Paul indicated that *all*, that is to say, all who had been filled with the Spirit, could speak (i.e., pray) in tongues.

Thus explicitly, as well as implicitly, the evidence indicates that *all* spoke with tongues as the evidence of their baptism in/filling with the Holy Spirit. On the other hand, to argue from the experience of Philip's Samaritan converts, or from the record of Paul's experience in Damascus, that all did not initially speak in tongues—and this is the point of the objection—therefore one need not speak in tongues now, is to argue from silence. Granted that the same objection may be urged against the use of these same

[64] I Cor. 14:6.

[65] I Cor. 11:23.

[66] The third class condition, *ἐὰν . . . πάντες λαλῶσιν γλώσσαις*, *if all speak in tongues*, cannot be dismissed as a wholly hypothetical case. It is no more hypothetical than the same third class condition in 14:14 where Paul wrote, *ἐὰν γὰρ προσεύχωμαι γλώσσῃ*, *if I pray in a tongue*. The fact that he was substantiating his point out of his own experience is shown by his acknowledgement in 14:18: "I thank God that I speak in tongues *more than you all*" (italics added).

[67] Acts 16:43, italics added.

scriptures to support the thesis that all did (and still do) speak in tongues. However, there is an important difference that gives the latter view the balance of probability. Reasoning from the experience of the disciples in Jerusalem, Caesarea, and Ephesus (where clearly *all* did speak with tongues when they were baptized in the Holy Spirit), it may be consistently argued that this was the normative pattern throughout the period covered by the New Testament.

Chapter 11

Concerning Spirituals

"NOW CONCERNING SPIRITUAL GIFTS, brethren, I do not want you to be uninformed."[1] It is a fundamental assumption of this study that the generally accepted translation of this text, i.e. "spiritual gifts" is misleading. In the course of this study, it will become self-evident that this is an interpretation rather than a translation in the strictest sense of the word. As a consequence, there is considerable misunderstanding among Christians of every theological persuasion concerning the nature and function of the Spirit's *gifts*. This is particularly so among Pentecostals and Charismatics.

Even a cursory reading of the literature on the subject suggests that the translation "spiritual *gifts*" has been influenced by theological assumptions suggested by other texts, rather than by a careful scrutiny of the immediate context. For example, the gifts of Christ[2] in Eph. 4:7ff. lend no support to the interpretation that the Holy Spirit's manifestations listed in I Cor. 12:8–11 are charisms bestowed by the Holy Spirit upon chosen individuals who are then responsible for their exercise in the Church. In the Ephesian passage the apostles, prophets, evangelists, and pastor-teachers ***are individuals who have been gifted with these special charisms, and in turn are gifted*** to the Church. However, the argument from analogy does not prove that the same is true in the Corinthian context, despite the fact that I Cor. 12:28 is a clear allusion to the text in Ephesians.

The fact that the word *gifts* is italicized in some of the older

[1] I Cor. 12:1, *περὶ δὲ τῶν πνευματικῶν*, "Now concerning spirituals."
[2] Eph. 4:7, *τῆς δωρεᾶς τοῦ Χριστοῦ*.

versions, including the King James, provides a clue, which properly noted, furnishes an insight into a more realistic understanding of the Holy Spirit's manifestations. What then is the significance of italicizing the word *gifts* in the English versions? It is commonly understood that the Old Testament was written in Hebrew and Aramaic, and the New Testament in Greek. Our English versions are translations of these original languages. It is a fact also well known, but perhaps too often overlooked, that when words are italicized in the English text, it indicates that they are not found in the original biblical languages. They have been added by the translators to clarify a felt ambiguity in the text.

What is not commonly recognized, except by specialists in the field of biblical translation work, is the number of ambiguities in the original text, both grammatical and theological, that confront the translator as he seeks to render the original text into a modern language. Italicized words are employed by the translator either to clarify, or to complete the sense of a passage not otherwise fully present in the original text. Such additions are not, however, introduced into the text arbitrarily. They are subject to clearly understood grammatical and exegetical principles. However, complete objectivity is never possible when the translator undertakes to resolve textual ambiguities. Preconceived ideas about the author's intention will, even unconsciously, affect the way in which any given text is understood.

A historical survey of the way in which successive English versions have interpreted I Cor. 12:1 is illuminating.[3] William Tyndale produced the first English version of the Bible translated directly from the Hebrew and Greek originals. His complete New Testament was published in 1526. The translation of I Cor. 12:1 reads as follows: "In spirituall thinges brethren I wolde not have you ignoraunt." The Great Bible, published in 1539 is associated with the name of William Coverdale. It followed closely the Tyndale version in its translation: "Concernynge spirituall thinges (brethren) I wolde not have you ignoraunt." In 1560 the Geneva Bible made its appearance. It achieved wide acceptance at once, and in popular use rivaled the later King James Version. Its trans-

[3] For the substance of this survey, and subsequent readings of the versions quoted, see Weigle, op. cit.

lation of the text in question follows: "Now concerning spiritual (giftes) brethren, I wolde not have you ignorant." The Bishops Bible followed in 1568. It retained the reading "giftes," first introduced in the Geneva Bible, e.g.: "Concerning spiritual *giftes* (*sic*) brethren, I would not have you ignorant." Roman Catholic scholars published an English version based on the Latin Vulgate, itself a translation from the Hebrew and Greek originals by Jerome. This was first published at Rheims in 1582, and was named after the place where it was published. It renders the text thus: "And concerning spiritual things, I will not have you ignorant brethren."

The King James Version followed in 1611. It retained the reading *gifts*, but printed it in italics, a precedent not always followed in subsequent reprintings, nor in subsequent revisions, e.g.: "Now concerning spiritual *gifts*, brethren, I would not have you ignorant." The Revised Version of 1881 was the joint effort of British and American scholars. The American edition, containing the translation preferences of the American committee, was published twenty years later in 1901 as the American Standard Version. It preserves a verbatim rendering of the King James in this place: "Now concerning spiritual *gifts*, brethren, I would not have you ignorant." This version was revised again, and published as the Revised Standard Version. The New Testament appeared in 1946, and the Old Testament followed in 1952. It retains the reading *gifts* of its predecessors, but fails to italicize it: "Now concerning spiritual gifts, brethren, I do not want you to be uninformed." The catalogue of versions could be drawn out further, but sufficient has been said to support the fundamental assumption that the translations are misleading by translating the text "spiritual gifts," especially when they fail to italicize the word *gifts*. The theological and practical consequences of this will be developed as the discussion proceeds.

A summary will set the discussion in sharper focus. It is important to recall that the "spiritual thinges" of the Tyndale (1526), Great Bible (1539), and Rheims (1582) versions was changed to "spiritual (giftes)" in the Geneva Bible. Followed in this translation by the Bishops Bible (1568) and the King James (1611), both indicated the tentative nature of the reading *gifts* in their respective versions. The hypothetical nature of this rendering is further indicated in the Revised Version (1881), and the American Standard Version (1901) by the use of italics. This is abandoned in later versions, including the Revised Standard Version (1946); consequently, the fact that a word (e.g. "gifts") is not a part of the original text in Greek is obscured.

What are the theological implications of this translation? It is commonly inferred that the Holy Spirit bestows upon specific individuals one or more of the charisms/gifts listed by the apostle Paul in I Cor. 12:8–10. These gifts are furthermore regarded as more or less permanent possessions of the individuals who receive them. The individuals thus *gifted* are responsible in turn for the exercise of "their gift(s)" in the church assembly.

What is merely implicit in most other versions, the Living Bible (1967) makes explicit in its paraphrase of the text: "And now, brothers, I want to write about the special abilities the Holy Spirit gives to each of you, for I don't want any misunderstanding about them." It could hardly be stated more clearly than this, but it is precisely this understanding of the text that is called in question here. Certainly the biblical text does not state this explicitly, nor does it represent unequivocally the intention of the context. It is simply an example of a theological a priori imposed upon the text.

Tedious though it may seem to the reader, this review of successive versions reveals the evolution and entrenchment of the commonly received translation of this text. The justification for such a survey, if justification be required, is not merely an exercise in pedantic curiosity, but a serious effort to provide a basis for a critical appraisal of the doctrinal and the practical implications of this translation for Pentecostal and Charismatic spirituality.

A literal reading of the Greek text of the passage makes it clear that what the apostle wrote was this: "Now concerning spirituals, brethren." Although it may seem redundant, it is nonetheless justifiable and necessary to call to the readers' attention the obvious fact that Paul did not write the word *gifts* in this verse. Necessary, because of the power of entrenched dogma to blind one even to the obvious. The result, in the present instance, is a prevailing tunnel vision among Christians in general, and Pentecostals and Charismatics in particular. Necessary also, because for the latter, life in the Spirit is, all too often, a restless quest for more and more gifts to exercise.

Gifts, Ministries, Workings

Examining the text more closely, the first question that confronts the reader is not, What is my gift?—the question most frequently asked—but, What did Paul mean by spirituals? As one reads the entire passage, the alert reader is struck by a seeming paradox between vv. 1 and 2 of I Corinthians 12. If one has accepted uncritically the common assumption that v. 1 refers to the *gifts* of the Holy Spirit, then they may fail to see the paradox. Observe how v. 2 begins: "You know that when you were heathen." What follows in the rest of vv. 2 and 3 is an allusion to their previous experience as idolaters with the manifestations of demonic spirits. Surely, if v. 1 is to be understood of the authentic gifts of the Holy Spirit, then the sudden and discordant reference to their former familiarity with demonic manifestations is a paradox, to say the least.

This disjuncture in Paul's thought, if disjuncture indeed it is, might be resolved as a parenthetical digression on the part of the apostle, although nothing in the context suggests that this is what the author intended. As a matter of fact, such an assumption contributes little to the understanding of the passage, rather it tends to obscure the intention expressed in the context.

As noted above, the substantive question raised by the passage is this: What did Paul mean by spirituals? The key to the interpretation of the context is provided by the grammatical form and function of the Greek word translated "spirituals."

The word "spirituals" is an adjective. Part of the function of adjectives is to serve as modifiers of nouns. Therefore, when the adjective is used, the reader normally expects to find the noun it modifies accompanying it. In New Testament Greek, this relationship is indicated, with greater precision than in English, by the inflectional endings of both the adjective and the noun (or nouns) that it modifies. In the present discussion it is important to note that the adjective "spirituals" in Greek is in the genitive case, that it is plural in number, and that it may be either masculine, feminine, or neuter—depending on the gender of the noun(s) that it modifies. The same case ending is used in the genitive plural for all three genders. However, gender in the adjective is not determined by form but by function, i.e., by the gender of the noun it modifies.

The rule to be observed then is that the adjective agrees with its noun in gender, number, and case. It may be observed in passing that the various translators, noting the absence of a noun with the adjective "spirituals," felt free to supply one in the interest of clarity. One cannot fault them for this, however, the questions remains, to what degree did their presuppositions about the intention of the author influence their choice of the word *gifts*?

Returning to the context of the passage in question, the student of the Greek New Testament will observe that in I Cor. 12:4–6 there are three nouns that meet the grammatical criteria above, agreeing with the adjective "spirituals" in gender, number and case. In 12:4 the text reads: "Now there are varieties of gifts, but the same Spirit." Verse 5 continues, "and there are varieties of service (ministries), but the same Lord." Lastly, v. 6 adds, "and there are varieties of working(s), but it is the same God who inspires them all in every one."

The agreement of the adjective "spirituals" with the three nouns ("gifts," "ministries," and "workings") in gender, number, and case supports the interpretation that the latter are the "spirituals" to which Paul referred in 12:1.[4]

Failure to observe the formal relationship between "spirituals," "gifts," "ministries," and "workings" has led interpreters to speculate whether the adjective "spirituals" is to be read as masculine or neuter. Those who have opted for the neuter—and these are by far the more numerous—have adopted the reading "spiritual *gifts*." Others, noting that the same genitive form serves also for the masculine, have suggested the translation "spiritual *men*." What is overlooked in the discussion, however, is that the *form* of the adjective may be all three genders, masculine, feminine, or neuter, depending upon the gender of the noun(s) it modifies. Hence, "spiritual gifts" is neuter, "spiritual ministries" is feminine, and "spiritual workings" is neuter. Subsequently, when the reading is suggested that seems to be most consistent with the intent of the context, it will be found that the noun in question is feminine.

In the light of this, one may ask, Why have Pentecostals and Charismatics persisted in speaking of the "nine gifts of the Spirit"

[4] By noting the identical endings on all four words, one can distinguish the agreement in form between *πνευματικῶν*, *χαρισμάτων*, *διακονιῶν*, and *ἐνεργημάτων*.

—with emphasis on the autonomous possession of one or more of these *gifts* as a personal enduement of which they are custodian and executor? The impression persists that this is in large measure a consequence of the tunnel vision fostered by the common rendering of 12:1 as "spiritual *gifts*"—with or without italics.

That such a view is at odds with the context becomes clearer when one listens to what the context is saying. This may be sharpened by asking several questions. For instance, of the so-called nine *gifts* of the Spirit, how many does Paul specifically identify as "gifts"? The answer to this one question sets the whole topic in a different light.[5] The question is answered in v. 9, "gifts of healings." Why then speak of "nine gifts of the Holy Spirit" when the apostle refers only to "healings" as "gifts"?

Certainly, in some significant measure, the insertion of the word *gifts* in v. 1 does serve to convey the translator's bias to the reader. In turn, the endless repetition of this teaching by Pentecostal and Charismatic teachers serves to reinforce it among the faithful. Thus the reader is preconditioned to understand the text in one way, and in one way only.

The first question prompts a second one. Who then "has" the gift of healing? Do those who pray for the sick, with or without the laying on of hands, "have" the gift of healing to dispense? This is a common assumption; however, what the context suggests is that those who pray and lay on hands for healing are simply channels who mediate the *gift of healing* from the divine Healer to the sick person. Consequently, it is the sick person who *receives* the gift of healing.[6] Of more immediate concern is a third question presented by the context.

As already noted, in the context there are two more words that are modified by the adjective "spirituals." One of these is called *working(s)*: How many of the so-called *gifts* of the Spirit does the apostle designate as *workings*? Only one, "working of miracles." By parity of reasoning, the question arises then whether or not one might refer with equal propriety to the "nine workings" of the Spirit? Would it not be equally appropriate to speak of the "nine ministries" of the Spirit?

[5] If our experience over the past twenty-five years with Pentecostal and Charismatic groups is any criterion, then the question has not even been raised.

[6] I am indebted to David du Plessis who first called this insight to my attention.

Concerning Spiritual Manifestations

Grammatical analysis of the context has shown that the "spirituals" of I Cor. 12:1 are the "gifts" (v. 4), "ministries" (v. 5), "workings" (v.6) of the Holy Spirit. The subsequent list, i.e., "wisdom," "knowledge," "faith," etc., lends specificity to these larger categories. The apostle clearly defined their source and dynamic thus: "To each is given the manifestation of the Spirit for the common good" (v. 7).

It is important to note what the text says, as well as what it does not say, e.g.: "To each is given the *manifestation*[7] of the Spirit." It does not say, although this is commonly inferred, that "to each is given the *gifts* of the Holy Spirit." The misconception, as pointed out above, is attributable to the pervasive, although generally unrecognized, power of preconceived ideas to mold faith and conduct. Taken collectively, "gifts," "ministries," and "workings" are *manifestations* of the Holy Spirit (12:7).

The discussion has progressed far enough to suggest an alternative translation, more representative of the context, for the "spiritual *gifts*" of I Cor. 12:1. The perceptive reader will have already anticipated us in this. As must by now be reasonably obvious, in place of the word *gifts*, the context itself (v. 7) supplies the word manifestations, i.e., "Now concerning spiritual *manifestations*, brethren, I do not want you to be uninformed."

By their very nature, the manifestations of the Spirit are not permanent enduements. They are transitory expressions of the Holy Spirit's presence and power in the midst of the Christian assembly. They are not private gifts to be exercised by the *gifted* at their will or whim. They are designed by the Spirit to minister to present needs in the community of believers.

In addition to the transitory nature of the Spirit's manifestations, it cannot be overemphasized, that they appear at His sovereign pleasure: "All these [spiritual *manifestations*] are inspired by one and the same Spirit, who apportions to each one individually as he wills." Thus "spiritual *manifestations*" are manifested in accordance with the divine will, not at the will of those who consider themselves as gifted with "special abilities."

[7] The judgment of Bauer, Arndt, Gingrich here must be rejected on contextual grounds, i.e., "the expr(ession) means the same thing as χάρισμα." On the contrary, it means the same thing as πνευματικῶν.

The experience of the apostolic community on the day of Pentecost confirms our fundamental thesis. They received not *gifts*, but "the Gift of the Holy Spirit."[8] In the Spirit-filled life, therefore, the spirituals of I Cor. 12:1ff. are simply the manifestations of the one Gift of the Holy Spirit as He reveals His presence and power in the Spirit-filled community.

Finally, the translation "spiritual *manifestations*" resolves the paradox already referred to between the "spirituals" (v. 1), and their former experience as pagans with demonic manifestations—"You know that when you were heathen, you were led astray to dumb idols" (vv. 2, 3). If, as advocated above, Paul addressed the subject of "spiritual manifestations" in general, then his reference to their prior experience as heathen represents an implicit polarity between the demonic manifestations to which they were accustomed and their subsequent experience as Christians with the authentic manifestations of the Holy Spirit.

Excursus on the Gender of Πνευματικῶν

As has been observed already, the form of the adjective *πνευματικῶν* may be masculine, feminine, or neuter, depending on the gender of the noun it modifies. Scholarly opinion has oscillated between the masculine and the neuter. If it is taken as masculine, then the subject is "spiritual persons." Suggested translations have been advocated such as "concerning the inspired,"[9] and "concerning men of the Spirit,"[10] and even "speakers in tongues."[11] Several considerations support this view.

(1) In the larger context, the apostle dealt with "the mutual relations and behaviour of its members within the society."[12] He sought first to regulate the decorum of women in the public assembly.[13] Then he rebuked the libertines who were drunken at the Lord's table.[14] Consequently, his reference to the *πνευματικῶν*

[8] Acts 2:38, *τὴν δωρεὰν τοῦ ἁγίου πνεύματος*.

[9] Hilgenfeld quoted by H. A. W. Meyer, *Critical and Exegetical Hand-Book to the Epistles to the Corinthians*, trans. D. D. Bannerman and W. P. Dickson (5th German ed.; New York: Funk and Wagnalls, 1884), p. 175.

[10] Ewald, quoted by Meyer, loc. cit.

[11] Meyer, loc. cit., in a comment on Ewald.

[12] Findlay, op. cit., II, p. 870.

[13] I Cor. 11:2–16; 14:33b–36.

[14] I Cor. 12:1ff.

(12:1) may be construed as directed toward the conduct of the charismatically endowed persons in the assembly. Some have seen this as the whole point of Paul's instructions in chapters 11 through 14.

(2) It is noteworthy that "in the immediate context the references are all to persons."[15] The repeated use of the pronoun "you" in vv. 1 through 3, along with the pointed reference to the "one speaking by the Spirit of God" (v. 3), illustrates this assertion. Then too, in v. 7 the "manifestation of the Spirit" is given to *each* one. In v. 11, the Spirit "apportions to each one individually" the Spirit's manifestations. It is, therefore, quite "possible that what the Corinthians had asked about was the position of a *spiritual person* and his testing."[16]

(3) Paul's whole counsel in chapters 12 through 14 is directed, not to an exposition of the nature of the Spirit's manifestations in themselves, but to the regulation of the conduct of the charismatically endowed individuals in the public assembly at Corinth. His is preeminently a practical concern.

In I Cor 14:37, the apostle addressed himself to certain charismatically endowed individuals in these words: "If any one thinks that he is a prophet, or spiritual, he should acknowledge that what I am writing to you is a command of the Lord." Here πνευματικός, "spiritual" (masculine gender) does unquestionably refer to certain individuals, but to what kind of individuals? Is it simply a general reference to one "gifted with the Spirit," as Moffatt translated it?[17] Or does the antecedent "prophet" suggest that the "spiritual *one*" is also a specific designation for another category of charismatically endowed persons, as is the prophet. Robertson's comment on this verse—"The prophet or the one with the gift of tongues"[18]—makes it clear that he regarded πνευματικός as equivalent to a "tongues-speaker." One might logically ask then, that if this is its meaning in this place, why not the same meaning in 12:1?

[15] R. St. J. Parry, *The First Epistle of Paul the Apostle to the Corinthians*, ed. R. St. J. Parry, *The Cambridge Bible for Schools and Colleges* (Cambridge: University Press, 1916), p. 127.

[16] Ibid.

[17] *The First Epistle of Paul to the Corinthians*, ed. J. Moffatt, *The Moffatt New Testament Commentary* (New York: Harper & Brothers, [n.d.]), p. 230.

[18] *Word Pictures*, IV, p. 185.

On the one hand, there is a respectable body of scholarly opinion, therefore, supporting the interpretation that *πνευματικῶν* in 12:1 is to be understood as masculine in gender. If this is so, the resultant translation would be, "Now concerning spiritual *persons*." Furthermore, if it is accepted that the sense of *πνευματικός* in 14:37 is "one endowed with the gift of tongues," a further refinement in the translation is suggested, namely, "Now concerning speakers in tongues."

On the other hand, a significant group of commentators, whose opinion is reflected in the "spiritual *gifts*" of the English versions, translate *πνευματικῶν* as neuter in gender. There is support also for this view in the context, for unquestionably *πνευματικά* in 14:1 is neuter in gender, and logically modifies a neuter noun, hence the translation, it is assumed, must be "spiritual *gifts*." However, this solution is too simplistic, for it does not take into account all the grammatical, syntactical, and contextual factors involved. For example, the question of syntax in I Cor. 14:1 is more complex than a simple matter of form, i.e., gender. The idiom *τὰ πνευματικά* is a neuter articular adjective used substantively.[19] A comparison of its use in another text in Paul's epistles casts light on its use here.

In Eph. 6:12, the antecedents of *τὰ πνευματικά τῆς πονηρίας*, "the spiritual hosts[20] of wickedness," are *τὰς ἀρχάς*, "principalities," *τὰς ἐξουσίας*, "powers," and *τοὺς κοσμοκράτορας*, "world rulers." The genders of the antecedents are both feminine and masculine, thereby indicating that the noun complement of the neuter articular adjective may be either feminine or masculine. As Meyer points out, "the adjective neuter, singular or plural, is collective, comprehending the beings in question according to their qualitative category as a corporate body.[21]

In the comparable idiom in I Cor. 14:1, the context defines the "spirituals" as "speaking in tongues" (v. 2), "prophesying" (v. 3), and "interpreting tongues" (v. 13). The cognate nouns of all three are feminine. Logically then the noun complement of the

[19] Robertson and Davis. op. cit., p. 205: "The articular neuter adjective is often used in the same sense as an abstract."

[20] As a matter of fact, the noun *hosts* (RSV), *στρατιά*, is feminine in Greek.

[21] H. A. W. Meyer, *Critical and Exegetical Hand-Book to the Epistle to the Ephesians*, trans. M. J. Evans, ed. and rev. W. P. Dickson (4th German ed.; New York: Funk and Wagnalls, 1884), p. 539.

adjective ought to be feminine. The nouns modified by *τῶν πνευματικῶν*, I Cor. 12:1, are *χαρισμάτων*, "gifts" (v. 4), *διακονιῶν*, "ministries" (v. 5), and *ἐνεργημάτων*, "workings" (v. 6). "Gifts" and "workings" are neuter, while "ministries" is feminine. The articular neuter adjective comprehends all of these qualities as a corporate whole irrespective of gender, and I Cor. 12:7 summarizes them under the comprehensive term "manifestations."[22]

We conclude, therefore, that the translation "spiritual *manifestations*" satisfies the criteria of grammar, syntax, and context, and represents a viable solution to the problem of I Cor. 12:1.

Excursus on the Use of the Word "Gifts"

In the light of the foregoing discussion, it would be more accurate to use Paul's collective designation, "spiritual manifestations." However, the word "gifts" is too firmly entrenched in the literature and in vernacular usage to effect a change here without ambiguity. Thus, to avoid needless confusion, the word "gifts" will be retained with the understanding that it comprehends all that the word "manifestations" connotes.

[22] The agreement between the substantive and the adjective is often determined by *sense* rather than *form*, cf. *τὰ ἔθνη ἐσκοτωμένοι* (Eph. 4:17) (Robertson and Davis. op. cit., p. 202). Also Dana and Mantey, op. cit., p. 116.

Chapter 12

Speaking by the Spirit of God

PAUL'S NEXT WORDS also have a bearing on the discussion of "spirituals." As already noted, it would be begging the question to assume that what follows is a departure from his announced subject of "spirituals." In developing this theme, (I Corinthians 12:2–3) he appealed to a contrast in their own experience:

> You know that when you were heathen you were led astray to dumb idols, however you may have been moved. Therefore I want you to understand that no one speaking by the Spirit of God ever says "Jesus be cursed!" and no one can say "Jesus is Lord" except by the Holy Spirit.

Note the contrast: "when you were heathen you were led astray[1] to dumb idols," but now "I want you to understand, as Christians."[2] Thus past bondage to silent idols is contrasted with their present experience with an articulate Holy Spirit.

The phrase, "speaking by the Spirit of God," is significant, and requires closer inspection. The use of the dative case with the preposition "in" ("speaking in/by the Spirit of God")[3] is a common idiom. Depending on the context, the preposition "in (ἐν) may be used either of sphere or instrumentality."[4] However, "active influence rather than surrounding element seems to be implied here."[5] This is the view of the translators of the New

[1] Robertson and Plummer, op. cit., p. 260. "Here only is ἀπάγειν found in the N.T., except in the Synoptics and Acts; and there the common meaning is lead away by force, rather than by seductive guile."

[2] Phillips, NTME.

[3] ἐν πνεύματι θεοῦ λαλῶν.

[4] Robertson, *Word Pictures*, IV, p. 167.

[5] Robertson and Plummer, op. cit., p. 261. A. T. Robertson, *Grammar*, p. 590, contends that "all the N.T. examples of ἐν can be explained from the point

English Bible which reads "speaking under the influence of the Spirit of God."

What then is meant by the phrase "speaking by the Spirit of God?" The suggestion that the expressions, "*Jesus is anathema, Jesus is Lord* are battle-cries of the spirits of error and of truth contending at Corinth,"[6] echoes a judgment expressed by Chrysostom. Writing against the background of a contemporary pagan culture he remarked that their idols "though dumb themselves, yet had their oracles, and prophets, and soothsayers, who professed to have *spiritual gifts*, such as the Pythia at Delphia; but do not be deceived," he warned, "their *gifts* may easily be distinguished from ours."[7]

Important though this suggestion is, further consideration of Chrysostom's "contrasting Christian inspiration with the frenzy of the Dionysiac and other mysteries"[8] must be postponed for now. As we shall endeavor to demonstrate, in the reconstruction of certain religious movements in the environment of the early Church, the influence of the mystery cults, in Gnostic guise, does affect one's understanding of the "spirituals."

The question that now presses for an answer is this: What relationship does "speaking by the Spirit of God" sustain to the subject under discussion in the context, namely, "spirituals."

Paradoxically, broadening the examination of the context helps to narrow the possible interpretations. In I Cor. 12:8–10, Paul listed nine supernatural manifestations of the Holy Spirit. These are the "word of wisdom," "word of knowledge," "faith," "gifts of healings," "workings of miracles," "prophecy," "discerning of spirits," "tongues," and the "interpretation of tongues."

Again in chapter 14 he specifically identified two of these, i.e., "prophesying" and "speaking in tongues," as "spirituals." Moffatt translated I Cor. 14:2 thus: "For he who speaks in a 'tongue' addresses God, not men; no one understands him; for he is talking of divine secrets *in the Spirit*."[9] Note that *Spirit* is capitalized

---

of view of the locative."

[6] Findlay, op. cit., p. II, p. 886.

[7] Wordsworth, op. cit., II, p. 126.

[8] Robertson and Plummer, op. cit., p. 260.

[9] Italics added. The RSV and New American Catholic Bible agree with this reading. Tyndale, Great Bible, Geneva Bible, Bishops' Bible, Rheims, KJV, ASV, NASV, and the NIV read *spirit*.

indicating that the translator understood that the Holy Spirit is in view here. The Revised Standard Version supports this interpretation, for it reads, "but he utters mysteries *in the Spirit*."[10] The New English Bible paraphrased it thus: "When a man uses the language of ecstasy he is talking with God, not with men, for no man understands him; he is no doubt inspired, but he speaks mysteries." There is, therefore, scholarly support for the judgment that the phrase, "in the Spirit," refers to a supernatural manifestation of the Holy Spirit, namely, "tongues-speech."

As already indicated, there are other versions that do not capitalize "spirit" in 14:2, thereby implying that the "spirit" spoken of is the speaker's own spirit, as distinct from the Holy Spirit. Among commentators who accept this view, support for it is adduced from I Cor. 14:14: "For if I pray in a tongue, my spirit prays but my mind is unfruitful." It is important to notice precisely what Paul said in this place. He is not here contrasting the human spirit with the divine Spirit, much less implying any antagonism between them, as has been suggested by some commentators. Rather, he contrasted the spirit (πνεῦμα) with the understanding (νοῦς). The contrast is between the rational and the suprarational (certainly not the irrational). The perceptive comment of Henry Alford underscores this when he says, "his spirit is the organ of the Holy Spirit."[11] The translators of the New English Bible avoided the wooden literalness of a word for word translation, choosing instead to convey the sense of the passage by rendering it thus: "If I use such language in my prayer, *the Spirit in me prays*, but my intellect lies fallow."[12]

It is a fair conclusion then, that whether the word Spirit is capitalized or not, the meaning is essentially the same. In both I Cor 14:2 and 14:14, the Holy Spirit is the author of the speaking. They spoke "as the Spirit gave them utterance." Significantly, in both verses, "speaking in/by the Spirit" is equivalent to saying "speaking in tongues."

The correspondence between "speaking by the Spirit" (12:3),[13] and "speak(ing) in the Spirit" (14:2)[14]—compare also "I

[10] Italics added.
[11] Op. cit., II, p. 590.
[12] Italics added.
[13] ἐν πνεύματι θεοῦ λαλῶν.
[14] πνεύματι δὲ λαλεῖ.

will pray with the Spirit" (14:15)[15]—is striking. In the light of contextual evidence, it is a reasonable conclusion that Paul's reference to "speaking by the Spirit of God" in 12:3 is also an allusion to "speaking in tongues."

One naturally wonders why the apostle should introduce his discussion of spiritual manifestations by the assurance that "no one speaking by the Spirit of God ever says 'Jesus be cursed!'" The tone is one of reassurance, as though it were a reply to a troubled questioner. As a matter of fact, it is probably a reply by Paul to a question sent to him by the Corinthians. This is suggested by the formula with which he introduced the subject. The same formula occurs first in 7:1: "Now concerning the matters about which you wrote." From the content of chapter 7, it is clear that one of the things about which they had inquired was the question of celibacy versus marriage. Each subsequent use of this formula serves to introduce a subject about which they had raised questions. In 8:1 he wrote, "Now concerning food offered to idols." As already noted, 12:1 opens with the words: "Now concerning spirituals." Finally, the offering for the church at Jerusalem was broached: "Now concerning the contribution for the saints" (16:1).

Precisely because of these queries from the Corinthians to Paul, much is known about the internal affairs of the church there. The frankness of their questions, and the equal candor with which he answered them, has often made this assembly of Christians the butt of unwarranted slanders. All too often they have been stigmatized as the most immature and carnal of all the churches which Paul founded. Certainly, it is a more charitable and balanced judgment that says: "All the problems of a modern city church come to the front in Corinth."[16] Nor are the Spirit's manifestations in operation there evidence of the immaturity of these primitive saints.

On the contrary, it is because the Holy Spirit operated so powerfully in their midst that their sins were exposed. It is not the manifestations of the Spirit's charisms that constitute evidence of their immaturity. It was their very human propensity for disagreements, leading to schism that revealed their spiritual immaturity.[17]

[15] προσεύξομαι τῷ πνεύματι.
[16] Robertson, *Word Pictures*, IV, p. 69.
[17] I Cor. 1:5ff.; 3:1ff.

Though it is clear that the Corinthians wrote to Paul for instructions concerning "spirituals," the situation that prompted their query is open to speculation. Is there a suggestion of reassurance in the apostle's words? Were they troubled by misgivings, aggravated by taunts from adversaries of the Holy spirit's manifestations, lest they unwittingly blaspheme the Lord in tongues-speech? Were there, as Chrysostom says, counterfeit manifestations that raised questions about the validity of the genuine? A paraphrase helps to focus the issue more clearly: "I want to reassure you that no Spirit-filled Christian, speaking in tongues as the Spirit of God gives utterance, will ever blaspheme Jesus."

Natural or Supernatural Manifestations?

A further word of explanation is needed to clarify some of the common misunderstandings surrounding the character of the "spirituals." These charisms are supernatural manifestations of the Holy Spirit. They are not natural talents. They are supernatural inasmuch as the operation of any and all of them is contingent on the divine initiative. Miracle working, except as a manifestation of the Holy Spirit's initiative and power, trespasses on the psychic and occult, the word of wisdom is simply accumulated philosophic and scientific learning, the word of knowledge is but the product of human intellectual effort. This distinction between natural talents and supernatural manifestations must be kept in the forefront of the discussion, if the nature of the "spirituals" is to be understood.

Stated negatively, the "gift" of tongues is not a shortcut to the mastery of a foreign language. "As the Spirit gave utterance" indicates that the vocabulary, syntax, and content expressed in tongues-speech are in the mind of the Holy Spirit and not in the mind of the individual speaking. Neither is the interpretation of tongues the ability to translate foreign languages. Much less is prophesying a natural talent for preaching the Gospel. It is rather a numinous awareness of the divine counsels, supernaturally revealed and spontaneously uttered for the "edification, and exhortation, and consolation"[18] of the assembled worshippers. The supernatural nature of these manifestations is verified by at least three lines of evidence.

[18] I Cor. 14:3.

(1) The Holy Spirit is referred to directly nine times in I Cor. 12:1–11 in relation to His manifestations.[19]

(2) A cursory survey of the context in I Corinthians 12–14 reaffirms the Spirit's authorship of these charismatic enablings. In this context, the manifestations of the Spirit are discussed in relation to (a) the unity of Christ's body, the Church (observe the parallelism between one Spirit, many gifts, and one Body, many members), 12:12–26; (b) the preeminence of love, 13:1ff.; and (c) the use of the charisms in Christian worship, especially tongues and prophesying, 14:1ff. In this context, the supernatural nature of these manifestations is reiterated in the explanation appended to one of these charisms, namely, "faith." It is not saving faith, but wonder-working faith "so as to remove mountains."[20]

(3) The supernatural origin of these manifestations is emphasized by the use of the adjective "spirituals."[21] A recognition of the supernatural origin of these "spirituals" is necessary for a proper understanding of their true nature and function. Of these spiritual manifestations, the one most frequently misunderstood and misrepresented is tongues. The common assumption that biblical glossolalia is the result of pathological emotional states is exegetically indefensible. It is a supernatural expression of the Holy Spirit's personal presence.

It is an unwarranted assumption to assert that the tongues in evidence at Corinth are

> the gift of men, who rapt in an ecstasy and no longer quite masters of their own reason and consciousness, pour forth their glowing spiritual emotions in strange utterances, rugged, dark, disconnected, quite unfitted to instruct or to influence the minds of others.[22]

Were this true, then the self-control counseled by Paul—"if there is no one to interpret, let each of them keep silence in church and speak to himself and to God"[23]—would be impossible. Quite the

[19] "by the Spirit of God" (v. 3); "by the Holy Spirit" (v. 3); "the same Spirit" (v. 4); "the manifestation of the Spirit" (v. 7); "through the Spirit" (v. 8); "the same Spirit" (v. 8); "in the same Spirit" (v. 9); "by the one Spirit" (v. 9); "one and the same Spirit" (v. 11).

[20] I Cor. 13:2.

[21] I Cor. 12:1; 14:1.

[22] Grimm, Wilke, Thayer, p. 188.

[23] I Cor. 14:28.

contrary, the tongues-speaker is in complete control of all his faculties at all times. His "mind is unfruitful"[24] because he does not understand the words he utters by the Spirit, not because he has lost control of himself.

The Holy Spirit never violates the integrity of one's personality. He exercises no coercion save the coercion of love; e.g., "If you love me," said Jesus, "you will keep my commandments."[25] The fallacy in the interpretation quoted above is its uncritical correlation of the "gifts" of the Holy Spirit with the psychic phenomena encountered in pagan religions, or in spiritism, the inspiration of which is demonic.

Always and everywhere, the Bible distinguishes between the activity of the Holy Spirit and the activity of demonic spirits. This is clearly reflected in the previous discussion of the context, i.e., I Cor. 12:2–3. The attempt to link biblical glossolalia with the cataleptic trance states of mediums, or other pagan devotees of demonic spirits, reflects unfavorably on Paul's discernment. It implies that he could not distinguish one from the other. Certainly Paul's counsel to regulate the Spirit's gifts of tongues and prophecy at Corinth indicates that he did not regard them as spurious. Paul never "regulated" demonic manifestations, he exorcized the spirits behind them.[26] Still the attempt to correlate biblical tongues with psychic counterfeits is repeatedly made. The following is just such an instance: "There is no doubt about the thing referred to, namely the broken speech of persons in religious ecstasy. The phenomenon, as found in Hellenistic religion, is described esp(ecially) by E. Rhode . . . and Reitzenstein."[27] The conclusion is, however, a category mistake, namely, correlation does not prove causation.

The tongues at Pentecost were recognizable dialects, or languages. They were not the incoherent ravings of men in a trance state. Neither were they akin to the maudlin mouthings of intoxicated men. When the cynics of that day tried to "shrug it off" as such, Peter was at pains to rebut the rationalization, saying, "these men are not drunk, as you suppose."

On the day of Pentecost they spoke dialects known to many

[24] I Cor. 14:14.
[25] John 14:15.
[26] Acts 16:16ff.
[27] Bauer, Arndt, Gingrich, p. 161.

of their auditors "as the Spirit gave them utterance." Luke ascribed these utterances to the direct agency of the Holy Spirit. In Corinth, they spoke different kinds of languages[28] as a manifestation of the Holy Spirit. In both cases, the Holy Spirit is the one with whom the languages originated. If there is any difference in the nature or expression of the respective utterances, this difference originated with the Holy Spirit, not with the persons doing the speaking.

Paul further identified the languages at Corinth as the "tongues [languages] of men and of angels."[29] They were the vehicle for expressing the praise and worship of men, who in full possession of all their faculties, had discovered that there are levels of communication with God that transcend the finite limitations of the purely rational. They are not, however, subrational; they are supraratíonal.

There is, furthermore, continuity in biblical glossolalia. There is no difference in kind in the various references to this phenomenon in Scripture. A. T. Robertson, in commenting on the Pentecostal manifestation, wrote

> the gift of tongues came also on the house of Cornelius at Caesarea (Acts 10:44–47; 11:15–17), the disciples of John at Ephesus (Acts 19:6), the disciples at Corinth (I Cor. 14:1–33). It is possible that the gift appeared also at Samaria (Acts 8:18). . . . The experience is identical in all four instances, and they are . . . for adoration and wonder and worship.[30]

Henry Alford also affirmed that the tongues are "one and the same throughout."[31]

[28] I Cor. 12:10, γένη γλωσσῶν. "Calvin flatly states that *tongue* 'means a foreign language.'" Quoted by, W. F. Orr and J. A. Walther, *I Corinthians A New Translation*, ed. D. N. Freedman, et al., *Anchor Bible*, Vol. 32 (New York: Doubleday 1976), p. 280.

[29] I Cor. 13:1.

[30] *Word Pictures*, III, p. 22.

[31] Op. cit., II, p. 122. Acts 10:45:

The λαλεῖν γλώσσαις here is identified with the λ(αλεῖν) ἑτέραις γλ(ώσσαις) of ch. ii.4, by the assertion of ch. xi.15 . . . and this again with the ἐλάλουν γλώσσαις of xix.6:—so that the gift was *one and the same throughout*.

How is this ἑτέραις γλώσσαις λαλεῖν releated to the γλώσσῃ λαλεῖν afterwards spoken of by St. Paul? I answer that they are *one and the same thing*. γλωσσῃ λαλ(εῖν) is to speak in a language, as above explained; γλώσσαις (ἑτέραις, or καιναῖς, Mark xvi.17) λαλ(εῖν), "to speak in *languages* under the same circumstances" (p. 15.)

Chapter 13

Last Therefore Least

"BUT EARNESTLY DESIRE the higher gifts."[1] With this exhortation, Paul summarized his discussion of the diversity of "spiritual *manifestations*." It is commonly assumed that these charisms are listed in the order of their relative importance. Consequently, those mentioned first must be the more important, while those that are least are placed last. Based upon this premise, the conclusion is accepted, without critical examination, that tongues are the least of the Holy Spirit's manifestations, because they are mentioned last.

This line of reasoning proceeds syllogistically in somewhat the following manner. Major premise: the gifts of the Holy Spirit are always listed in the order of their relative importance. Minor premise: tongues are mentioned last. Conclusion: tongues are least, because they are recorded last.

The truth of the syllogism does not rest on the consistency of its deductions, but on the validity of the premises from which it reasons. It may be formally correct, but substantively wrong in its conclusions. If either the major or the minor premise is factually wrong, its conclusions will, of necessity, be wrong no matter how cogent its logic may be. Consequently, the conclusion drawn in the syllogism above can only be true if its premises are true. This can only be determined by a critical evaluation of the evidence.

In I Cor. 12:28, Paul does list tongues last, and only above the interpretation of tongues in I Cor. 12:10. On the basis of this evidence, one can say, at least for the time being, that the minor premise is substantially correct. However, this alone cannot justify the conclusion that tongues are the least of the Spirit's manifes-

[1] I Cor. 12:28.

tations. The entire assumption hinges on the validity of the major premise.

This raises the question, does the Apostle Paul list the manifestations of the Holy Spirit in the order of their importance? To answer this, it will be necessary to determine whether or not such a value judgment is either stated or implied by a comparison of the various enumerations of the charisms in his writings. As to the first, it can be answered categorically that he does not make such a statement. In fact, his express statements point in the opposite direction. In answer to the second, his scattered enumerations of the Spirit's manifestations are arranged schematically in the following seven lists. This arrangement is adopted to facilitate analysis. It is self-evident that if there is consistency in the order of the various listings, this in itself will suggest such a value judgment.

I Cor. 12:8–10

1. "word of wisdom" (λόγος σοφίας)
2. "word of knowledge" (λόγος γνώσεως)
3. "faith" (πίστις)
4. "gifts of healings" (χαρίσματα ἰαμάτων)
5. "workings of miracles" (ἐνεργήματα δυνάμεων)
6. "prophecy" (προφητεία)
7. "discerning of spirits" (διακρίσεις πνευμάτων)
8. "kinds of tongues" (γένη γλωσσῶν)
9. "interpretation of tongues" (ἑρμηνεία γλωσσῶν)

I Cor. 12:28

1. "apostles" (ἀποστόλους)
2. "prophets" (προφήτας)
3. "teachers" (διδσκάλους)
4. "miracles" (δυνάμεις)
5. "gifts of healings" (χαρίσματα ἰαμάτων)
6. "helps" (ἀντιλήμψεις)[2]
7. "governments" (κυβερνήσεις)[3]
8. "kinds of tongues" (γένη γλωσσῶν)

[2] Robertson, *Word Pictures*, IV, p. 174. "Probably refers to the work of the deacons." Robertson & Plummer, op. cit., p. 281; "the work of the diaconate, both male and female."

[3] Robertson, *Word Pictures*, IV, p. 174: "Probably Paul has in mind

I Cor. 12:29–30

1. "apostles" (ἀπόστολοι)
2. "prophets" (προφῆται)
3. "teachers" (διδάσκαλοι)
4. "miracles" (δυνάμεις)
5. "gifts of healings" (χαρίσματα ἰαμάτων)
6. "tongues" (γλώσσαις)
7. "interpretation" (διερμηνεύουσιν)

I Cor. 13:1, 2

1. "tongues" (γλώσσαις)
2. "prophecy" (προφητείαν)
3. "knowledge" (γνώσιν)
4. "faith" (πίστιν)

I Cor. 13:8

1. "prophecies" (προφητεῖαι)
2. "tongues" (γλῶσσαι)
3. "knowledge" (γνῶσις)

Eph. 4:11

1. "apostles" (ἀποστόλους)
2. "prophets" (προφήτας)
3. "evangelists" (εὐαγγελιστάς)
4. "pastors" (ποιμένας)
5. "teachers" (διδασκάλους)

Rom. 12:6–8

1. "prophecy" (προφητείαν)
2. "ministry"[4] (διακονίαν)
4. "exhorting" (ὁ παρακαλῶν)
5. "giving" (ὁ μεταδιδούς)

---

bishops (episcopoi) or elders (presbuteroi)." Robertson & Plummer, op. cit., p. 281: "This probably refers to those who superintend the externals of organization . . . may be equivalent to ἐπίσκοποι and πρεσβύτεροι.

[4] Grimm, Wilke, Thayer: "The office of deacon in the primitive church . . . Rom. xii.7." Bauer, Arndt, Gingrich, "the *office of a deacon* Ro 12:7."

3. "teaching" (ὁ διδάσκων)
6. "ruling" (ὁ προϊστάμενος)[5]
7. "mercy" (ὁ ἐλεῶν)

"Last, therefore least" can only be valid as an interpretive principle, if it can be proven to be applicable to each subsequent situation. If there is consistency in the listing of the manifestations of the Holy Spirit, it will argue for the truth of such a presumed rule of last mention. On the other hand, if the various lists of spiritual gifts are not consistent in their order, this would serve to discredit the assumption that the lesser gifts are mentioned last. Furthermore, if such a rule of interpretation is applied only in special cases to support a priori prejudices against tongues, then it is not a valid exegetical rule. It is simply special pleading, and may be dismissed as such without the formality of an apology.

Even a cursory reading of the schematic arrangement of these seven lists reveals a number of omissions, transpositions, and substitutions in Paul's tabulation of the Spirit's charisms. A comparison of the initial list in I Cor. 12:8–10 with the second list in 12:28 shows several substitutions in the latter. The "word of wisdom," "the word of knowledge," and "faith" are dropped from the first three places, and "apostles," "prophets," and "teachers" are substituted. There are obvious correspondences between the latter and the list of gifts in Eph. 4:11, e.g., Christ's "gifts were that some should be apostles, some prophets, some evangelists, some pastors and teachers."

Important too is the fact that Paul in I Cor. 12:29 combined charismatic manifestations of the Holy Spirit with the ministry gifts of Christ. These ministry and administrative gifts[6] are included under the charismata in I Cor. 12:28, 29 as the more comprehensive category of God's supernatural "gifts of grace."[7] Nevertheless, there is a valid distinction between them that must neither be blurred nor lost.

[5] Robertson, *Word Studies,* IV, p. 36: "Literally, those who stand in front of you, your leaders in the Lord, the presbyters or bishops and deacons." Probably not the deacons here since they are singled out for mention in v. 7.

[6] Eph. 4:7, τῆς δωρεᾶς τοῦ Χριστοῦ is used in a collective sense here, and particularized as δόματα in 4:7b, a quotation from Ps. 68:18.

[7] Grimm, Wilke, Thayer, χάρισμα.

The charismata are "the operation(s) which manifests the Spirit."[8] The gift(s) of Christ are ministries and offices in the Church. The former are miraculous enablements for the Church's worship and witness. The latter are ministries designed by our Lord "for the work of ministry . . . until we all attain to the unity of the faith and of the knowledge of the Son of God."[9] The charismata are apportioned "to each one individually"[10] as the Spirit wills for the edification of the whole assembly of believers. The δωρεά is Christ's gift of individuals called, equipped, and "gifted" to the Church as ministers and administrators. In the charismata, the stress is upon the charism itself as a manifestation of the Holy Spirit. In the δωρεά, the emphasis is on the persons who exercise these gift-ministries.[11] In a word, the charismata are manifestations, the δωρεά are persons. Their common denominator is the fact that both are "*a gift of grace*; *a favor which one receives without any merit of their own*."[12]

Referring again to the first two lists, one notes that "miracles" and "gifts of healings" have been transposed. In addition, "prophecy" and "discerning of spirits" are omitted from the second compilation of gifts in favor of "helps" and "governments." If one accepts the view that "helps" refers to the work of the deacons, and "governments" is an allusion to the ministry of bishops, or elders, then their transposition argues against the proposition that the gifts are tabulated in order of importance. The office of deacon is hardly greater than the office of the bishop, or elder. It may also be noted in passing, that the "interpretation of tongues" is omitted in the second catalogue of gifts.

The third list of gifts in I Cor. 12:29–30 follows the arrangement of the second for the first five gifts, e.g., "apostles," "prophets," "teachers," "miracles," and "gifts of healings." Four that are included in the second are omitted in the third, viz., "faith," "discerning of spirits," "helps," and "governments."

The fourth catalogue of the Spirit's gifts in I Cor. 13:1, 2

[8] Robertson & Plummer, op. cit., p. 264: "in ἡ φανέρωσις. . . τοῦ πνεύματος, the genitive is probably objective, 'the operation which manifests the Spirit,' rather than subjective, 'the manifestation which the Spirit produces.'"

[9] Eph. 4:12, 13.

[10] I Cor. 12:11.

[11] Salmond, op. cit., III, p. 329.

[12] Grimm, Wilke, Thayer, χάρισμα.

places "tongues" first, even before "prophecy" and "knowledge," with "faith" put in last place. Then the apostle *transposed* this order in 13:8 with "prophecies" in first place, "tongues" second, and "knowledge" last. If the supposititious rule of last mention was valid, one would have to argue that "knowledge" was least in 13:8.

In Rom. 12:6–8, the order of spiritual gifts, also deviates from the order found in I Corinthians 12–14. The office of the "deacon"[13] is placed second, following "prophecy," but preceding both "teaching" and "ruling," i.e., before the office of the bishop or elder. "Exhorting" is listed as a separate manifestation in Rom. 12:8, but in I Cor. 14:3 it is described as a function of "prophesying." Romans 12:8 adds spiritual gifts not listed before, namely, "giving" and "mercy."

Thus a compilation and comparison of spiritual gifts listed by Paul shows no consistency in order or arrangement, with the notable exception of the ministry gifts of Christ.[14] The various transpositions, omissions, and substitutions in the order of the charismata suggests a random recital, rather than a discernible pattern. In the face of this evidence it is doubtful indeed that there is a rule of last mention operative in these lists of spiritual gifts. If it were then "faith" would be least, because last in I Cor. 13:2, "knowledge" would be least because last in I Cor. 13:8, while the function of the deacon would take precedence over the bishop or elder.

Desire Earnestly the Greater Gifts

From the foregoing analysis of Paul's listing of the gifts of the Holy Spirit, it is clear that he implied no value judgment upon their relative worth (or importance) by their placement in the several lists. There is, however, one noteworthy exception to this general observation which will be examined later.

First, though, several additional observations concern the rule of last mention deserve attention. Such an arbitrary interpretive principle not only defies consistent application to the various inventories of spiritual gifts, it cannot be applied consistently in the same context. For example, Paul wrote in I Cor. 13:13, "So

[13] διακονίαν.
[14] τῆς δωρεᾶς τôυ Χριστοῦ.

faith, hope, love abide, these three. . . ." If the rule of last mention was valid, then "love" would be the least of these spiritual virtues, simply because it is mentioned last. This is obviously not true, inasmuch as Paul expressly said that "the greatest of these is love." Perhaps one might be tempted to assume from this that the reverse is true, namely, that the least important is mentioned first, and the most important placed last for emphasis. As a matter of fact, this is precisely what some commentators have attempted to do.

It is unfortunate, not to add confusing, that scholars have involved themselves in painful contradictions by tacitly accepting either a rule of last mention, or its mirror image, a rule of first mention. In what is clearly a polemic against the charismatic gifts of the Irvingites, one scholar wrote of tongues in I Cor. 12:10: "Hence Paul placed this gift lowest of all. It created wonder, but did little real good."[15] Nor is this merely a passing comment, for the same writer repeated this "last, therefore least" judgment in a comment on tongues in 12:28, saying pointedly, "last again."[16] However, when confronted with tongues *in first place* in I Cor. 13:1, straightway he reversed himself, saying, "Mentioned first because really least.[17] It is a tortured logic that affirms as true mutually contradictory propositions.

Where logic fails special pleading is invoked by two other commentators in their interpretation of I Cor. 13:1. In their own words,

> The Apostle takes the lowest of these spiritual gifts first, because the Corinthians specially needed to be set right about them, and also because the least valuable of the special gifts made the strongest contrast to the excellence of love. . . . There is a climax in the succession γλῶσσαι, προφητεία, ψωμίσω καὶ παραδῶ.[18]

This is a reversal of the rule of last mention to accommodate the facts to prior biases. Apparently prejudice and consistency are incompatible. Tongues are to be condemned out of hand regardless of the reasons, or lack of facts, adduced. Attention must be directed to a twofold fallacy in this opinion.

[15] Robertson, *Word Pictures*, IV, p. 179.
[16] Ibid., p. 174.
[17] Ibid., p. 179.
[18] Tongues, prophecy, faith, to give away all one's property bit by bit, to give up, i.e., one's body to be burned (Robertson & Plummer, op. cit., p. 288.).

First of all, the above list omits "knowledge" which comes between "prophecy" and "faith" in the text of I Cor. 13:2. This omission is significant. In I Cor. 12:8–9 these gifts are listed as "knowledge," "faith," "prophecy," "tongues." An inverted order, therefore, should read "tongues," "prophecy," "faith," "knowledge." Such an inverted order would be necessary in any "climax in succession." Now notice that "knowledge" *precedes* "faith" in 13:2. If the order were inverted, the opposite should be true; "faith" should precede "knowledge." It is obvious then that there is no inversion in 13:2 in the order of "knowledge" and "faith." They occupy the same relative positions as in the original list in 12:8–9. The only way, therefore, that a "climax in succession" in the order of the gifts in 13:1–3 can be maintained is by omitting "knowledge." Furthermore, it cannot be argued that "all knowledge" in 13:2 is merely an expansion of the idea of "prophecy," for "knowledge" and "prophecy" are treated as separate and distinct charisms in the context.

In the second place, such a "climax in succession" is contradicted by the transposition of the order of these same manifestations in 13:8, e.g., "prophecy," "tongues," "knowledge," rather than "tongues," "prophecy," "knowledge," as in 13:1f. The whole idea of a "climax in succession" from least to greatest emerges as an exercise in special pleading.

These attempts to deprecate tongues as a spiritual gift are based upon arbitrary assumptions. They represent deductions from prejudice rather than induction from facts. If such invincible prejudices are accepted in lieu of evidence from facts, then tongues would be the least of the spiritual gifts no matter where they appeared in the various lists of the charismata. In effect, such preconceived opinions are simply saying, "My mind is made up, do not confuse me with the facts."

Overlooked heretofore is an explicit parallelism in Pauline thought that sets the whole matter in biblical perspective. In I Cor. 12:14ff., he likened the relationship of the members of Christ's body, the Church, to the various parts of the physical body, e.g., "God arranged the organs in the body" (v. 18). Applying the metaphor to the Church he added, "And God has appointed in the church first apostles, etc." As God has arranged the members in the body, so also He has appointed the gifts and ministries of the Holy Spirit in the Church. And as there are no inferior members in the body, so also there are no *inferior* gifts in the Church. One member may be subordinate to another for the sake of the functioning of Christ's body, the Church. The subordinate members are not, therefore, inferior. Jesus, in the days of His flesh became subordinate to the Father. He is not, therefore, inferior. The wife is subordinate to the husband. She is not, in consequence of that, inferior. So also, the subordination of one gift to another does not, by virtue of that fact, imply inferiority.

Remembering that Paul included the ministry gifts (Eph. 4:11) with the charismata in I Cor. 12:28–30 as the larger category, we are in possession of a clue to the identity of the "greater gifts." The use of the word δωρεά to characterize the ministry gifts suggests their importance, for this word "is reserved for the highest and best gifts."[19] In addition, in 12:28 Paul explicitly tabulated these ministry gifts in numerical order. This is the one exception to the apostle's random order in cataloguing spiritual gifts. It intimates that when he said, "*first* apostles, *secondly* prophets, *thirdly* teachers," he was expressing a value judgment upon this specific category of gifts. The apostles are, therefore, "possessors of the most important gift I Cor. 12:28f."[20]

It is the enumeration of these particular gifts that sets them apart from the rest of the charismata as the most important. Consequently, when Paul exhorted his readers to "desire earnestly the greater gifts,"[21] it is both logical and consistent with the context to interpret these "greater gifts" as the ones he has himself set off from the others by an arithmetical enumeration, e.g., "first . . . second . . . third." In the context of I Cor. 12:28ff., the "greater gifts" are "apostles," "prophets," and "teachers," in that order.

[19] W. Sanday & A. Headlam, *A Critical and Exegetical Commentary on the Epistle to the Romans*, ed. E. A. Briggs, et al., *The International Critical Commentary* (13th ed.; New York: Charles Scribner's Sons, 1911), p. 140.

[20] Bauer, Arndt, Gingrich, ἀπόστολος.

[21] I Cor. 12:31, ζηλοῦτε. The Corinthians are exhorted to be zealous for, i.e., to place the highest premium on the ministry gifts because of their relative value for the whole Church (cf. Eph. 4:11ff.). It is not an exhortation to seek individual manifestations, but to cultivate a corporate attitude toward the greater gifts.

Chapter 14

Prophets and Prophesying

A CONSIDERATION OF THE FIRST and third of the ministry gifts, i.e., apostles and teachers, need not detain us. In broad terms, their function is generally recognized. However, a further clarification of the second, i.e., prophets, is a practical necessity. The distinction between "prophecy" as a manifestation of the Holy Spirit in the worship of the community, and "prophecy" as a ministry gift of Jesus Christ to His Church needs to be clearly drawn. Their interrelations are such that some have assumed that they are one and the same. Nor is this assumption entirely amiss when they are considered solely from the standpoint of an oracular function of the Holy Spirit. But in their scope and application, there are important distinctions that must be taken into account.

The office of the prophet is a specific order of ministry in the apostolic Church. "The frequency with which they are referred to . . . and the place assigned to them next to the Apostles (Eph. iv.11) shows the prominent position they had in the primitive Church."[1]

From the biblical record certain definitive aspects of their ministry and influence can be gleaned. As in the case of the prophet Agabus—who journeyed from Jerusalem to Antioch prophesying a coming famine,[2] then later traveled from Judea to Caesarea, and in an acted parable predicted Paul's imminent imprisonment at Jerusalem[3]—the prophets were frequently itin-

[1] Salmond, op. cit., III, p. 299.
[2] Acts 11:27ff.
[3] Acts 21:10f.

erant.[4] At Antioch, Agabus "foretold by the Spirit" the impending famine.[5] In Caesarea, the prophetic declamation was enforced by a "Thus says the Lord."[6] However, their oracles were not delivered in an ecstatic or trance state, for "the spirits of the prophets are subject to the prophets."[7] In the worship services of the churches, their utterances were to be self-regulated, speaking by "two or three," and were subject to the discipline and discernment of the rest of the prophets.[8]

At Antioch, it was through them that the Holy Spirit called Barnabas and Saul into missionary service, and "the imposition of hands upon Paul and Barnabas—whether for a special mission or to a distinct order it matters not—was at the dictation of the prophets."[9] The prophets also played a part in the calling and ordination of elders.[10] It is in this sense that the words of Paul addressed to Timothy are to be understood, i.e., "in accordance with the prophetic utterances which pointed to you."[11] The prophecies referred to "are utterances of the prophets, such as Silas (and not excluding Paul himself) who were with St. Paul when the ordination of Timothy became possible; utterances which pointed out the young man as a person suitable for the ministry, *led the way to* him (R.V. marg.)."[12]

Furthermore, the offices of the prophet and teacher are noted separately in each instance. Though both gifts might be exercised alternately by the same person, they are nonetheless regarded as separate and distinct, as for example in Antioch where prophets and teachers were ministering together when the Holy Spirit called Barnabas and Saul to missionary service. This distinction is further maintained when Paul and Barnabas returned from the first Jerusalem council, convened to settle the legalistic questions

[4] Cf., *The Teaching of the Twelve Apostles*, Chap. VII, eds. A. Roberts and J. Donaldson, Vol. VII, *The Ante-Nicene Fathers* (rpt. Grand Rapids: Eerdmans, 1970), p. 380.

[5] Acts 11:28.

[6] Acts 21:11.

[7] I Cor. 14:32.

[8] I Cor. 14:29.

[9] N. J. D. White, *The First and Second Epistles to Timothy*, ed. W. R. Nicoll, Vol. IV, *The Expositor's Greek Testament*, (Grand Rapids: Eerdmans, [n.d.]), p. 100.

[10] I Tim. 4:14. Cf. Acts 16:23; Titus 1:15.

[11] I Tim. 1:18.

[12] White, op. cit., p. 100.

raised by the Judaizers. They were accompanied by two prophets, Judas and Silas, who "exhorted the brethren with many words and strengthened them."[13] The prophetic character of the speakers would, in the opinion of J. Rawson Lumby, "give to their words the force of revelation,"[14] thus making the terms of the Jerusalem settlement more palatable to both Jewish and Gentile converts in Antioch. After their departure, the continuing ministry of teaching was carried out by Paul and Barnabas.[15]

The comments of S. D. Salmond provide a fitting summary of the situation: "The prophets were preachers or exhorters to whom revelations of spiritual truth were imparted, and who spoke in the Spirit . . . but not in ecstacy [*sic*] or as one in a trance. . . . Further, he is usually, if not always, itinerant. This order of prophets continued to have a place in the Church for a considerable period."[16] They are mentioned frequently in the Didache, while Eusebius preserves the names of two of them at Philadelphia, Quadratus and Ammia respectively.[17]

In a more general sense, the manifestation of prophesying was not limited to a separate office. The prophetic promise of Joel quoted by Peter on the day of Pentecost, is this: "your sons and daughters shall prophesy," and "my menservants and my maidservants . . . shall prophesy."[18] Paul's promise to the Corinthian church echoes this prophetic promise—"you can all prophesy one by one."[19] True, some commentators would limit the "all" here to the order of the prophets. But the apostle Paul's exhortation to "desire the spiritual gifts, especially that you may prophesy,"[20] suggests that this gift was within the reach of the whole assembly, and not just the order of recognized prophets. All might aspire to prophesy in the worship services of the churches, but not all could be prophets in the technical sense of the term.

[13] Acts 15:32.

[14] *The Acts of the Apostles*, ed. A. Nairne, *The Cambridge Bible for Schools and Colleges* (1882, rpt.; Cambridge: University Press, 1934), p. 199.

[15] Acts 25:35.

[16] Op. cit., p. 330. "The statements made regarding them in the early non-canonical literature (*The Teaching of the Twelve*, *Clem. Alex.*, *Strom*., the *Shepherd of Hermas*, etc.) show how they continued to exist and work beyond the Apostolic Age" (p. 300).

[17] Ibid., p. 330.

[18] Acts 2:17–18.

[19] I Cor. 14:31.

[20] I Cor. 14:1.

This larger connotation of prophecy is reflected in the experience of the Ephesian converts of Paul who "spoke with tongues and prophesied"[21] after the Holy Spirit came upon them through the imposition of the apostle's hands. That tongues and prophecy were uttered spontaneously by those baptized in/filled with the Holy Spirit has already been discussed at length. It should suffice here simply to remind the reader that on the day of Pentecost, the tongues-speech of the disciples is described by a word used only of prophetic utterance in the Septuagint. The manifestation of tongues-prophecy will be expounded later in an examination of I Cor. 14:6. Suffice it to point out here that prophesying was apparently not restricted to those who were recognized as prophets. Nor should this seem strange, for the community of the new covenant is a prophetic community. When the Holy Spirit so moved them severally, or collectively, the divine afflatus would enable all to prophesy in "unpremeditated apocalyptic utterances in the Christian meetings."[22]

The case of the four virgin daughters of Philip the evangelist-deacon who prophesied[23] presents a special problem. Their experience has given countenance to the view that "with NT prophets we have also NT prophetesses."[24] Three considerations militate against this view.

(1) Paul explicitly forbade women to teach or to have authority over a man.[25] It seems fair to conclude that his reference is to the ministry gift of pastor-teacher which carried with it the authority and responsibility for authoritative pronouncements on doctrine. Logically, the same prohibition would extend to all the ministry gifts, including that of prophet. A. T. Robertson remarked that, "at any rate there was no order of women prophets or official ministers."[26]

(2) Aside from the problematical example of Philip's daughters, there is no instance of New Testament prophetesses. The prophetess Anna, daughter of Phanuel, who greeted the presentation of the infant Jesus in the temple with prophetic insight was an

[21] Acts 19:6.
[22] Robertson, *Word Pictures*, VI, p. 270.
[23] Acts 21:9.
[24] Salmond, op. cit., p. 329.
[25] I Tim. 2:12.
[26] Robertson, *Word Pictures*, III, p. 363.

Old Testament prophetess.[27] The only other instance in the New Testament in which the title prophetess is ascribed to a woman is Jezebel, whose claims are qualified with the disclaimer, "who calleth herself a prophetess."[28] The description of her activities makes it clear that she was a false prophet.

(3) It is said that the daughters of Philip prophesied, but in the same context Agabus is called a prophet. Although nothing is said directly about the content of their prophesying, the text does contain a hint. In each Christian assembly where Paul stopped on his journey to Jerusalem, their fellowship and worship was punctuated by recurrent revelations of the tribulation that awaited him at Jerusalem. The apostle confided this to the elders of the church at Ephesus during their hurried meeting at Miletus, the seaport of Ephesus, saying, "that the Holy Spirit testifies to me in every city that imprisonment and afflictions await me."[29] The disciples at Tyre, where Paul tarried for seven days, reiterated the warning "through the Spirit."[30] Agabus came down from Judea to Caesarea, and, perhaps in Philip's house, predicted Paul's imprisonment at Jerusalem. The prophetic burden of Philip's daughters was, perhaps, one more link in the recurring cycle of revelations of the apostle Paul's impending tribulations; "they prophesied with tears over the fate of Paul."[31] The context provides no clear evidence that they exercised the ministry gift of a prophet. Their experience falls within the provision made for women to exercise the gifts of the Spirit in the church's worship services, including "praying and prophesying."[32]

In conclusion it may be said, that it is in this dual sense that prophesying is presented in the New Testament: (a) as a charismatic manifestation of the Holy Spirit, open to every Christian, and (b) as the specific function of the prophetic office.

[27] Luke 2:36.
[28] Rev. 2:20.
[29] Acts 20:23.
[30] Acts 21:4.
[31] Spitta quoted by Knowling, op. cit., p. 445, 446.
[32] I Cor. 11:5.

Chapter 15

The Greatest of These Is Love[1]

CONTRARY TO A POPULAR misconception, love is not one of the "higher gifts"[2] that Paul exhorted his readers to desire. Strictly speaking, it is not one of the charismata at all. Love is rather a "fruit of the Spirit."[3] That this is neither a new nor a novel view of the facts is attested by the comment of Hermann Olshausen: "Chapter xiii clearly shows that love is no Charisma, it is contrasted with all the gifts."[4] In the natural order, fruit is the evidence of life. So also in the supernatural order, fruit is the evidence of supernatural life, that is, of the new birth, and every Spirit-begotten Christian will bear the "fruit of the Spirit" by virtue of their spiritual rebirth. On the other hand, the charisms of the Spirit are evidence of the baptism in the Holy Spirit.

Love is much more than a gift, for the gifts of God are love's bestowals. This lies at the heart of the gospel, "For *God so loved* the world that *he gave* his only Son, that whoever believes in him should not perish but have eternal life."[5] Thus eternal life is a gift of God's redemptive love. But His love is antecedent to all of His gifts, while His gifts are the manifestation of His love. In point of fact, there can be no gifts without the Giver, and love is the dynamic in all the divine gifts.

Though one speak with tongues, prophesy, have knowledge of the divine purposes, manifest supernatural faith, and even

[1] I Cor. 13:13.

[2] I Cor. 12:31.

[3] Gal. 5:22, καρπός, *fruit(s)*, a collective noun. Cf. Phil. 1:11, καρπόν (Byz. καρπῶν). RSV, *fruits*. Cf. also NEB "the harvest of the Spirit."

[4] *Biblical Commentary on the New Testament*, trans. A. C. Kendrick, VI (1st American ed.; New York: Sheldon & Company, 1860), p. 345.

[5] John 3:16, italics added.

suffer martyrdom, these are useless and worthless without love. Paul is saying that to manifest the gifts of the Spirit without love is to separate the gift from the divine Giver. Love is what God is in himself; His charisms are what He does supernaturally in and through His Church. Love is ontological, it is an attribute of the divine nature. His gifts are functional. Reluctant though some theologians may be to recognize metaphysical attributes in the deity, love is such an ontological distinction. In the profound simplicity of John's affirmation, "God is love."[6] A word of caution is in order, however. One cannot invert this declaration, and say that "love is God." The proposition may be convertible grammatically, it is not convertible theologically. Certainly, "love is an attribute of God,"[7] but God is greater than the sum of His attributes, and no one attribute encompasses all that God is.

Christians "come to share in the very being of God"[8] through regeneration, for in these words "Peter is referring to the new birth."[9] The divine nature is manifested in the "fruit of the Spirit," the highest expression of which is love. It cannot be emphasized too strongly that God's love, which "has flooded our inmost heart through the Holy Spirit,"[10] is the highest expression of the divine nature in which Christians "come to share" through the new birth—for "the greatest of these is love."

Paul does not draw a contrast between love and the Spirit's charisms (i.e., tongues, prophecy, knowledge, faith, etc.). The former is an expression of His nature, the latter are supernatural manifestations of His personality. Put in another way, love is an attribute of the divine essence, the gifts are the predicates of divine personality, whereby God reveals His identity and purposes in and through the worshipping, witnessing Church. Love initiates the gifts, the gifts reveal the love-source from whence they come. The reader will miss the point of Paul's panegyric on love in I Corinthians 13, if he regards it as an either/or option between love and gifts. Love does not exclude the operation of the Spirit's gifts; it is, rather, the source and dynamic whereby they are made effectual.

Paul qualified his exhortation, "earnestly desire the higher

[6] I John 4:8, 16.
[7] J. D. Jones, quoted by Robertson, *Word Pictures*, IV, p. 180.
[8] II Pet. 1:4, NEB.
[9] Robertson, *Word Pictures*, VI, p. 150.
[10] Rom. 5:5, NEB.

gifts," by adding, "I will show you a still more excellent way"[11] than simply desiring even the higher gifts. He then developed this theme of the "more excellent way" in a series of negative propositions.[12] These propositions are stated in a series of third class conditions, "a supposable case."[13] They read as follows:

> If I speak in the tongues of men and of angels, but have not love, . . . and if I have prophetic powers, and understand[14] all mysteries and all knowledge, and if I have all faith . . . but have not love, (and) if I give away all I have (i.e., to feed the poor), and if I deliver my body to be burned, but have not love. . . .

It should be noted that such conditions are not hypothetical assumptions for the sake of illustration. For instance, the condition as stated does not imply a doubt that the apostle spoke in tongues. He said categorically in another place, "I thank God that I speak in tongues more than you all."[15] Nor is his statement, "if I have prophetic powers," meant to imply that he did not prophesy, for Paul was a prophet. He did, furthermore, give evidence of miracle-working faith. His life was one of constant self-denial for the sake of others. His physical safety was continually in jeopardy; it is "the concurrent testimony of ecclesiastical antiquity, that he was beheaded at Rome."[16]

The force of the negative hypotheses, referred to above, rests in the dependent clause, "but have not love." He implied that it is possible to do all of these things without the motivation of love, but the consequences would be fruitless and barren. If speech in tongues be not energized by love, one is "a noisy gong or a clanging cymbal." The exercise of the other gifts of prophecy, knowledge, or faith without love, is to be nothing. Acts of benevolence, even the supreme sacrifice of martyrdom, gain nothing, unless they are motivated by love. Nor does this exhaust the application of this principle, for although Paul enumerated only five spiritual charisms, what he said of these applies equally to all the gifts of the Holy Spirit. For example, without love, the

[11] I Cor. 12:31.
[12] I Cor. 13:1–3.
[13] Robertson, *Word Pictures*, IV, p. 176.
[14] καὶ ἐάν or κἂν is understood before εἰδῶ.
[15] I Cor. 14:18.
[16] H. B. Hackett and E. Abbot, eds., *Dr William Smith's Dictionary of the Bible*, III (Boston: Houghton, Mifflin and Company, 1896), p. 239.

apostles are dictators;[17] the elders and deacons are merely busybodies; and the teachers are pedants.

The exposition of these gifts in their relation to love prompted a digression by Paul on the characteristics of love. In a moving encomium on love, he penned its noblest exposition to be found in Scripture. Briefly and incisely, he set forth the nature of love,[18] the immutability of love,[19] and the primacy of love over every gracement of the Spirit of God. Thus he concluded, "But now abideth faith, hope, love, these three: and the greatest of these is love."[20]

The words, "But now abideth," are logical not temporal in significance.[21] The importance of this needs to be underscored. Paul does not mean that "*for the present* Faith and Hope 'abide' with Love, but Love alone 'abides' forever."[22] It is not a contrast "between love which is imperishable and faith and hope which are perishable, but between ephemeral gifts and enduring graces."[23] He pointedly contrasted the "these three" of 13:13 with the "other three" of v. 8,[24] i.e., faith, hope, and love over against prophecies, tongues, and knowledge. Concerning the former, "Paul puts the three on the same footing in respect of enduringness . . . pointedly adding Faith and Hope to share and support the 'abiding' of Love; 'love is the *greater* among these' not more lasting."[25] Even in the eternal state "into which the charismata will not continue, Christians will not cease to believe, to hope, to love."[26] It is the permanence of "their abiding trust in the atonement which took place through the death of Christ" that "keeps the glorified in *continued possession* of salvation."[27]

Turning again to the negative propositions with which Paul began the development of his theme, the "more excellent way,"

[17] I am indebted to a friend and colleague, the Rev. William Wilson, for this trenchant observation.

[18] I Cor. 13:3–7.

[19] I Cor. 13:8–12.

[20] I Cor. 13:13, ASV.

[21] νυνὶ δὲ μένει, Findlay, op. cit., p. 901. Cf. also Robertson & Plummer, op. cit.: "The νυνὶ is not temporal but logical."

[22] Findlay, op. cit., p. 301.

[23] T. W. Chambers, Amer. ed., Meyer, *Critical and Exegetical Hand-Book to the Corinthians*, p. 311.

[24] Findlay, op. cit., p. 901.

[25] Ibid.

[26] Meyer, *Corinthians*, p. 309.

[27] Ibid., p. 308.

his argument may be illustrated in another way. Instead of stating these conditions negatively, they may be stated affirmatively, and the opposite conclusion drawn from them. For example, "If I speak in the tongues of men and of angels, and I have love also," what then should I conclude? Stated another way, if one combines the gifts of the Holy Spirit with the love of the Spirit, what then is the result? Unquestionably, the consequences are the opposite of those drawn when the hypothesis is stated negatively. Tongues coupled with love are both meaningful and edifying. Prophecy, knowledge, and faith united with love contribute substance and reality to Christian character and witness. Benevolence and martyrdom initiated by love bear eternal fruit in Christian experience and witness. Therefore, the combining of love with the gifts of the Holy Spirit is the "more excellent way" expounded by Paul. Love without the Spirit's charisms is not the choice the apostle offers to us. This is a false disjunctive. It is rather, love plus the gifts of the Spirit. There can be no reasonable doubt of this, for Paul says as much in his summation of this theme, e.g.; "Follow, then, the way of love, while you set your heart on the gifts of the Spirit."[28]

The frequent assertion that tongues are a mark of spiritual immaturity, which Paul here counseled the Corinthians to discard in favor of love, is not even remotely suggested in the text. Were this assumption applied with logical consistency to the whole passage, then prophecy, knowledge, faith, acts of charity, and martyrdom must too be discarded in favor of love. If love excludes tongues, then consistency demands that it exclude all the others. Even the most adamant critics of glossolalia dare not advocate such a drastic purge of the text, or of Christian experience, for that matter. As a matter of fact, to strip love of all of its individualized manifestations—prophecy, tongues, knowledge, faith, benevolence, sacrifice, etc.—would be to relegate this metaphysical attribute of God to the limbo of the unsearchable and the incommunicable. How then could the Church experience or express divine love? Consequently, the apostle Paul taught that the gifts of the Holy Spirit are never an end in themselves. They must be used to articulate the love of God.

Inasmuch as Paul wrote of these gifts in the same terms, to dismiss one is to dismiss all, to retain some is to retain all. Without compromise he declared that if one speaks in tongues without love

[28] I Cor. 14:1, Phillips NTME.

he is an empty echo. And if he is graced with prophecy, knowledge, and faith, yet is without love, he is nothing. Even though one should voluntarily endure martyrdom for his faith, but is devoid of love, it is of no profit to him. The unity of thought here is inescapable. Therefore, to dismiss tongues with the epithet "spiritual immaturity" is to stoop to the demagoguery of the shibboleth. To stigmatize one charism of the Spirit of God above all others, in so cavalier a fashion, cannot be dignified as exposition. It is polemics, pure and simple.

There is, furthermore, no scriptural justification for claiming that tongues were dividing the Corinthian church. As a matter of record, it was not tongues, it was teachers that introduced division and discord into the assembly at Corinth. As Paul wrote to the Corinthians:

> For, it has been reported to me by Chloe's people that there is quarreling among you, my brethren. What I mean is that each one of you says, "I belong to Paul," or "I belong to Apollos," or "I belong to Cephas," or "I belong to Christ." Is Christ divided? Was Paul crucified for you? Or were you baptized in the name of Paul?[29]

True to human nature, a parallel situation developed in the contemporary charismatic renewal of the churches. The ecclesiastical censures of bishops, synods, conventions, or commissions are unambiguous repudiation of the apostolic decree, "do not forbid speaking in tongues."[30] Actually the import of this prohibition is even stronger than this translation conveys. Glossolalia per se is not nearly as divisive as the dogmatic pronouncements of sundry teachers on the subject.

As already pointed out by Paul himself, it is in the ordered operation of the gifts of God's Spirit as interpersonal ministries, that the unity of the Church is ideally manifested.[31] All of the Spirit's manifestations are given "for the common good."[32] They are to be sought for "building up the church,"[33] for the ultimate goal of all of God's gifts is that "we all attain to the unity of the faith and of the knowledge of the Son of God."[34]

[29] I Cor. 1:11–13.
[30] I Cor. 14:39.
[31] I Cor. 12:12ff.
[32] I Cor. 12:7.
[33] I Cor. 14:12.
[34] Eph. 4:13.

Chapter 16

Paul's Attitude Toward Tongues

TO SPEAK IN TONGUES, or not to speak in tongues! Where did the apostle Paul stand in relation to this vexed question?

That the utterances given by the Holy Spirit are under the volitional control of the speaker is quite clear from his counsels to both the tongues-speaker and prophet. The former is to "keep silence in the church and speak to himself and to God" (i.e., in tongues) "if there is not one to interpret."[1] Such an admonition obviously presupposes voluntary control of the speech organs by the one(s) speaking in tongues. This very fact exposes the fallacy of the assertion that tongues "was supposed to represent a divine monologue, bursting through the lips of the unconscious enthusiast."[2]

Nor was the oracular speech of the prophet an uncontrollable outburst in an ecstatic state. The same counsel applies to the prophets as well as to the speaker in tongues. They are to speak by two or three in succession,[3] but "if a revelation is made to another sitting by, let the first be silent."[4] Added to this is the unqualified declaration that "the spirits of prophets are subject to prophets."[5]

It is this very rational and voluntary control by the Spirit-filled Christian that distinguishes the charismata of the Holy Spirit from the cataleptic states of trance mediums and pagan psychics. The charismatic manifestations of the Holy Spirit involve a recip-

[1] I Cor. 14:27–28.
[2] Moffatt, *Corinthians*, p. 208.
[3] I Cor. 14:29.
[4] I Cor. 14:30.
[5] I Cor. 14:32.

rocal relationship between the Holy Spirit and the human spirit. The only coercion the Spirit of God uses is the coercion of love. The Spirit-filled Christian is permeated with, not invaded by, the divine Spirit. The charismatic manifestations of the Spirit are voluntary responses, not involuntary reactions, to the Holy Spirit's initiatives. Confusion in the expression of the Spirit's gifts results from lack of discipline, not loss of consciousness. Such confusion is not inherent in the operation of the gifts themselves, but in the lack of restraint of the individual worshipper.

The point at issue here is this: There is nothing inherently emotional in glossolalia. Some individuals display more emotion than others during glossolalia, but in general, no more than when speaking their vernacular tongue under similar circumstances.[6] The emotional overtones are inherent in the speaker's temperament, not in the gifts themselves. The utterance in other tongues is a manifestation of the Holy Spirit's personality. The emotional response that may, or may not, accompany it is a manifestation of the speaker's personality.

Did Paul, therefore, deprecate the intrinsic value of speaking in tongues because he counseled restraint in their use in the worship of the Christian assembly? Of course not! As well say that he depreciated the value of prophecy because he counseled discipline in its manifestation. Paul's attitude toward glossolalia, as revealed by his actual pronouncements, merits a more sympathetic and objective appraisal than critics of tongues have been so far willing to concede. It is the better part of wisdom to allow Paul to speak for himself.

I Cor. 14:5—"Now I Want *You All to Speak in Tongues"*[7]

An appraisal of Paul's attitude toward tongues begins logically with an assessment of the meaning of his exhortation, "Follow after love; yet desire earnestly spiritual gifts, *but rather*[8] that ye may prophesy." The translation "but rather" of the American

[6] One of the most unrestrained worship services this writer ever attended was a prayer meeting in which every worshipper prayed simultaneously in English with considerable display of both noise and emotion. Their expression of an intensely revivalistic fervor was non-charismatic in character. Denominationally, the same group is unabashedly antitongues.

[7] I Cor. 14:5. italics added.

[8] I Cor. 14:1, ASV, italics added; μᾶλλον δὲ.

Standard Version implies an antithesis between speaking in tongues and prophesying. This implied opposition between tongues and prophecy suggests, at face value, a judgment by the apostle upon the intrinsic inferiority of the former to the latter. Pressed out of context, some read into it the total exclusion of tongues in favor of prophecy. But is this what Paul really said?

The implied adversative force of the translation, "but rather," merits closer scrutiny. Actually the antithetical force is not an inherent part of the meaning of this phrase, for the Greek idiom "introduces an expression or thought that supplements and thereby corrects what has preceded."[9] Note well that "supplements" cannot be stretched to mean "excludes." The idiom can have the sense "instead of," if it follows a negative—as for example in Eph. 4:28; "Let the thief no longer steal, but rather let him labor, doing honest work with his hands."

This it precisely the point at issue in the use of this idiom in I Cor. 14:1, 5 where, in neither instance is *μᾶλλον δὲ* used with a negative. The adversative force may be ruled out of the interpretation of both of these verses in I Corinthians.[10] The basic comparative force of the adverb comes to the fore, and this may be expressed more clearly by translating it "to a greater degree."[11]

This point is more clearly illustrated by the use of this phrase in Rom. 8:34; "It is Christ Jesus that died, *yea rather*, that was raised from the dead."[12] Once again, the New English Bible rendering of this idiom is more precise; "It is Christ—Christ who died, and more than that was raised from the dead." Here the clause introduced by *μᾶλλον δὲ*, "and *more than that*, was raised from the dead," is not in opposition to (i.e., does not exclude) the first clause, "It is Christ—Christ who died." The idiom "supplements and thereby corrects" by the addition of a supplementary

[9] Bauer, Arndt, Gingrich, p. 490.

[10] The Greek phrase is identical in 14:1 and 14:5, i.e., *μᾶλλον δὲ ἵνα προφητεύητε*. The translation of the various versions lacks consensus on 14:1. The Great Bible, Bishop's Bible, Rheims, KJV, AV, ASV, and NASV introduce the clause with the adversative conjunction "but." Tyndale, Geneva Bible, and NEB read "and" in place of "but." The RSV, New American Catholic Bible, and NIV omit the conjunction altogether. However, in their translation of 14:5 all of these versions, without exception, introduce the phrase with the adversative "but." This latter consensus suggests an overriding theological bias against tongues.

[11] *μᾶλλον* is the comparative of the adverb *μάλα*.

[12] ASV, italics added.

fact. The fact that Christ was raised from the dead is not set in antithesis to the fact that He died.

What effect do these grammatical insights have upon one's understanding of I Cor. 14:1 and 5? Applied to the translation of 14:1, it may justifiably be translated: "Follow after love; and desire earnestly spiritual gifts, ***and more than*** that, that you may prophesy." The Revised Standard Version says essentially the same thing, e.g., "especially that you may prophesy." As already noted,[13] there is no consensus of the versions consulted supporting the adversative "but" in 14:1. However, in the translation of 14:5, the same versions are unanimous in support of the adversative "but." However, in conformity with the grammatical insights discussed above, it may be translated more accurately thus: "Now I would have you all speak with tongues, and more than that, that you should prophesy also." It may be concluded then, that Paul did not imply that prophesying excluded tongues, or any other spiritual charism for that matter.

The primacy apparently attributed to prophecy over the other spiritual gifts, specifically tongues, is not an unqualified preeminence. It must be borne in mind that Paul speaks here of prophecy and tongues in a given context, namely, the services of the worshipping community of believers. This imposes certain limitations upon what he said regarding prophecy, or, for that matter, any of the other gifts of the Spirit. The apostle's concern is a very practical one. Inasmuch as prayer in tongues edifies only the one speaking,[14] therefore, prophecy, which ministers "edification, and exhortation, and consolation" to the assembled worshippers, is preferred in the church services.[15]

Paul's endorsement of prophecy over tongues is, consequently provisional, for he wrote: "He who prophesies is greater than he who speaks in tongues, *unless*[16] someone interprets, so that the church may be edified."[17] Thus the apostle Paul qualified his value judgment on prophecy in two respects.

[13] Cf. n. 10.

[14] I Cor. 14:4.

[15] I Cor. 14:3.

[16] Findlay, op. cit., p. 903: "*ἐκτὸς εἰ μὴ* is a Pauline pleonasm . . . consisting of *ἐκτὸς εἰ* (*except if*) and *εἰ μὴ* (*unless*) run together." Did Paul use the lengthened form for emphasis?

[17] I Cor. 14:5, ASV, italics added.

(1) Prophecy is greater than tongues in the worship services of the Church, because it is readily intelligible to all. Later in the same chapter, he wrote: "I thank God that I speak in tongues more than you all; nevertheless, in church I would rather speak five words with my mind, in order to instruct others, than ten thousand words in a tongue."[18] Knowing experientially the power of tongues for self-edification, Paul apparently reserved tongues for his private devotions.

(2) Tongues accompanied by interpretation are equal to prophecy, for,

> The power to interpret ***superadded*** to the glossolalia . . . puts the mystic speaker on a level with the prophet: first "uttering mysteries" . . . and then making them plain to his hearers, he accomplished in two acts what the prophet does in one.[19]

The prophet was known "as proclaimer and interpreter of the divine revelations."[20] In this sense too, the "prophetic"[21] utterance in tongues with interpretation was as much prophecy as the speaking forth of divine mysteries in the vernacular.

Apart from an a priori assumption, it is difficult to detect a Pauling prejudice against tongues in his words: "Now I would have you all speak in tongues."[22] The Revised Standard Version rendering of this verse is even more explicit than the one just quoted: "Now I want you all to speak in tongues." It is only fair to say that he valued tongues as a charism of the Holy Spirit. The preference expressed for prophecy was dictated by the practical concerns of corporate worship. Prophecy in the language(s) current among them inspired and edified because it was immediately understood. Tongues, with interpretation, did not do this. The value judgment thus expressed is a utilitarian one, not an assessment of intrinsic worth.

I Cor. 14:6—"If I Come to You Speaking in Tongues"

A certain ambiguity veils the interpretation of the next passage to be considered, but it is an ambiguity that must be resolved if one is

[18] I Cor. 14:18–19.
[19] Findlay, op. cit., p. 903.
[20] Bauer, Arndt, Gingrich, προφήτης.
[21] Acts 2:4.
[22] Acts 14:5, ASV.

to be fair to Paul's attitude toward tongues. The text in question is I Cor. 14:6: "Now, brethren, if I come to you speaking in tongues, how shall I benefit you unless I bring you some revelation or knowledge or prophecy or teaching?"

To begin, it will be necessary to analyze the sentence structure, and to define the relationship of the parts to the whole. The sentence is a compound one in which the several clauses "may be either coordinate (*paratactic*) or subordinate (*hypotactic*)."[23] This means that its individual statements or clauses may be either "parallel with each other or dependent on one another."[24]

Thus two possibilities are open to the interpreter. In the first place, the clauses may be regarded as coordinate. Then the sense of the passage could be understood thus: "If I come speaking with Tongues, instead of speaking either in the way of revelation, etc.,"[25] "how shall I benefit you?" This view not only interprets the clauses making up the sentence as independent, but by the translation "instead of" introduces a disjunctive element into the translation. This view injects a mutually exclusive contrast between the tongues-speech of the first clause and revelation etc., (spoken in the vernacular) of the third clause. If this interpretation is embraced, then it could be argued that Paul disparaged tongues-speech as unprofitable. The corollary is then plain. If the assembly is to receive revelation, knowledge, prophecy, or teaching, then speaking in tongues must be abandoned in favor of the language(s) spoken in any given congregation. However, the weakness of this view resides in its introduction of a false disjunctive into the author's thought.

The second interpretation regards the third clause, "unless I speak to you either by way of revelation, etc.," as subordinate to the first clause. Again much hinges upon the significance of the conditional conjunction (*ἐὰν μὴ*) which joins the third clause to the preceding ones. Grammatically, this conjunction indicates that the clause which it introduces is subordinate to the initial clause.[26] As a subordinate clause, it does not introduce a new

[23] Robertson & Davis, op. cit., p. 203.
[24] Ibid.
[25] Robertson & Plummer, op. cit., p. 307.
[26] Meyer, *Corinthians*, p. 316:
the key to the interpretation which is in accordance with the context and logically correct lies in this, that the two uses of *ἐὰν* are not *co-ordinate*

subject (i.e., "revelation, etc.," spoken in the vernacular), but elaborates some fact, or facts, relating to the subject of the initial clause, namely, tongues-speech. The translation of the New English Bible is in harmony with this view: "unless what I say contains something by way of revelation, etc." The effect of this translation on the interpretation of the verse may be sharpened by asking, "unless what I say"—How? The answer is obvious, namely, "unless what I say in tongues."

Paul might have phrased it differently, and written, "if I come unto you speaking in tongues, how shall I benefit you, unless you understand the revelation, etc., which I have spoken in tongues." The apostle acknowledged, with thanksgiving, that he exercised the gift of tongues, and he might just as well have been his own interpreter.[27] Paul "*specifies* the two *kinds* of discourse in which he might give ***an interpretation of his speech in tongues***, and says: ***If I shall have come to you speaking with tongues, what shall I profit you, if I shall not have spoken to you*** (for the sake, namely, of expounding my speech in tongues, ver. 5), either in revelation, etc."[28]

This second interpretation shows no contrast between speaking in tongues and revelation, etc., in the vernacular dialects. Instead, tongues are the vehicle for conveying revelation, knowledge, prophecy, and teaching. For this reason, Paul summarized his instruction in this section (vv. 5–13), with the inferential conjunction "therefore" (διὸ); e.g., "Therefore, he who speaks in a tongue should pray for the power to interpret." The conjunction looks back to v. 5, and concludes this section of the apostle's thought.

In essence he said that since tongues with interpretation is equivalent to prophecy, therefore, the one who speaks in a tongue (in the corporate worship service) should pray that he may inter-

---

(which was my own former view), so as in that way to give to the principal clause *τί ὑμᾶς ὠφελήσω*, two parallel subordinate clauses . . . ; but, on the contrary, that *ἐὰν μή*, corresponding to the *ἐκτὸς εἰ μή*, ver. 5, is ***subordinated*** to the first *ἐὰν*. Paul might, forsooth, instead of *ἐὰν μὴ* . . . *διδαχῇ* have written simply: *ἐὰν μὴ ὑμῖν διερμηνεύσω*.

[27] Ibid. "The apostle possessed the gift of glossolalia (ver. 18), but might also be his own *διερμηνευτής*, and might apply to the *διερμηνεύειν* the other apostolic charismata which belonged to him for teaching, prophecy, and *διδαχῇ*."

[28] Ibid. ". . . not four, but two charismatic modes of teaching are here designated—*prophecy* and ***didascalia***. For the former, the condition is *ἀποκάλυψις*; for the latter, *γνῶσις*."

pret, in order that the revelation, knowledge, prophecy, or teaching contained in the tongues-speech may be made intelligible to all the worshippers. Speech that is not understood is to the hearer an unintelligible barbarism. This is true of tongues unless they are interpreted. Paul did not, for that reason, advise the discontinuance of tongues-speech, rather he urged them to pray for the interpretation of such speech.

I Cor. 14:1—"Desire Earnestly Spiritual Gifts"

Divine initiative always courts a human response. Nonetheless, the assumption is often made that the Christian is not to seek the manifestations of the Spirit. It is frequently phrased something like this: "If God wants me to have them, He will give them to me." On the surface, this affirmation sounds convincingly pious. Actually, it is merely platitudinous. There is a rather obvious error in the tacit assumption that grace operates irresistibly upon the passive, even indifferent child of God. The ancient Psalmist, for instance, knew nothing of such pious self-deception when he sang: "As the hart panteth after the water brooks, so panteth my soul after thee O God."[29] To this heart cry, the words of Jesus read like the divine requital of the Psalmist's ardor: "Blessed are those who hunger and thirst after righteousness, for they shall be satisfied."[30] So too, in the bestowal of the Holy Spirit's gifts and graces, there is a divine/human synergism. The divine initiative does not function by arbitrary decree. Spiritual gifts are not God's decrees, they are His promises, contingent upon our response to certain conditions clearly stated in the Scriptures. God's gifts are for those who earnestly desire them, or Paul's words are meaningless, e.g., "desire earnestly spiritual gifts,"[31] and "desire earnestly to prophesy."[32]

The apostle Paul counseled an active appropriation of the charisms of the Holy Spirit in I Cor. 14:12. Here he amplified his exhortation to include the controlling motivation prompting the desire for the Spirit's manifestations, saying, "since you are zeal-

[29] Ps. 42:1, 2, KJV.
[30] Matt. 5:6.
[31] I Cor. 14:1, ASV.
[32] I Cor. 14:39, ASV.

ous of spiritual gifts, seek that you may abound unto the edifying of the church."[33]

Here too, there is some obscurity in the English translations. It may be observed in the translation above, that the verb "seek" has no direct object expressed. The purpose clause[34] which follows, i.e., "that you may abound," is not the object of the verb. Actually, the verb in the purpose clause is also without an expressed object. It is important for the interpretation of the verse to note that both verbs find their "object supplied beforehand in the previous clause,"[35] that is, by "what was previously meant by *πνευμάτων*, spiritual gifts."[36] The meaning of the verse may be paraphrased thus: "since you are zealous of spiritual gifts, seek spiritual gifts that you may abound in them[37] to the edifying of the church." Another rendering that comes closer to reproducing the word order, and emphasis of the original reads: "for the edifying of the church seek (them, i.e., spiritual gifts) that ye may abound therein."[38]

Paul's endorsement of seeking spiritual gifts is here a general one, embracing all of the Spirit's gifts. The New English Bible paraphrase of this verse sharpens the emphasis: "You are, I know, eager for gifts of the Spirit; then aspire above all to excel in those which build up the church." In the next verse, interpretation of tongues is one of the gifts "which build up the church." Note again the sequence of thought: "So also you, since you are zealous of spiritual gifts, seek them that you may abound therein to the edifying of the church. Therefore, let him that speaks in a tongue pray that he may interpret."

It cannot be argued convincingly, therefore, that tongues and interpretation of tongues were excluded by the apostle from the gifts to be used for the edifying of the Church. The gift that does not edify the assembly at worship is tongues *without* interpretation. As already pointed out, tongues plus interpretation is equivalent to prophecy, and is to be used for the edification of the

[33] ASV, edited.

[34] Findlay, op. cit., p. 905: "ἵνα (περισσεύητε) bears its ordinary sense as conj. of *purpose*."

[35] Ibid.

[36] Meyer, *Corinthians*, p. 321.

[37] Grimm, Wilke, Thayer, op. cit., περισσεύω.

[38] Findlay, op. cit., p. 905.

assembled worshippers. The assumption that Paul counseled abstention from tongues in the corporate worship is inaccurate. As I Cor. 14:26–28 and 39 show, Paul did not forbid the use of the gift of tongues. He simply sought to regulate its use in the public services of the churches.

I Cor. 14:15—"I Will Pray with the Spirit"

The clearest appraisal by the apostle of the part played by tongues in his own spiritual experience is related in I Cor. 14:14–18. "If I pray in a tongue," wrote Paul, "my spirit prays but my mind is unfruitful." A relevant fact needs to be underscored here before proceeding, i.e., prayer in tongues is prayer on a suprarational level. Therefore, when he added, "I will pray with the spirit," he referred to prayer in tongues. By the same token, when he continued, "I will pray with the mind also," he referred to prayer in the vernacular. Henry Alford explained that by the words, "I will pray with the (my) spirit: I will pray also with the mind," the apostle meant, I "will interpret my prayer for the benefit of myself and the church."[39] This is a possible interpretation, however, anyone who prays in tongues is aware that while praying, one may switch from tongues to one's own language, and back again into tongues. The vernacular portion of the prayer is not necessarily an interpretation of the accompanying tongues.

Amplifying this thought, Paul continued, "I will sing with the spirit," that is to say, "in tongues," and "I will sing with the mind also." Following Alford's suggestion, this may be a reference to an interpretation of the song previously sung in tongues. Singing in tongues with an accompanying "sung" interpretation is encountered more or less frequently in the present charismatic renewal, and the edifying power of this mode of worship must be experienced to be appreciated.

Paul continued his autobiographical comments thus: "Otherwise, if you bless (i.e., 'God'[40]) with the spirit," that is to say, in tongues, "how can anyone in the position of an outsider say the

[39] Op. cit., II, p. 594. Interpretation was not (and is not) indispensable to the edification of the one praying in tongues. Such prayer, whether understood or not, edifies the one praying. Cf. I Cor. 14:4, "He who speaks in a tongue edifies himself." Also 14:28.

[40] Findlay, op. cit., p. 907.

'Amen' to your thanksgiving when he does not know what you are saying?" By the "outsider" (τοῦ ἰδιώτου), the apostle alluded to "the one destitute of the gift of tongues,"[41] or to "a kind of proselyte or catechumen."[42] Hence, "prayer with the understanding," i.e., in the vernacular languages, was necessary for the sake of these proselytes or catechumen. Certainly, no censure for such charismatic prayer is even hinted at in what follows. On the contrary, Paul pointedly said, "For you are giving thanks well enough, but the other man is not edified."[43] Contextually it is clear that he meant by that prayers of thanksgiving in tongues.

While prayer in tongues, without an accompanying interpretation, is inadequate for the mutual edification the corporate worship should provide, this cannot be construed to mean that tongues are intrinsically inferior to the other gifts of the Spirit. Such disparagement of this charism cannot be deduced legitimately from Paul's statements in this (or for that matter) any other context. After all "speaking in other tongues, as the Spirit gives utterance,"[44] is a manifestation of the Holy Spirit's personality. One wonders at the presumption that would arrogate to itself the right to make disparaging value judgments upon the workings of God's own Spirit. In the final analysis, only God himself can pass judgment on His own workings.

I Cor. 14:18—"I Thank God That I Speak in Tongues More Than You All"

Perhaps no other verses in these three chapters (I Corinthians 12–14) have been the subject of more tortured exegesis than 14:18, 19. Apart from invincible prejudice, it is incomprehensible how Paul's words can be misconstrued so as to assert that he depreciated on the one hand what he praised on the other. But let him speak for himself: "I thank God that I speak in tongues more than you all." Obviously, as the sequel indicates, tongues played a significant role in his private devotions, and the apostle speaks with reverence and gratitude of this manifestation of the Holy Spirit in his own experience.

[41] Grimm, Wilke, Thayer, ἰδιώτης.
[42] Bauer, Arndt, Gingrich, ἰδιώτης.
[43] I Cor. 14:17.
[44] Acts 2:4.

It is faulty exegesis that would warp these words to read, "I thank God that I speak more languages than you all," meaning, thereby, learned languages, not charismatic utterances. This translation is grammatically wrong because it misconstrues the word "more" as an adjective modifying the noun "tongues." It is not an adjective, it is a comparative adverb modifying the verb "speak." The clause is correctly translated, "I speak in tongues more than you all."[45]

Though the above mistranslation of the text has been widely disseminated recently, its roots apparently go back to patristic sources. "Jerome, in his Notes, refers the *μᾶλλον to the other (Ap(ostles)* as though P(aul) exulted in being a better linguist than any of the Twelve."[46] This is text out of context exegesis. The comparison is drawn between the charismatic experience of Paul, and the charismatic experience of the Corinthians, and not between himself and the other apostles. "Here we have strong evidence that Tongues are not foreign languages. He does not say that he speaks 'in more tongues.'"[47]

Most comments critical of tongues, sooner or later, appeal to Paul's word's in 14:19, and are more a matter of emphasis than of exegesis. This verse is at times pressed out of context in an attempt to make it nullify what the apostle had already said in a positive vein about tongues in the preceding verse. For this, if for no other reason, the question raised by v. 19 must be dealt with.

After the doxology for tongues in v. 18, to what extent, and in what direction, did he modify this by saying, "nevertheless, in church I would rather speak five words with my mind, in order to instruct others, than ten thousand words in a tongue"? Was he taking back with his left hand what he had previously proffered with his right? Is this ipso facto evidence that Paul did not really value tongues, but was deftly accommodating himself to the situation in Corinth in hopes of remedying presumed abuses? The assumption does not really do justice to the context, nor to Paul's

[45] Bauer, Arndt, Gingrich, *μᾶλλον*. "I can speak in tongues more than you all."

[46] Findlay, op. cit., p. 908: "The V(ulgate), omitting *μᾶλλον*, reads ***omnium vestrum lingua loquor***, making P(aul) thank God that he could speak in every language used at C(orinth)." The Challoner-Rheims Version reflects the Vulgate: "I speak with all your languages."

[47] Robertson & Plummer, op. cit., 314.

integrity. For example, in the pattern of primitive Christian worship outlined in 14:26–33, provision is made for every manifestation of the Holy Spirit. Here the apostle wrote; "When you come together, each one has a hymn, a lesson, a revelation, a tongue, or an interpretation." From this representative sampling it may be justifiably concluded that every charism of the Holy Spirit would be in evidence during the corporate worship services of the Christian assembly. Paul simply counseled the ordering of these manifestations that would be most beneficial to all those present, namely, "Let all things be done for edification."

Everyone baptized in, i.e., filled with the Spirit, may pray in tongues—abiding evidence of the Spirit's fulness. But not everyone will be prompted by the Holy Spirit to speak in tongues, with an accompanying interpretation in the corporate worship of the congregation, by way of "revelation or knowledge or prophecy or teaching."

When Paul said, "I would rather speak five words with my mind, in order to instruct others than ten thousand words in a tongue," he was simply implementing his own advice to "earnestly desire the higher gifts"—of which, he said, the third in order of importance was the gift of "teacher." Without deprecating tongues, he was setting this gift (*χάρισμα*) of the Holy Spirit in its proper relation to the greater gift (*δωρεά*) of Christ, namely, that of "teacher."

In summary then, the evidence indicates that Paul did not depreciate tongues as a lesser charism. He thanked God for the full measure of the gift in his own devotional life, for therewith he edified himself. This edification was manifested in the efficacy of his service for Jesus Christ. Concerning the use of tongues in public worship, he counseled restraint for the sake of the uninitiated or the catechumens. Coupled with interpretation, it will edify the church. Without interpretation it edifies only the one so worshipping. As will be pointed out subsequently, Paul also counseled restraint for the sake of the "unbeliever" who might be present in the service. It cannot be deduced, however, from the context that Paul was simply "honing an ax" in these chapters against the gift of tongues. Even when there is no interpretation, he instructed the one praying in tongues not to stop entirely, but to continue to pray in tongues silently, "speak(ing) to himself and to God."

If more Christians would act upon the apostle's advice, renewal could come to the churches. If the worshippers at any given service of worship would pray "ten thousand words in a tongue" before they went to church, they would need only five words in the vernacular from the preacher to get the job done. Hyperbole? Perhaps! But experience teaches us that there is more than a grain of truth in it.

If the Church today covets apostolic results, let it begin with an apostolic experience: "I thank God that I speak in tongues more than you all."

Chapter 17

Whence the Party Strife at Corinth?

"TONGUES ARE LEAST." So say the critics; yet Paul devoted more space, in the Corinthian context, to a discussion of tongues than to the discussion of love. Was this a paradox or a polemic on his part? Was it because, as so many have assumed, he was doing some "knuckle rapping" over a childish absorption with tongues by immature Corinthian converts? Was it then an overindulgence in tongues-speech that he sought to correct? Or was Paul confronted with a diametrically opposite situation in Corinth? It will be the task of these final chapters to suggest an answer.

The Corinthian church was divided. The apostle Paul castigated this party spirit as carnal and immature.[1] He pleaded with them to cease and desist from this flagrant disunity, or else he threatened to come and to deal personally with the partisan instigators responsible for it. He warned them, saying, "Some are arrogant, as though I were not coming to you. But I will come to you soon, if the Lord wills, and I will find out not the talk of these arrogant people but their power."[2] It is this schismatic spirit in Corinth that underscores the apostle's discussion of the body, the Church[3]— a unity ideally evidenced in the body-ministry supplied by the gifts of the Spirit. It is likely that he again addressed himself to this very party spirit when he exhorted them "in wicked disposition[4] to be as babes."[5] That is to say, "be a child as far as

[1] I Cor. 3:1ff.
[2] I Cor. 4:18, 19.
[3] I Cor. 12:12ff.
[4] Grimm, Wilke, Thayer, *κακία*.
[5] I Cor. 14:20.

wickedness is concerned."[6] To which Paul added, "but in thinking (φρεσίν) be men." The subtle nuance between "thinking" (φρεσίν) here, and "mind" (νοῦς) in v. 14 is suggestive.

The νοῦς is "the reflective consciousness."[7] the intellect, or reason. Φρεσίν means "*the heart*,"[8] as the seat of the passions,[9] thence, "the *heart* or *mind*, as the seat of the mental faculties, perceptions or thought."[10] Thus it relates "thinking" (φρεσίν) more to the emotional nature than to the purely intellectual faculty. The following paraphrase will serve to sharpen Paul's meaning here: "Brethren, do not be childish in *heart*; in wicked disposition be childlike, but in heart be mature."

In the light of the party strife that blighted the Corinthian church, the impression grows that Paul, in the choice of φρεσίν juxtaposed to νοῦς in the context, was taking notice again of the passions that clouded sober judgment among the Corinthians. He was pleading for emotional maturity and a gentle disposition, not for intellectual attainment per se. As a matter of record, some among them already prided themselves upon an intellectualized "wisdom" rejected by Paul, who spoke "not in plausible words of wisdom, but in demonstration of the Spirit and power."[11] Unquestionably, this was a *charismatic* "demonstration of the Spirit and power" to which he was to refer again in his epistle to the Romans 15:19, e.g., "by the power of *signs and wonders*, by the power of the Holy Spirit, so that from Jerusalem and as far round as Illyricum I have fully preached the gospel of Christ."[12] In a nutshell, violent partisan passions must not corrupt the manifestations of the Holy Spirit's gifts.

Inasmuch as the party strife in the Corinthian church must have affected its whole life, two questions press for an answer. First, what was the nature of these warring factions? Second, what effect did these parties have on the manifestation of the Spirit's gifts? An answer to the first question will be offered in this chapter; the second will be addressed in the next chapter.

[6] Bauer, Arndt, Gingrich, κακία.

[7] Cremer, op. cit., p. 456.

[8] Grimm, Wilke, Thayer, φρήν: "Septuagint several times in Prov. for *leb* [heart]."

[9] Liddell and Scott, φρήν.

[10] Ibid.

[11] I Cor. 2:4.

[12] Italics added.

There are numerous suggested answers to the first question, however, Robertson and Plummer were close to the truth when they suggested that the Corinthian parties were the results of influences which showed themselves at work elsewhere in the New Testament, distinguished

> respectively as St. Paul and his Gospel, Hellenistic intellectualism (Apollos), conciliatory conservatism, or "the Gospel of the circumcision" (Kephas), and "zealots for the law," hostile to the Apostleship of St. Paul. These last were the exclusive party.[13]

The Pauline and the Petrine "parties" are sufficiently clear from other scriptures and need not be elaborated on here. However, the enigmatic figure of Apollos (Hellenistic intellectualism), and the elusive "Christ" party demand further investigation.

What little is known biblically about Apollos is contained in a few scattered references. From Acts 18:24–19:1, it is clear that he was a Jew of Alexandria, well-versed in the Scriptures, eloquent in speech, and knowing the baptism of John (consequently the doctrine of John). After being instructed by Priscilla and Aquila, he left Ephesus for Corinth. Furthermore, in I Cor. 1:12; 3:4–6, 22; and 4:6 his name is linked with one of the sectarian parties in Corinth. Next, in I Cor. 16:12, it is recorded that he refused Paul's importunity to return to Corinth. The final reference to him is found in Paul's instructions to Titus (3:13) to assist Zenas, the lawyer, and Apollos in their preparations for a journey.

Little enough to go on, to be sure, but in addition to the suggestion that his name is linked with those espousing a Hellenistic intellectualism, there are several other provocative implications at hand. As an Alexandrian Jew, he would have been exposed to the syncretistic philosophy of Philo who sought to reinterpret the Old Testament in terms of Greek philosophical speculations.

Apollos would be, therefore, representative of diaspora Judaism which to a considerable extent had adopted Greek culture. Their Bible was the Greek translation of the Hebrew known as the Septuagint. They not only adopted Greek names, but also adopted the Greek language in their worship. Their communal organizations were influenced to some extent by Hellenistic prototypes. Fired by an intense missionary zeal, they ardently sought to con-

[13] Op. cit., p. 12.

vert their pagan neighbors, for "the Jews of the Diaspora were possessed with the conviction that they were destined to realize the prophetic word, 'I have set thee for a light of the nations.'"[14] Apollos' instruction in the Scriptures would be that of diaspora Judaism rather than that of "normative" Palestinian Judaism.

Nor is this suggested influence of an Alexandrian theology on the Corinthian church an isolated phenomenon. It was, in fact, anticipated in the following reconstruction of the Colossian heresy.

> The most probable view, therefore, seems to be, that some Alexandrian Jew had appeared at Colossae, professing belief in Christianity, and imbued with the Greek "philosophy" of the school of Philo, but combining with it the Rabbinical theosophy and angelology which afterwards were embodied in the Kabbala, and an extravagant asceticism, which also afterwards distinguished several sects of the Gnostics.[15]

The parallels with the situation at Corinth will be drawn out in the subsequent discussion.

In addition to the synopsis of the theological influences of Alexandrian theology already given, there was a strong messianic emphasis in Apollos' preaching—"he spoke and taught accurately the things concerning Jesus"[16]—which derived from the teaching of John the Baptist. Although, "he knew only the baptism of John," he had imbibed the strong messianic expectations of the Forerunner. As a disciple of John, he would reflect to a greater or lesser degree the emphases of his ministry, and "it is generally recognized that John forms the most important channel through which eschatological and soteriological ideas and practices passed from Essene or proto-Gnostic sources into Christianity."[17]

Apollos' rhetorical polish was an added touch of Greek sophistication, and it contrasts sharply with the avowed simplicity of Paul's own preaching at Corinth concerning which he wrote: "When I came to you, brethren, I did not come proclaiming to

[14] G. H. Box, "The Historical and Religious Background of the Early Christian Movement," *Abingdon Bible Commentary*, ed. Frederick Carl Eiselen, et al. (New York: Abingdon-Cokesbury Press, 1929), p. 847.

[15] W. J. Conybeare and J. S. Howson, *The Life and Epistles of St. Paul*, II (New York: Charles Scribners and Co.), p. 383.

[16] Acts 18:25.

[17] Albright, op. cit., p. 377.

you the testimony of God in lofty words or wisdom."[18] How far the influence of Alexandrian theology and "proto-Gnostic" elements influenced his ministry after he had been instructed by Priscilla and Aquila is a moot question. It is reasonable to assume —and the Corinthian epistle(s) of Paul bear out this assumption—that he did not divest himself of these influences entirely, for his contact with Priscilla and Aquila suggests an intellectual reorientation, rather than the radical change that conversion would imply. Indeed it is stated expressly by Luke, that they "expounded to him the way of God more accurately."[19] As this hypothesis suggests, Alexandrian influences though sublimated, may well have exerted an effect, either directly or indirectly, upon the party strife in Corinth.

The party whose watchword was "I am of Christ" is even more difficult to classify than the former. Worthy of consideration is the suggestion that

> the cry, therefore, seems to voice a party which may be identified . . . with some ultraspiritual devotees or *high-flying gnostics* who made a mystical Christ, no human leader, the centre of religion.[20]

Thus the cry, "I am of Christ," may well denote early christological speculations which characterized Gnostic teachings.

Some thirty years after Paul wrote the Corinthian epistles, the Docetic and Cerinthian Gnostics championed clearly defined views of the person of Christ. The former "denied the actual humanity of Christ," while "the Cerinthian Gnostics distinguished between the man Jesus and the *aeon* Christ that came on him at his baptism and left him on the Cross."[21] In the second and third-century Valentinian Gnostic system, the aeons which made up the *plērōma*, or fulness of the Godhead numbered thirty.[22]

The Gnostic systems all shared a dualism in which spirit was conceived as good, and matter as evil. The incarnation was, therefore, an impossibility, because the divine essence could not come

[18] I Cor. 2:1.

[19] Acts 18:26.

[20] Moffatt, op. cit., p. 10, italics added.

[21] Robertson, *Word Pictures*, VI, p. 200.

[22] W. R. Nelson, *The Interpretation of the Revelation of John in Valentinian Gnosis and the Evangelium Veritatis*. An unpublished manuscript study tracing the philosophical, mythological, and magical expansions of this system of gnostic thought, especially in relation to the Apocalypse of John, circa, 1961.

into direct contact with matter. The aeons were a hierarchy of being that mediated the contact of the spiritual with the material. For the "Christian" Gnostics this posed a fundamental problem in Christology. Indeed, for them the incarnation of the Christ was in appearance only. This became known as the Docetic Gnosticism referred to above from the Greek word meaning "to seem," or "have the appearance." Cerinthus added the view that Jesus and Christ were not one and the same being. According to him, Jesus was

> a mere man, at the time of his baptism the Celestial Christ descended —"he came by water . . . and used him as medium for his revelations; although the words were Christ's the voice was that of Jesus, so no one could really hear Christ speak, while he certainly could not be seen or touched. . . . When Christ concluded his message, he left Jesus and the latter was crucified, an event that had no religious significance, as Christ was not involved; "he did not come by blood," according to Cerinthus.[23]

Paul's words in I Cor. 12:3 may well point in the direction of some such heresy, e.g., "no man can say, 'Jesus is Lord' except under the influence of the Holy Spirit."[24] The fact that "the Gnostics would not call Jesus 'Lord,'"[25] suggests that Paul's words represented a convenient rule of thumb for distinguishing Spirit-filled Christians from such "proto-Gnostics" as the "Christ" party at Corinth.

It was fashionable for earlier commentators to date Gnosticism as a late heresy, equating it with its developed literary forms in the second and third centuries. In fact, Godet's conjecture that the Christ party at Corinth "were Gnostics before Gnosticism," was considered "an anachronism" by Findlay.[26] However, other scholars recognized that Gnosticism was a "type of religious thought widespread in the world into which Christianity came."[27]

[23] B. S. Easton, "The Epistle of John," *Abingdon Bible Commentary*, p. 1350.

[24] NEB.

[25] J. Alex. Robertson, "Philippians," *Abingdon Bible Commentary*, p. 1239.

[26] Findlay, op. cit., p. 765. The growing literature on the Nag Hammadi texts considerably broadens the context of the discussion.

[27] C. H. Dodd, "Colossians," *The Abingdon Bible Commentary*, p. 1250. E. Pagels, *The Gnostic Gospels* (New York: Random House, 1979), p. xvii.

Professor Helmut Koester of Harvard University has suggested that the collection of sayings in the *Gospel of Thomas*, although compiled c. 140,

Nor have more recent studies altered fundamentally this viewpoint. From his examination of the *Evangelium Veritatis* by Valentinus, William Nelson concluded that

> this authentic Gnostic source has given us a clearer picture of the great current of spiritual life with which Christianity came into contact in its earliest years as it grew towards a World Church.[28]

As a religious system, Gnosticism was an eclectic blend of Greek intellectualism and mystical elements derived from the oriental mystery cults. C. H. Dodd characterized it as "a mixture, or syncreticism, of Greek and Oriental religions, supported by a kind of philosophy or pseudo-philosophy borrowing largely from Platonism and Stoicism."[29] As such, the name

> is vague, as it describes a method rather than a result, and covers all sorts of systems. Gnostics might be ascetic and puritannical to the last degree, or they might be debased libertines who quite literally gloried in their shame. They might be men of high mental attainments—some of the second-century Gnostics were able speculative thinkers—or they might be intellectually beneath contempt.[30]

The very name Gnosticism, derived from the Greek word meaning *knowledge*, "implies the possession of a superior wisdom, which is hidden from others."[31] In the theosophical speculations which characterized it, a distinction was introduced between esoteric and exoteric doctrines. For the vulgar, that is the uninitiated, blind faith was sufficient, "while knowledge is the exclusive possession"[32] of the Gnostic initiate.

Historically, the question of proto-Gnostic and Judaeo-Gnos-

---

may include some traditions *older* than the gospels of the New Testament, "possibly as early as the second half of the first century" (50–100)—as early as, or earlier, than Mark, Matthew, Luke and John.

William Bousset, who traced gnosticism to ancient Bablonian and Persian sources, declared that "gnosticism is first of all a pre-Christian movement which had roots in itself. It is therefore to be understood . . . in its own terms, and not as an offshoot or byproduct of the Christian religion" (Pagels, op. cit., p. xxx).

[28] Loc. cit.

[29] Op. cit., p. 1250.

[30] Easton, op. cit., p. 1350.

[31] J. B. Lightfoot, *Saint Paul's Epistles to the Colossians and to Philemon* (London: Macmillan, 1892), p. 75.

[32] Ibid.

tic sources is an elusive one. This is in large measure due to the fact that its documentary remains come largely from the second century and later. There are, however, evidences of its greater antiquity.

Scarcely had the Church reached beyond the boundaries of Jerusalem and Judaea, when it was confronted with Gnosticism in a developed form. In Samaria, Philip the evangelist-deacon came into contact with Simon the sorcerer.[33] According to Irenaeus and Hippolytus, he was "the earliest Gnostic known"[34] to them. In this regard, the claim that Simon Magus was "the father of Gnosticism,"[35] must be modified. In a particular sense, this contains a measure of truth, for Simon Magus is credited with "the first known Gnostic system."[36] However, in a general sense, this claim is misleading, for "there is now direct evidence that some of the central ideas of the Gnostic system go back into the ancient Orient."[37] The most then that can be claimed for Simon is that he systemized ideas already current in the intellectual ferment of his day.

The role of magic in Gnosticism, vis-à-vis orthodoxy, is provocative of independent study. Suffice is to point out here, that Simon is described as a sorcerer, while one, Marcus a magician, is known to have been a follower of Valentinus a century or more later.[38] Is it coincidence, or as is more likely, did the theosophical speculations of Gnosticism provide a fertile soil in which magic thrived?

In the apocryphal Wisdom of Solomon, the author sets God in contrast with matter in an essentially Gnostic manner, and treats the body as the soul's prison which exists before birth, and

[33] Acts 8:9ff.

[34] Albright, op. cit., p. 370. Cf. Hippolytus, *Refutation of All Heresies*, ii.

[35] Jean Daniélou, *The Dead Sea Scrolls and Primitive Christianity* (New York: New American Library, 1958), p. 94.

[36] Albright, op. cit., p. 371.

[37] Albright, op. cit., p. 370. Cf. Pagels, op. cit., pp. xx, xxi.
Does not such teaching—the identity of the divine and human, the concern with illusion and enlightenment, the founder who is presented not as Lord, but as spiritual guide—sound more Eastern than Western? Some scholars have suggested that if the names were changed, the "living Buddah" appropriately could say what the *Gospel of Thomas* attributes to the living Jesus. Could Hindu or Buddhist tradition have influenced gnosticism?

[38] Nelson, loc. cit.

after death. This would imply that in the first century B.C., a Jewish Gnosis had begun to crystallize.[39] Certainly, the material for such was at hand by the middle of the first century A.D., when Simon Magus is reputed to have formulated such a system. Though a younger contemporary of Philo in Alexandria, there is no evidence that he drew directly from the latter. Rather each seems to have been influenced by "a common proto-Gnostic background."[40] In addition to Simon, the Talmud names a Johanan ben Zakkai, also a contemporary of the apostle Paul, as the "earliest Jewish scholar with Gnostic tendencies."[41]

The polemic against Gnosticism is quite pronounced in some of Paul's epistles. The epistle to the Colossians, written some eight or ten years after I Corinthias reflects these influences to such a degree that "one cannot understand Colossians without knowledge of Gnosticism."[42] The heretics in Colossae introduced the worship of angels, suggestive of the aeons that mediated between matter and spirit in Gnostic speculations. Coupled with this was a form of asceticism, and a *gnōsis* (γνῶσις) derogatory of Jesus Christ. They added rigid observances of Jewish festivals and sabbaths suggestive of a Judaic Gnosticism. All these elements were apparently "combined by some of the early Gnostics."[43]

In the Pastoral Epistles, the "myths and endless genealogies,"[44] the "godless and silly myths,"[45] and the "Jewish myths,"[46] were probably "fanciful myths concerning the origin and emanation of spiritual beings,"[47] which the Gnostics of the second century systematized into hierarchies of intermediate beings, or aeons, between "the Absolute God and evil matter."[48] In the Kabbala, a collection of Jewish mystical theology, in which

[39] Albright, op. cit., p. 370. Cf. Pagels, op. cit., p. xxx: "Professor M. Friedlander, maintained that gnosticism originated in Judaism: the heretics whom the rabbis attacked in the *first* and second centuries, said Friedlander, were Jewish gnostics." Italics added.

[40] Albright, op. cit., p. 371.

[41] Ibid., p. 371.

[42] Robertson, *Word Pictures*, IV, p. 472.

[43] Conybeare & Howson, op. cit., I, p. 383.

[44] I Tim. 1:4.

[45] I Tim. 4:7.

[46] Titus 1:14.

[47] Conybeare & Howson, op. cit., I, p. 451.

[48] C. T. Wood, *The Life, Letters, and Religion of St. Paul* (2nd ed.; Edinburgh: T. & T. Clark, 1932), p. 367.

Jewish theosophy and Gentile speculation blended, there are "many fabulous statements concerning these emanations."[49]

We conclude from this that though most of the literary remains of Gnosticism date from the second century and later, it had a much more ancient origin. Its influence appears in the history of the Church as early as Philip's encounter with Simon the sorcerer, at the outset of the Church's worldwide missionary endeavors. A recognition of this helps to explain much that otherwise may be obscure in Paul's counsels to the Corinthian church.

The challenge of this subtle, alien religious force was intensified as Christianity reached out to the Diaspora, and thence to the Gentile world. The evidence suggests a determined effort to infiltrate the new Christian communities, and to subvert them into Gnosticism. It was not until near the end of the first century that an orthodox apologetic began to crystallize a separation between the two. However, in the Corinthian context to which Paul wrote, orthodoxy and Gnostic heterodoxy existed side by side in the form of rival parties in the church.

[49] Conybeare & Howson, op. cit., I, p. 451.

Chapter 18

Gnostic Influences at Corinth

EVIDENCE OF THE CONFRONTATION between Christian orthodoxy and Gnostic heterodoxy in the Corinthian church is not lacking in Paul's first Corinthian epistle.

I Cor. 2:6ff.—"We Speak Wisdom"

Paul's discussion of "wisdom" in this passage may well be a refutation of incipient Gnostic tendencies in the Corinthian assembly: e.g., "We speak wisdom, however, among them that are fullgrown: yet a wisdom not of this world . . . but we speak God's wisdom in a mystery." The very phraseology suggests "an allusion to the technical language of mystical initiation"[1] common among the Gnostics. The difference between men in spiritual attainment is recognized by Paul, but "it is vital to notice that he does not erect a barrier between the advanced Christian and the babe in Christ (as the Gnostics did, for instance)."[2]

I Cor. 5:1ff.—"Immorality Such as Even the Pagans Do Not Tolerate"

A second illustration may be seen in the enormity of the guilt, over against the inexplicable apathy of the church, of the man guilty of gross immorality—"the union of a man with his father's wife."[3]

[1] Robertson and Plummer, op. cit., p. 35.

[2] C. T. Wood, op. cit., p. 181. Cf. Pagels, op. cit., p. 147. "While the gnostic saw himself as 'one out of a thousand, two out of ten thousand,' the orthodox experienced himself as one member of the common human family, and as one member of a universal church." Cf. also Irenaeus: "The multitude, however, cannot understand these matters, but only one out of a thousand, or two out of ten thousand" (*Against Heresies*, I, 24, 6).

[3] I Cor. 5:1ff. NEB.

Granted, Corinth, with its thousand prostitutes dedicated to Aphrodite, the goddess of love, was one of the most licentious cities of the ancient world. Almost every student of the New Testament, sooner or later, discovers that "the very name to Corinthianize meant immorality."[4] But this is hardly sufficient to explain the apostle's strong language—"immorality such as even pagans do not tolerate."

In view of the gravity of the situation, it is hardly appropriate to understand his words here as exaggeration for the sake of emphasis. After all, genuine conversion involves a "new birth." It does imply a new moral consciousness, and a changed lifestyle. It was not only the enormity of the moral delinquency, but even more, the local congregation's benign attitude of tolerance that beggars the explanation that prior pagan habits, plus the contaminating moral climate of Corinth, are sufficient to explain the situation. Rather the moral turpitude with which Paul charged the Corinthian assembly may well reflect the licentious attitude of an influential Gnostic element there.

As already noted, some of these advocated a rigid asceticism, while others reacted against ascetic practices, and went "to the opposite extreme of unrestrained licentiousness."[5] Both reactions were the result of a false conception of matter as intrinsically evil. Only a moral depravity as extreme as that practiced by some Gnostics is sufficient to explain the local congregation's pride in such degrading immorality. Such unnatural vice cannot be explained as an immature regression to pre-Christian habits. Paul's words indicate that it was abnormally debased, even for the dissolute society of Corinth. Judged in the light of the biblical ethic, it was intolerable. There can be no compromise between revealed morality and a social ethic debased to the lowest common denominator of self-gratification. Without the philosophical and religious speculations of some such system as Gnosticism provided, the tension with revealed morality would have condemned it out of hand in the Corinthian assembly.

[4] Robertson, *Word Pictures*, III, p. 294.

[5] J. B. Lightfoot, *Saint Paul's Epistles to the Colossians and to Philemon* (London: Macmillan, 1892) p. 78. Cf. Irenaeus, *Against Heresies*, I, 25, 3: "Others of them yield themselves up to the lusts of the flesh with the utmost greediness, maintaining that carnal things should be allowed to the carnal nature, while spiritual things are provided for the spiritual."

I Corinthians 7—Celibacy Versus Marriage

A double moral standard is implied also in the discussion of celibacy versus marriage in I Corinthians 7. Here a rigid asceticism, such as that advocated by certain Gnostics, would place a premium upon celibacy over marriage as the ideal spiritual state. If this seems like condoning incest on the one hand, and advocating celibacy on the other—it must be understood that these extremes were advocated by rival schools of thought among the Gnostics themselves. Both extremes were plausible within the presuppositions of a neo-Platonic metaphysics.

In a world view in which matter was believed to be intrinsically evil, it was important to know how to keep one's higher spiritual nature unsullied by escaping the hurtful influences of contact with matter.[6] It is understandable then that celibacy would commend itself to some as reducing some of the grosser defilement of matter. In this aspect, at least, man's sensual nature would be subdued, "and the spirit thus set free, would be sublimated, and rise to its proper level."[7]

Opposed to such celibate views is the attitude of the Old Testament on the desirability of marriage, a view espoused by Peter and Paul himself. Paul, as a matter of fact, branded the "forbidding to marry" as one of "the doctrines of demons."[8] The resultant friction between the proponents of these two opposed points of view on so sensitive an issue would contribute to the fragmentation of the Corinthian church already referred to in I Cor. 1:11ff.

The celibate idea has always been alien to normative Judaic tradition. Essene asceticism is not typical of normative Judaism, or at least of the type of Old Testament piety that triumphed in post-exilic Judaism. The genius of Essene monasticism was messianic and apocalyptic, not unlike the underlying assumptions in Paul's solution to the question of celibacy versus marriage at Corinth, viz., "I think that in view of the impending distress it is

[6] Lightfoot, *Colossians*, p. 77.

[7] Ibid.

[8] I Tim. 4:1–3. Cf. Hippolytus, *Refutation of all Heresies*, VIII, 13, on the Encratites. Also, Irenaeus, *Against Heresies*, I, 24, 2: "They [Saturninus, et al.] declare also, that marriage and generation are from Satan."

well for a person to remain as he is."[9] If married, do not seek a divorce; if unmarried, do not marry for "the appointed time has grown short."

This tension between traditional Jewish views of marriage and the celibate state has not changed even today. In Herbert Wiener's insightful chronicle of religious encounters in contemporary Israel, Father Jochanan, a Catholic priest, commented on the difficulty he encountered in explaining the celibate idea to contemporary Israelies. In discussions in the kibbutzim, he was repeatedly asked how he could reconcile celibacy with his faith in the Torah whose first commandment is "to be fruitful and multiply."[10]

I Cor. 8:1–10:33—"Concerning Things Sacrificed to Idols"

Radically conflicting views come to the fore again in Paul's discussion of the eating of meats sacrificed to idols.[11] It was the antagonism of the legalists in the Church that forced the church in Antioch to appeal to the apostles and elders in Jerusalem to resolve the question: Must Gentile converts to Christianity assume the yoke of the ceremonial law of Judaism as a prerequisite to conversion? Their answer was a memorandum initiated by James, and endorsed by the Jerusalem council which read in part,

> it has seemed good to the Holy Spirit and to us to lay upon you no greater burden than these necessary things: that you abstain from what has been sacrificed to idols and from blood and from what is strangled and from unchastity.[12]

At Corinth the question of eating "what has been sacrificed to idols" apparently precipitated a conflict between Gnostic libertinism and Judaic scrupulosity. Paul placed his answer on the highest level of love when he concluded: "All things are lawful, but not all things are profitable. All things are lawful, but not all things edify. Let no man seek his own good, but that of his neighbor."[13] Corinth was not the only place where the same influences produced tensions over the same question. In Colossae

[9] I Cor. 7:26–29.
[10] *The Wild Goats of Ein Gedi* (New York: Meridan, 1961) pp. 88, 89.
[11] I Cor. 8:1ff.
[12] Acts 15:28, NEB.
[13] I Cor. 10:23.

the ascetic tendencies of Gnosticism gained the upper hand. There the apostle Paul was obliged to "condemn the ascetic practices of the Gnostics."[14] On the other hand, the libertine influence triumphed later in Thyatira where "Jezebel, who calls herself a prophetess . . . is teaching and beguiling my servants to practice immorality and to eat food sacrificed to idols."[15]

The nature of the group at Corinth to whom Paul addressed his remarks about eating meats sacrificed to idols is suggested in his opening words: "'Knowledge'[16] puffs up, but love builds up." Note that it is "knowledge" that he thus rebuked as the source of pride. This same "knowledge" caused them to treat with "arrogance" rather than censure the man guilty of gross immorality.

I Corinthians 15—The Resurrection of the Dead

Finally, the discussion of the resurrection[17] becomes clearer when seen against the backdrop of Gnostic speculation. It is in this direction that Paul's words point: "Now if Christ is preached as raised from the dead, how can some of you say that there is no resurrection of the dead?"[18] Those who challenged the doctrine of the resurrection

> were not skeptics or Christians of a Sadducean temper. . . . they were mystical enthusiasts of the Greek type who could not see anything relevant to spiritual Christianity in any doctrines which drew upon Jewish belief about bodily resurrection after death as needful to immortal life.[19]

This description can be crystallized in one word, Gnosticism. This assumption is supported by Paul's extended description of the resurrection body, which begins as an explicit rebuttal of a heret-

[14] Robertson, *Word Pictures*, IV, p. 578. Cf. Irenaeus, *Against Heresies*, I, 24, 2: "Many of those who belong to his [Saturninus] school abstain from animal food, and draw away multitudes by a feigned temperance of this kind."

[15] Rev. 2:20. Cf. Irenaeus, *Against Heresies*, I, 6, 3. Wherefore also it comes to pass, that the "most perfect" among them addict themselves without fear to all those kinds of forbidden deed of which the Scriptures assure us that "they who do such things shall not inherit the kingdom of God." For instance, they make no scruple about eating meats offered in sacrifice to idols, imagining that they can in this way contract no defilement.

[16] I Cor. 8:1, *γνῶσιν* = Gnostic (?).

[17] I Cor. 15:1ff.

[18] I Cor. 15:12.

[19] Moffatt, op. cit., p. 240.

ical assertion: "But some one will ask, 'How are the dead raised? With what kind of body do they come?'"[20] It is difficult to sidestep the conclusion that the heretics addressed here were Gnostics who typically would not "assign a body to the exalted Christ or to glorified believers."[21]

The foregoing evidence, admittedly incomplete, is nonetheless adequate to indicate clearly that the Apollos party and the Christ party at Corinth represented Gnostic influences and speculations. The Apollos party probably reflected two streams of influence coming through Apollos; first, as one adept in Philonian (Alexandrian) philosophy, and second, as a disciple of John the Baptist with his Essene contacts. The Christ party is more elusive; however, it may well have embodied more pronouncedly Gentile influences from Greek philosophy and Oriental theosophy. These convergent streams of Gnostic influence provide a viable explanation for the problem of extreme licentiousness and asceticism addressed in Paul's epistles to Corinth and elsewhere.

[20] I Cor. 15:35.

[21] J. A. Robertson, op. cit., p. 1239. Cf. Pagels, op. cit., p. 11. "Some gnostics called the literal view of the resurrection the 'faith of fools.'"

Chapter 19

Do Not Forbid Speaking in Tongues

THE WAY IS NOW CLEAR to apply the insights provided by the preceding study to the second question propounded in chapter 17. What effect did the various parties at Corinth have upon the manifestations of the charisms of the Holy Spirit—especially "tongues" and "prophesying"? The crux of the matter is to be found in I Cor. 14:39. Here the English translations have contributed to some ambiguity in the interpretation of the passage.

The conclusion to Paul's discussion of *the spirituals*[1] is summarized in two brief injunctions: "So, my brethren, earnestly desire to prophesy, and do not forbid speaking in tongues."[2] Here the English translation(s) do not adequately reproduce the force of the idiom in the original language. In Greek the word translated "forbid" is a present imperative with the negative "not" preceding it.[3] The import of this idiom is prohibitive. It is not concessive, as is often tacitly assumed. This may be illustrated by the following paraphrase. "Desire earnestly to prophesy (as the greater charism), and if (by reason of your childish infatuation with glossolalia) you must speak in tongues then you may indulge yourselves a little." But the apostle neither said nor implied this. Quite the contrary, for the present imperative in a prohibition does not support such an assumption.

It is important to note that "a prohibition in the present imperative demands that *action then in progress* be stopped."[4] For

[1] I Cor. 12:1, *τῶν πνευματικῶν*.
[2] I Cor. 14:39.
[3] *μὴ κωλύετε*, *do not forbid*.
[4] Dana and Mantey, op. cit., p. 301.

example, the American Standard Version rendering of Matt. 7:1 is, "Judge not, that ye be not judged." The import of the idiom could be more accurately translated, "Stop judging, lest you be judged." Another illustration is Rev. 5:4, 5: "and I wept much. . . . then one of the elders said to me, 'Weep not.'" More precisely rendered it means, "I was weeping. . . . then one of the elders said to me, 'Stop weeping.'"

Therefore, to do justice to the idiom, I Cor. 14:39 should be translated, "Stop forbidding speaking in tongues."[5] The "action then in progress" that Paul bade them to stop was not speaking in tongues. On the contrary, it was the *forbidding* to speak in tongues that he admonished them to stop. This suggests that the apostle Paul addressed a practice then current in the Corinthian assembly, namely, the prohibiting of speech in other tongues. He was not generalizing a future contingency, i.e., "if anyone should speak in tongues, do not stop them." The implication is rather that there was an influential party at Corinth which sought to forbid speaking in tongues, and Paul enjoined the continuance of this practice. His words may be paraphrased thus: "Stop your current practice of forbidding the speaking in tongues."

This interpretation prompts then the question: Whence did this practice of forbidding tongues-speech originate? The answer lies at hand in the party strife that fragmented the Corinthian church on so many other issues.[6] James Moffatt defined the issue clearly when he wrote: "Some sober-minded Christians in the local church, as at Thessalonica, evidently were shocked; *they desired to check the habit* (xiv. 39)."[7] Lest the allusion to Thessalonica be overlooked, let the reader take note that Corinth was not the only church disturbed by the activities of an anticharismatic faction. In Corinth it was "forbidding tongues-speech," while at Thessalonica it was "despising prophesying"—a fact to be commented on subsequently.

[5] The objection of Robertson & Plummer, op. cit., p. 328 to this rendering is not well taken. The passages in I Tim. 4:14 and 5:22 cited against it may be cited with equal appropriateness in favor of this translation. In the final analysis, the implication remains that their rebuttal rests not so much on exegetical considerations as upon a theological bias against speaking in tongues.

[6] I Cor. 1:11ff.

[7] Op. cit., p. 211, italics added.

In the light of the historical and religious context, the question posed by Moffatt needs to be sharpened a little more. Someone at Corinth was trying to stop speaking in tongues, but did this result from the scruples of some "sober-minded Christians," or was it a more fundamental clash in viewpoint between factions already identified at Corinth? The latter alternative is more consistent with the historical and religious context to which the Corinthian epistles were addressed.

Such an anticharismatic influence would hardly come from the avowed followers of Peter, for he had been present at Pentecost, and his subsequent charismatic ministry is spelled out in the book of Acts. Nor is it reasonable thus to indict the Pauline party, for Paul magnified the richness of his own charismatic endowments. The alternative then is either the party of Apollos, or the Christ party—or a coalition of these parties. As already argued, both of these represented Gnostic influences.

Is it possible that the anticharismatic agitation originated with them? Quite probably. Why? Here the nature of Gnosticism furnishes a further clue. It was not simply a rational, speculative system of philosophy. Its religious expressions were frequently orgiastic. It even boasted esoteric knowledge "derived in part from ecstatic experiences."[8]

As already observed, Paul's opening remarks on the Holy Spirit's charismatic manifestations[9] may contain more than a hint here of a contrast between the authentic manifestations of the Spirit and counterfeit charisms of an essentially demonic nature. "The air was full of the mystery cults like the Eleusinian mysteries, Mithraism, the vogue of Isis,"[10] and the mystery cults in Gnostic guise do affect one's understanding of the religious context of the charismata in the primitive Church. Chrysostom warned that their idols

> though dumb themselves, yet had their oracles, and prophets, and soothsayers, who professed to have *spiritual gifts* such as the Pythia at Delphi; but do not be deceived, their gifts may easily be distinguished from ours.[11]

[8] Easton, op. cit., p. 1350.
[9] I Cor. 12:1–3.
[10] Robertson, *Word Pictures*, IV, p. 471.
[11] Wordsworth, op. cit., II, p. 126.

The rendering of the New English Bible makes such a contrast explicit: "You know how, in the days when you were still pagans, you would be seized by some power which drove you to those dumb heathen gods."[12] Paul was saying that "those of you who were brought up as pagans are familiar with the frenzied cries of the cults. You know the religious impulses that once swept you into seances where devotees had their experiences of divine (?) [demonic] possession."[13]

The implications for one's understanding of the manifestations of the Holy Spirit deserve to be probed more deeply in the light of these facts. Was the charismatic exuberance of Spirit-filled believers offensive to "some sober-minded Christians," as Moffatt suggested? Or were counterfeit "ecstatics" alarmed at the threat of exposure by the spontaneous vitality of the Holy Spirit's manifestations? Did Paul suggest as much when he wrote:

> But if all prophesy, and there come in one unbelieving or unlearned,[14] he is reproved by all, he is judged by all; *the secrets of his heart are made manifest*; and so he will fall down on his face and worship God, declaring that God is among you indeed.

Obviously this is not prophesying that ministers "edification, and exhortation, and consolation"[15] to the Christian assembly. Rather this is prophesying that exposes the deceit and duplicity of the heart, as, for instance, in the case of Ananias and Sapphira.[16] With this aspect of prophesying at work in Corinth, and also in Thessalonica, the consequences may have been just as drastic for the dissemblers in these churches as they were for Ananias and Sapphira, who paid with their lives for lying to the Holy Spirit.

Furthermore, this punitive aspect of prophecy is hinted at in Paul's sentence passed *in absentia* upon the man in the Corinthian assembly who was guilty of gross immorality:

[12] I Cor. 12:2.

[13] Moffatt, op. cit., p. 178.

[14] ἰδιώτης, I Cor. 14:24, ASV, italics added. "In I Cor. 14:23f ἰδιῶται and ἄπιστοι together form a contrast to the Christian congregation. The ἰδ. are neither similar to the ἄπιστοι . . . nor are they full-fledged Christians; obviously they stand betw. the two groups as a kind of proselytes or catechumens" (Bauer, Arndt, Gingrich).

[15] I Cor. 14:3, ASV.

[16] Acts 5:1ff.

> For though absent in body I am present in spirit, and as if present, I have already pronounced judgment in the name of the Lord Jesus on the man who has done such a thing. When you are assembled, and my spirit is present, with the power of our Lord Jesus, you are to deliver this man to Satan for the destruction of the flesh, that his spirit may be saved in the day of the Lord Jesus.[17]

Before this reconstruction is brushed aside, it would be well to remind oneself that the anticharismatic spirit exposed itself outside of the Corinthian assembly. As already noted, the apostle Paul wrote to the Thessalonians: "Quench not the Spirit; despise not prophesyings."[18] Only an arbitrary redefinition of prophesyings could deny that the apostle here meant the same charismatic manifestation of prophesying to which he also referred in his Corinthian epistle.

The very words, "despising"[19] and "forbidding,"[20] indicate something of the intensity of the opposition to the Holy Spirit's ministries of "prophesying" and "tongues." In Thessalonica prophesying was under fire, and in Corinth tongues—which with "interpretation of tongues" is equivalent to prophecy—was under the ban. It is suggestive that opposition crystallized against charisms that are in part, at least, revelatory.

Within the context of this anticharismatic attitude, Paul's words, "earnestly desire spirituals"[21]—and the spirituals singled out for discussion in I Corinthians 14 are prophecy and tongues—sets these charisms in a new perspective in the Corinthian church. It is obvious that the admonition to the Corinthians, "earnestly desire . . . that you may prophesy,"[22] is the affirmative counterpart of his prohibition addressed to the Thessalonians, "stop despising prophesyings." Both say essentially the same thing. In both instances, Paul reversed the judgment of the anticharismatic party.

There is another possible reconstruction of events in Corinth

[17] I Cor. 5:3, 5.

[18] I Thess. 5:19, 20, ASV. The idiom is the same as in I Cor. 14:39, i.e., a present imperative in a prohibition. It means "Stop an action already in progress."

[19] I Thess. 5:18.

[20] I Cor. 14:39.

[21] I Cor. 14:1.

[22] I Cor. 14:1.

that fits the facts. It is possible that the sober-minded Christians, with or without the cooperation of Gnostic elements of more speculative bent of mind, may have initiated the prohibition against tongues in the worship of the assembly. Alarmed at the patently unspiritual excesses of Gnostic "ecstatics," and being unable to cope with such counterfeit manifestations, they may have consented to the radical expedient of forbidding all "spiritual" manifestations. This solution may have represented a counsel of expediency which Paul sought to counter by reinstating tongues and prophesying to their proper place in the worship of the church where "each one has a hymn, a lesson, a revelation, a tongue, or an interpretation."[23]

There are those today who also advocate "throwing out the baby with the bath water," but this was not Paul's solution. He defined the bona fide operations of the Holy Spirit, especially with regards to tongues and prophesying. Then he hedged each with certain safeguards. Tongues are to be manifested in the public worship when accompanied by the companion gift of interpretation. prophesying is subject to the discernment of the order of prophets. In every case, self-control is the dominant note, for "the spirits of prophets are subject to prophets."[24] Contemporary descriptions take note of the fact that such self-control was lacking in the orgiastic ecstacies of the mystery cults. Hence, these safeguards would protect the church by distinguishing counterfeit ecstacies from the genuine manifestations of the Holy Spirit.

[23] I Cor. 14:26ff.
[24] I Cor. 14:32.

Chapter 20

The Uninstructed or Unbelieving[1]

THE IDENTIFICATION OF THE Apollos party and the Christ party at Corinth with Gnosticism sheds light on Paul's quotation from the prophet Isaiah in I Cor. 14:21: "In the laws it is written, 'By men of strange tongues and by the lips of foreigners will I speak to this people, and even then they will not listen to me, says the Lord.'" Was this quotation of Isa. 28:11 simply a loose verbal application, or a midrash of two otherwise unrelated scriptures? Or is there an inner logic at work here, a statement of a general principle valid in both contexts?

In Isaiah, the prophet addressed Jerusalem and her scoffing rulers as "this people." The unintelligible tongues of foreign invaders were to be a sign of divine judgment upon them. Paul declared that the "tongues" in Corinth were a sign to the unbelievers there. In both instances, the common denominator was the sign value of the tongues used. What connection is there then between the "sign" of tongues to "this people" in Isaiah, and the "sign" of tongues to the "unbelievers" in Corinth? But one ought to ask first, who were these "unbelievers." Were they, as Moffatt claimed, "outsiders at Corinth [who] did not belong to the Lord's people"?[2] Or were they unbelievers who had attached themselves to the church there, and masqueraded as Christians? A survey of the uses of the term "unbeliever" in the Pauline epistles suggests some provocative answers.

[1] I Cor. 14:23
[2] Op. cit., p. 223.

"Out of sixteen occurrences of the word ἄπιστος in the Pauline epistles, fourteen are found in the Epp. to the Corinthians."[3] Often the apostle designated the heathen by it. However, in several instances, he used the term to describe false teachers. For example, "Be not unequally yoked with unbelievers,"[4] may be a contrast with the heathen, or it may be a reference to the false teachers who "bring you into bondage."[5] Throughout these epistles the apostle apparently has in mind certain individuals anonymously referred to as "the many" who are "peddlars[6] of God's word," i.e., false teachers within the church. The suggestion is all the more plausible in the light of the sectarian spirit alluded to in I Cor. 1:11ff. In Titus 1:15 the reference "to the corrupt and unbelieving" is a descriptive comment on those who taught "Jewish fables, and commandments of men." As already suggested, these were perhaps false teachers of a Judaeo-Gnostic persuasion.

This use of the term "unbeliever" as an epithet for "teachers of error,"[7] recurs in the subapostolic age in the epistles of Ignatius, bishop of Antioch, *To the Trallians*, 10, and *To the Smyrnaeans*, 2, 5. Both epistles were probably written in the first decade, or decade and a half, of the second century (ca. A.D. 107, or A.D. 116),[8] the former from Smyrna, the latter from Troas, while Ignatius was on his journey to Rome where he suffered martyrdom.

In the shorter version of the letter to the Trallians, he wrote: "But if, as some that are without God, that is the unbelieving, say, that He only seemed to suffer, . . . then why am I in bonds?"[9] The Docetic Gnosticism that Ignatius was rebutting here is made even more explicit in the longer version of his letter:

> But if, as some that are without God, that is, the unbelieving, say, He became man in appearance [only], that He did not in reality take unto Him a body, that He died in appearance [merely], and did not

[3] J. H. Barnard, *The Second Epistle to the Corinthians*, ed. W. R. Nicoll, Vol. III, *The Expositor's Greek Testament* (Grand Rapids: Eerdmans, [n.d.]), p. 60.

[4] II Cor. 6:14, ASV.

[5] II Cor. 11:22, ASV.

[6] II Cor. 2:17, καπηλεύοντες, "the word comes to mean almost *adulterate* (so Vulg. Syr. Goth.)."

[7] Bauer, Arndt, Gingrich, ἄπιστος, 2.

[8] *Apostolic Fathers*, eds. A. Roberts and J. Donaldson, Vol. I., *Ante-Nicene Christian Library*, (Edinburgh: T. & T. Clark, 1876) pp. 143, 144.

[9] Trallians, 10.

> in very deed suffer, then for what reason am I now in bonds, and long to be exposed to the wild beasts?[10]

Again in his epistle to the Smyrnaeans, his allusion to Gnostic teachers is equally obvious in this statement: "And He suffered truly, even as also He truly raised up Himself, not, as certain unbelievers maintain, that He only seemed to suffer, as they themselves only seem to be [Christians]."[11] He returned to the same subject saying; "For what does anyone profit me, if he commends me, but blasphemes my Lord, not confessing that He was [truly] possessed of a body?"[12] The longer version of this place reads as follows: "For what does it profit, if anyone commends me, but blasphemes my Lord, not owning Him to be God incarnate?" Ignatius concluded this section of his epistle by writing: "Yea far be it from me to make any mention of them, until they repent and return to [a true belief in] Christ's passion, which is our resurrection."

How deep was his alarm at the influence of these insidious Gnostic teachers may be judged from his description of them as "beasts in the shape of men, whom you must not receive, but if it be possible, not even meet with; only you must pray to God for them, if by any means they may be brought to repentance, which, however, will be very difficult."[13] Ignatius' concern for the repentance of these false teachers echoes Paul's burden in a similar situation in Corinth:

> I fear that when I come again my God may humble me before you, and I may have to mourn over many of those who sinned before and have not repented of the impurity, immorality, and licentiousness which they have practiced.[14]

In the interpretation of the "unbelievers" at Corinth there are now two possibilities. One, the usual view that they were heathen who, for one reason or another, entered the Christian services. It is not, however, clear that the outsider was casually admitted to these Christian assemblies, as this view assumes. They may have been admitted to them as they were to the synagogue. On the

[10] Smyrnaeans, 2.
[11] Loc. cit., 2.
[12] Op. cit., 5.
[13] Op. cit., 4.
[14] II Cor. 12:21.

other hand, since the Eucharist was an integral part of every service, and the Christian worship services were conducted largely in private homes, outsiders were not likely to be admitted indiscriminately.[15] In v. 23 the "unbeliever" is linked with the "unlearned"[16] as having access to the Christian assembly.

If the "thanksgiving" referred to in vv. 16 and 17 is an allusion to the Lord's Supper[17]—and the corporate "Amen" referred to there "was a prominent feature of the Eucharist"[18]—it shows that the "unlearned" were present at the Communion Service as well as the "unbelievers." The custom of excluding the catechumen—if this is what is meant by the "unlearned"—from the celebration of the Eucharist may be a later development; however, the exclusion of the heathen from the Eucharist, the celebration of the central mystery of the Christian faith, is a foregone conclusion. Therefore, the view that the "unbelievers" at Corinth was casual outsiders is not convincing.

Alternatively, the abuses which Paul rebuked at the Lord's Supper in Corinth reflect the libertine tendencies associated with certain Gnostic influences already seen at work in the Corinthian church. This introduces the second possibility, namely, that these "unbelievers" were adherents of Gnostic ideologies there, e.g., the "Christ" party, who, being outwardly identified with the church, had access to its services of worship.[19] In the light of Paul's use of the term "unbeliever" as a designation for false teachers within the Christian assembly, this identification is not unreasonable. Furthermore, the reaction of the "unlearned" and "unbelievers" to tongues is essentially the same as that of the anticharismatics at Corinth and Thessalonica, namely opposition.

A general observation points also in this direction. In this epistle, Paul dealt with the various aspects of the party strife, and its effect upon the church's life and worship. He was not concerned with the problems affecting the pagan community except

[15] Robertson and Plummer, op. cit., p. 318.

[16] I Cor., 14:16, ἰδιῶται, "proselytes or catechumens" (Bauer, Arndt, Gingrich).

[17] Wordsworth, op. cit., II, p. 133.

[18] Parry, op. cit., pp. 152, 153.

[19] Irenaeus identified Simon the magician (Acts 8:9–24) as the founder of a Gnostic sect that bore his name. His successor was Menander, followed by Saturninus and Basilides. Gnosticism was a vital religious current in the Hellenistic world antedating Christianity (*Against Heresies*, I, 23; I, 24).

as these affected the experience of the Corinthian church, e.g., meats sacrificed to idols, etc.

This brings the discussion back to the question of the sign value of tongues, and the connection between the "sign" of tongues to "this people" in Isaiah, and to the "unbelievers" in Corinth.[20]

A clue to this question is to be found in Isaiah's prophecy. In the Old Testament passage,

> the prophet in the name of the Lord is threatening drunken priests and prophets of Jerusalem that he will speak to them through the unintelligible language or babble of foreign invaders, though even that punishing experience will not induce them to obey the Lord.[21]

Herein lies the point of contact between the prophecy of Isaiah and Paul's application of the prophecy to the situation in Corinth. In Isaiah, the alien tongues were to be a sign that God had spoken through his prophet. Their response would be a scornful disregard both of the oracle and its "tongues sign." By analogy, therefore, just as the "tongues" in Isaiah hardened apostate Israelites in unbelief, so also the "tongues" in the Corinthian assembly would harden these "unbelievers" and "unlearned" (novices) in unbelief and disobedience.

Observe the parallelism. If the entire assembly speaks in tongues, "and some uninstructed persons or unbelievers should enter, will they not think you are mad?"[22] This is just what had happened at Pentecost when the newly Spirit-filled believers spoke in tongues, and some of their auditors mocked them, saying, "They are filled with new wine."[23] In Isaiah's day "they [would]

[20] Paul's allusion to tongues as a sign for "unbelievers" rather than "believers" (14:22) has caused some difficulty for expositors. For example, the solution offered by J. B. Phillips for the felt contradiction in the verse is too radical. He felt himself constrained "from the sense of the next three verses," to regard Paul's words in v. 22 as "either a slip of the pen on the part of Paul, or more probably, a copyist's error." (NTME, fn. to I Cor. 14:22). The "sign" of tongues on the day of Pentecost was likewise to the unsaved multitude, not to the disciples. It was confirmation for all to hear and see the Holy Spirit's supernatural presence and power. Tongues are also among the "signs" in Mark 16:17ff., and are, as the context makes clear, a "sign" to unbelievers. Cf. aso H. M. Ervin, *This Which Ye See And Hear* (Plainfield: Logos International, 1972), pp. 89–94.

[21] Moffatt, op. cit., p. 223.

[22] I Cor. 14:23, NEB.

[23] Acts 2:13.

not hear the Lord," for the "tongues sign" simply hardened them in unbelief. In Jerusalem at Pentecost, perverse Israelites mocked the disciples, accusing them of drunkenness. At Corinth, Paul warned, intractable "unbelievers" would scorn them as "mad."[24]

In both cases, "this people" of Isaiah's day, and the "uninstructed" and "unbelievers" of Corinth, outwardly, at least, were identified with the covenant community. They were *in* but not *of* these communities, hence, they neither understood nor responded in faith to God's "charismatic" manifestations in the midst of His people.

It is important to note here that when Paul wrote, "If, therefore, the whole church assembles and all speak in tongues," he referred to tongues used devotionally. If all pray with tongues without interpretation, there will be no exposure of sin, consequently no call for repentance. However, as already pointed out, on the basis of I Cor. 14:6, tongues *with* interpretation is equivalent to prophecy. Thereby, God does communicate "revelation or knowledge or prophecy or teaching." Even as prophecy in the vernacular may expose "the secrets of the heart," so also tongues *with* interpretation may accomplish the same end.

[24] Did this reflect a judgment already articulated by those opposed to tongues? It is understandable that the otherwise unidentified ἄπιστοι, who stressed γνῶσις, or esoteric knowledge as the path to spiritual attainment, would thus rail at such spiritual manifestations among their less sophisticated coreligionists.

Chapter 21

Let All Things Be Done For Edification

IF TONGUES WERE INTRINSICALLY WRONG, Paul would not have included them in his epitome of primitive Christian worship, nor would he have restricted them to two or three utterances with interpretation. He would simply have forbidden them altogether.

His summary of charismatic worship is presented in I Cor. 14:26: "What then, brethren? When you come together, each one has a hymn, a lesson, a revelation, a tongue, or an interpretation. Let all things be done for edification." This description provides an insight into normative Christian worship in the apostolic age. The comment of B. B. Warfield is to the point here: "There is no reason to believe that the infant congregation at Corinth was singular in this. He [Paul] even makes the transition to the next item in his advice in the significant words, 'as in all the churches of the saints.'"[1]

Paul's admonition, "be filled with the Spirit, addressing one another in psalms and hymns and spiritual[2] songs," may be understood as an allusion to worship in the apostolic churches.[3] Along with the almost identical passage in Col. 3:16, it bears the stamp of charismatic worship. These evidences support the opinion, that

> we are justified in considering it characteristic of the Apostolic churches that such miraculous gifts should be displayed in them.

[1] *Counterfeit Miracles*, (New York: Charles Scribner's Sons, 1918), p. 5.

[2] Eph. 5:18, 19, πνευματικαῖς, cf. I. Cor. 12:1.

[3] "πνευματικαῖς defines the songs *as proceeding from the Holy Spirit*, as Θεοπνεύστους" (Meyer, *Epistle to the Ephesians*, p. 507). It may also suggest a correlation with Paul's words in I Cor. 14:14: "I will sing with the Spirit," i.e., in tongues.

The exception would be, not a church *with*, but a church *without* such gifts.[4]

If all the gifts of the Holy Spirit are to manifest the Spirit's presence and power for the edification of the whole community "for the common good,"[5] the absence of these supernatural enablements of the Spirit is a mute, but nonetheless eloquent, commentary upon the impoverished worship experience of much of contemporary Christianity. Critics of charismatic worship are quick to point to the apostle's admonition, "all things should be done decently and in order,[6] without pausing to realize that the "ordering" Paul counseled applies to the manifestation of the charisms of the Holy Spirit. Such apostolic order can only apply where the gifts of the Spirit of God are in operation. Where there are no gifts of the Spirit manifested, there is nothing thus to "order."

Measured by the biblical norm, contemporary "giftless" worship services lack the divine "order" counseled by the apostle. As a matter of fact, there is little to set in apostolic order. They are largely the conventionalized memorabilia of the long past charismatic activities of the Holy Spirit. For example, confirmation is a reminiscence of the early days when Spirit-filled men laid their hands on converts, and they too were filled with the Spirit, and spoke in other tongues, guided supernaturally in their utterances by the Spirit of God. The holy chrism recalls the ancient healing ministry of the Church, when Spirit-filled elders responded to the call of the sick, and prayed the prayer of faith over them after having first anointed them with oil in the name of the Lord,[7] and they were healed.

The spontaneous, unpremeditated, apocalyptic utterances of the prophetic community of believers have been largely stilled. Unlike ancient Israel, the Church no longer "kills the prophets,"[8] it simply ignores them. The demoniacs have been psychodynamically labeled, and remain in their wretched bondage, a witness to a Christianity that is charismatically impotent. Not only have some theologians undertaken to write God's epitaph, but others

[4] Warfield, op. cit., p. 5; italics added.
[5] I Cor. 12:7.
[6] I Cor. 14:40.
[7] James 5:14.
[8] Luke 11:47.

have relegated devil and demons to the never, never land of pious myth. The revelatory "word of wisdom and word of knowledge" have been traded off for the cultured ratiocinations of an antitheistic humanism. To believe in miracles . . . much less to confess that one has experienced them!—this is the height of naivete. The sophisticated "modern" Christian is embarrassed by what he deems to be mythical regressions in the Scriptures. Holy Writ must be demythologized to void the intellectual embarrassment of its supposedly unscientific world view.

In compromising the biblical metaphysic, the Church's Sadducean counselors would make the gospel relevant to modern society by negating "the stumbling block of the cross"[9] (and of Pentecost), and by worldly wisdom would make "the cross of Christ . . . void."[10] But a Christ without a cross (and a resurrection) is no Christ at all, and the divine Spirit without supernatural manifestations is robbed of the attributes of personality.

The plea to maintain an open mind to truth from every and any source to blatant hypocrisy on anyone's lips, unless and until that one too is willing to have an open mind to what the Holy Spirit is saying charismatically to the Church today. If love has a language all its own, so too does faith—"He who has an ear, let him hear what the Spirit says to the churches."[11]

On the day of Pentecost, Peter waited in the upper room with the 120 disciples still tarrying in Jerusalem after Christ's ascension. With the rest of Jesus' followers there, he too was "filled with the Holy Spirit and began to speak in other tongues, as the Spirit gave them utterance." Having praised God in tongues, he turned to the assembled multitude, and in the midst of a Spirit-filled, charismatically endowed community of faith, he preached the gospel with supernatural power, and "there were added [to them] that day about three thousand souls."[12]

Then this Galilean fisherman, accompanied by John, went up to the temple at the hour of prayer. Seeing there a lame man sitting at the gate called Beautiful, he answered his plea for alms with the unforgettable words: "Silver and gold have I none; but what I have, that I give thee. In the name of Jesus Christ of Nazareth,

[9] Gal. 5:11.
[10] I Cor. 1:17, ASV.
[11] Rev. 3:22.
[12] Acts 2:41.

walk."[13] This same Peter had quailed before the accusing finger of a serving maid, and denied his Master, not once, but three times, and that with cursing. Yet summoned before the same Sanhedrin that had condemned Jesus, he amazed them with his boldness and wisdom. And so the record runs. . .

Baptized in, that is to say filled with the Spirit, he testified with power to the multitude, spoke in faith the word of healing to the impotent man, answered with boldness the charges of the authorities. Does not his example say to the present age, that the Church needs an apostolic experience to achieve apostolic results in an apocalyptic age?

[13] Acts 3:6, ASV.

Chapter 22

Rivers of Living Water

DURING A MOMENTARY LULL in the temple service on the last, or great day of the Feast of Tabernacles, A.D. 26 or 29,[1]

> Jesus stood up and proclaimed, "If any one thirst, let him come to me and drink. He who believes in me, as the scriptures has said, Out of his heart shall flow rivers of living water." Now this he said about the Spirit, which those who believed in him were to receive; for as yet the Spirit had not been given, because Jesus was not yet glorified.[2]

On the day of Pentecost, this river of the Spirit, promised by Jesus, began to flow, for so we understand Peter's words: "This Jesus God raised up. . . . and having received from the Father the promise of the Holy Spirit, he has poured out this which you see and hear."[3] It is no merely academic question then: Does the Pentecostal "river" still flow with the same supernatural manifestations and results?

A brief reconstruction of the occasion on which Jesus uttered His prophecy of the outpouring of the Spirit enhances its dramatic effect. In the midst of the solemn temple ceremonies, two priests mounted the altar, one to pour wine, the other to pour water from the Pool of Siloam into two silver funnels on the west side of the altar. As symbolic of the outpouring of the Holy Spirit, this pouring of the water was the central point of the service. Jesus' words have a special appropriateness combined with this ritual act. The pouring of the water was immediately followed by the singing of the Hallel. Then followed a short pause for the preparation of

[1] A. T. Robertson, *A Harmony of the Gospels for the Student of the Life of Christ* (New York: Harper & Brothers, 1950), p. 114.

[2] John 7:37–39.

[3] Acts 2:32, 33.

the festival sacrifices. It was at this moment that Jesus' voice reverberated through the temple. However, "He interrupted not the services, for they had for the moment ceased: He interpreted, and fulfilled them."[4] Thus Jesus declared that this liturgical act of pouring out the water drawn from the Pool of Siloam found its fulfillment in Him. The epexegetical commentary of the evangelist, John, explains the meaning of His words more fully. It was symbolic of the Pentecostal effusion of the Holy Spirit that was yet to come.

Specifically, John's explanatory comment, "for as yet the Spirit had not been given, because Jesus was not yet glorified," is "a clear reference to the great Pentecost."[5] His glorification was not His death, but, as Jesus himself declared, it was "the glory which I had with thee [the Father] before the world was made."[6] It was from His ascended "glory" that the Son "poured out" the "river of living water" which He "received from the Father."[7] This is known theologically as the doctrine of the procession of the Holy Spirit. It is probably more accurate to say, that "the Spirit proceeds from the Father *through* or *by* (not 'and') the Son."[8]

As this "river" of the Holy Spirit poured forth, He manifested His person and presence in supernatural charisms. The first of these to be manifested was prophetic utterance in other tongues, i.e., Spirit-given languages of praise and adoration, a supernatural vehicle for lauding the "magnificence" of God. There followed in

[4] A. Edersheim, *The Life and Times of Jesus the Messiah*, II (4th ed.; New York: A. D. F. Randolph and Co., [n.d.]), p. 156ff. In the midst of conflicting views, we have chosen to follow Edersheim here.

[5] Robertson, *Word Pictures*, V, p. 132.

[6] John 17:5.

[7] John 2:33.

[8] A. H. Strong, *Systematic Theology* (Philadelphia: Judson Press, 1907), p. 323. Cf. T. Ware, *The Orthodox Church* (1963; rpt. Baltimore: Penguin Books, 1972), p. 58.

Originally the creed [Nicene-Constantinopolitan] ran:

> "I believe in the Holy Spirit the Lord, the Giver of Life, *who proceeds from the Father*, who with the Father and the Son together is worshipped and together glorified." This, the original form, is recited unchanged by the east to this day. But the west inserted an extra phrase "and from the Son" (in Latin *filioque*), so that the Creed now reads, "who proceeds from the Father and the Son."

Cf. also Pierre Loret, *The Story of the Mass*, trans. Dorothy Marie Zimmerman (Liguori: Liguori Publications, 1982), p. 77: "The *filioque* had already been added to the Creed in Spain at the insistence of the Council of Toledo in 589." It was apparently added as a defense against Arianism.

rapid sequence a spiritual repertoire of miraculous manifestations of which the "word of wisdom," "the word of knowledge," "faith," "gifts of healings," "workings of miracles," "prophecy," "discerning of spirits," "tongues," "and interpretation of tongues" is only a partial listing.[9] The book of Acts is an inspired chronicle of this spiritual "river" as the Holy Spirit flowed irresistibly and supernaturally in and through the apostolic community.

Pentecost was God's river in spate. Succeeding generations have been prone to regard it as a flash flood, lacking continuity, but this is not the biblical view. The mighty manifestations of the Holy Spirit continue as an integral part of the Church's life and witness. As such, they are to continue until Jesus comes again.

Acts 2:38, 39—"To All That Are Far Off"

In response to the guilt-stricken query of those who heard his "Pentecost" sermon—"Brethren, what shall we do"—Peter replied,

> Repent, and be baptized every one of you in the name of Jesus Christ for the forgiveness of your sins; and you shall receive the gift of the Holy Spirit. For the promise is to you and to your children and to all that are far off, every one whom the Lord our God calls to him.[10]

As already argued, "the gift of the Holy Spirit" cannot be confined to the work of the Spirit in regeneration. In the context, Peter interpreted for his auditors the meaning of the Pentecostal phenomena they were witnessing. The phrase refers expressly to the supernatural manifestations of the Holy Spirit "which they were seeing and hearing." The experience of Cornelius and his household, upon whom "the gift of the Holy Spirit had been poured out,"[11] confirms the charismatic connotations of this phrase, "the gift of the Holy Spirit."[12]

Peter's allusion to "the promise" in this context can only refer to the baptism in the Holy Spirit promised by Jesus in Acts 1:4,

[9] I Cor. 12:8–10.

[10] Acts 2:38, 39.

[11] Acts 10:45.

[12] Knowling, op. cit., II, p. 91. "The word [τὴν δωρεὰν] is used specially of the gift of the Holy Ghost by St. Luke four times in Acts, viii.20, x.45, xi.17, but by no other Evangelist (cf., however, Luke xi.13), cf. Heb. vi.4 (John iv.10)."

and it is the scope of "the promised baptism in the Spirit that refutes the attempt to confine the Pentecostal experience to the apostolic age. "The promise" is first to the assembled multitude of Jews. Then it embraces their descendants, "sons and daughters of verse 17."[13] Finally, "the horizon widens and includes the Gentiles. Those 'afar off' from the Jews were the heathen."[14]

"The promise" of Jesus, even "the gift of the Holy Spirit" in Pentecostal fulness and power, is indeed for "all that are far off, every one whom the Lord our God calls to him." The universality of "the promise" is abridged only by the prior condition of repentance, and its concomitant saving faith in Jesus Christ as Savior and Lord. The Lord is still calling. His "promise" is still in effect. The Pentecostal/Charismatic revival of the churches is thoroughly consistent with the biblical evidence.

I Cor. 13:8—"Tongues Will Cease"

Attempts to limit the Pentecostal charisms to the apostolic age are repeatedly advanced on exegetical grounds. First Corinthians 13:8 is frequently pressed out of context for this purpose, i.e., "Love never ends; as for prophecies, they will pass away; as for tongues, they will cease; as for knowledge, it will pass away." It has been argued from this that tongues, as one of the "sign gifts," ceased at the end of the apostolic age. But the argument is erroneous. Here the Greek words translated respectively, "they will pass away," (*καταργηθήσονται*, future passive), and "they will cease" (*παύσονται*, future middle), are used synonymously.[15] There is no exegetical significance in the use of either the passive or the middle voices with these verbs. The lexicons list no current uses of the word *καταργέω* in the middle voice. It is consistently used in the passive instead. By the same token, *παύω* is used consistently in the middle voice.[16] The use of these two forms reflects grammatical and stylistic considerations rather than dogmatic concerns. The writer simply chose the forms currently used for each word. It cannot, therefore, be deduced from the forms of

[13] Robertson, *Word Pictures*, III, p. 36.

[14] Ibid.

[15] Bauer, Arndt, Gingrich.

[16] Bauer, Arndt, Gingrich, *παύω*. They list only one passive form, the 2nd aorist infinitive, *παῆναι* in the postbiblical Hermas, *Vision*. This form is a verbal noun.

these verbs that tongues "will stop themselves" at the end of the apostolic age, while prophecy and knowledge will continue indefinitely. Certainly, no terminus is fixed by the use of either word. That these three charisms will come to an end is clearly affirmed by the text. When they will cease can only be deduced from the context.

While the verse itself does not tell when these gifts will terminate finally, the context does indicate it, namely, "when that which is perfect is come."[17] The temporal clause here refers to an "indefinite future time."[18] "That which is perfect," in the opinion of G. G. Findlay, "is brought about at the *παρουσία*—it 'comes' with the Lord from heaven."[19] As a matter of fact, "the Apostle is saying nothing about the cessation of *χαρίσματα* in this life."[20] Paul did say "that these charismata generally, as being designed only for the aeon of the partial, and not in correspondence with the future aeon of the perfect, will cease to exist at the Parousia."[21] Most comments on the passage are deeply dyed with the stated, or implied, assumption that there was something intrinsically suspect with the manifestation of tongues at Corinth. As a result, some commentators have gone out of their way to derogate them. It is certainly a more charitable, and scriptural, judgment to conclude that "Great as is the value even of prophecy, knowledge, and 'tongues,' their function is confined to the brief interval till the Lord returns."[22]

In addition, the words of the apostle Paul in I Cor. 13:12 are often overlooked or misconstrued in this connection: e.g., "For now we see in a mirror dimly, but then face to face. Now I know in

[17] I Cor. 13:10, ASV.

[18] Robertson, *Word Pictures*, IV, p. 179: "*Hotan elthei* is second aorist subjunctive with *hotan*, temporal clause for indefinite future time."

[19] Op. cit., II, p. 900.

[20] Robertson and Plummer, op. cit., p. 297:

> We might have expected St. Paul to put it in this way, yet he does not. He does not say, "But when we shall have come to the perfection of the other world, " etc. He is so full of the thought of the Second Advent, that he represents the perfection as coming to us. "*When* it shall have come"; then, but not till then. The Apostle is saying nothing about the cessation of the *χαρίσματα* in this life. . . . All that he asserts is, that these things will have no more use when completeness is revealed; and therefore they are inferior to Love.

[21] Meyer, *Corinthians*, p. 305.

[22] Moffatt, op. cit., p. 200.

part; then I shall understand fully, even as I have been fully understood." These words scarcely admit of any other conclusion than, that "unquestionably the time alluded to is that of *the coming of the Lord* . . . and this applies to ***all these***, not to the last (γνῶσις) only."[23]

Expediency and/or apologetic intent have led some to define "that which is perfect"[24] as the completed canon of Scripture. In support of this view, the charisms of "prophecy" and "knowledge" are restricted in operation to revelatory gifts given for the sole purpose of communicating the New Testament revelation. However, the whole thesis is devastated by the argument *reductio ad absurdum*. A simple paraphrase of Paul's words will serve to illustrate this contention, e.g.: "Now," wrote Paul, "I know in part; but then (when the canon of the New Testament is completed) shall I know fully even as also I was fully known." The absurdity of this is readily apparent. The apostle was dead, martyred, before the corpus of the New Testament was completed. By way of contrast, he spoke specifically of himself, and of his own expectations when he said, "then shall I know." He anticipated the time when his own partial knowledge—"seen in a mirror dimly"—would be completed. Clearly, he was looking forward to the second coming of our Lord and Savior Jesus Christ when he penned these words, at which time, his own fragmentary knowledge would be completed.

The apostolic age began with miraculous signs and wonders. After the day of Pentecost, "tongues" were followed in rapid succession by all, and more, of the charisms of the Holy Spirit enumerated in I Corinthians 12–14. And it is the plain testimony of Scripture that these supernatural manifestations of the Holy Spirit were to continue throughout the whole of the Church age, terminating only at the second advent of our Lord Jesus Christ.

[23] Alford, op. cit., II, p. 587.

[24] Robertson and Davis, op. cit., p. 205. "The articular neuter adjective [τὸ τέλειον] is often used in the same sense as an abstract."

Postscript

If the book of Acts bears witness to normative Christian experience—and it indubitably does—then, by every biblical standard of measurement, contemporary church-life is subnormal. As a consequence, it does not speak meaningfully, much less authoritatively, to our fragmented modern world. Well may a tormented humanity, staggering on the brink of an apocalyptic abyss, cry out to a Church that knows neither health nor wholeness, "Physician! Heal thyself!"

It is precisely at this point that the Holy Spirit, through the present charismatic awakening of the fragmented Christian community, speaks urgently to the whole Church on the ecumenical, the denominational, the congregational, and the personal levels of a unity of spirit and life. Only out of the plenitude of its own charismatic "fulness" can the modern Church confront redemptively an alienated world.

It has been said that "everywhere the apostle Paul went, he had a riot or a revival," and often both. The book of Acts is a book full of just such "revivals." The significant, and frequently overlooked fact, is that these were "Pentecostal" revivals. The gospel was preached in a context of charismatic signs—tongues, healings, miracles, exorcisms, etc. This is the biblical pattern of revival. This is the only pattern of revival commensurate with the challenges and opportunities of our day.

Greek Word Index

Scripture Index

Author Index

Subject Index